WHAT OTHERS ARE SAYING ABOUT THE SOUL CARE LEADER

I recently told Rob that while I a[m] personal transformation and depth teaching and ministry the piece I'm most thankful for is the ability to pass this on and lead others into freedom. That's why I'm so glad Rob wrote this book. From practical and reproducible guidance to new understandings about Spiritual authority and power, this book will be an essential tool in the ministry leader's toolbox. This will be used widely and effectively across cultures and generations. I'm excited for all who will read this but mostly I'm simply grateful for the gift of Rob and this material to the world and to the Kingdom!

—**Dr. Tim Meier**, Vice President, Christian and
Missionary Alliance

"The need for healthy leadership in the church is receiving growing attention around the Christian world. While preparing for ministry I wish I had been taught what Dr Rob teaches. In this book Dr Rob has brought Biblical truth, applicable principles and personal insights into the life walk and role of the Christian leader. He writes as one who has pursued and wrestled with God and found keys to being a healthy leader and shares insights on how to inspire and encourage other leaders to be healthy leaders. This work challenges and encourages leaders to that deeper journey with Jesus and to be effective cultural change agents in their ministry. It is for the leader, teacher, student, preacher or proclaimer of faith in Christ."

—**Rev Ken Graham**, Regional Coordinator, Asia Pacific
Region, Alliance World Fellowship
President, Christian and Missionary Alliance of Australia

Through his own spiritual story and experience Rob shares what is possible through a life lived by the power of the presence of God. He invites those who desire more peace, authority and fullness to pursue their intimacy with God. Rob clearly calls those who desire real life change and want to help others experience this genuine change, to engage in a spiritual life rhythm that develops them carrying a greater presence of the Father.

As the saying goes "we can only take others as far as we have gone ourselves", Rob has passionately and humbly led the way in living out spiritual principles that can ignite revival in a church. In "The Soul Care Leader" Rob helps us by passing on valuable wisdom and experience that God has taught him. The question is what will we do with the gift of this wisdom and invitation to engage in the quest for spiritual revival in our churches?

—JOHN HUTCHINSON, Executive Minister
   Churches of Christ in WA

"Discovery Church has been so profoundly impacted by Soul Care that we re-engineered and re-labeled the ministry we had in place for soul care purposes to 'Soul Care.' Over the last few years, hundreds of people have found new levels of freedom in Christ, in relationships with others, and in life overall. So significant has the impact been that we are bringing even more resources to our Soul Care Ministry in the coming ministry year. After 46 years in church ministry, I have witnessed enough to know what kind of ministry truly bears fruit, and this is one that truly does. I'm "all-in" on Soul Care and encourage you to be as well.

—DON COUSINS, Lead Pastor Discovery Church

"In the rich tradition of 'Care of the Soul' Dr Rob Reimer makes a significant contribution for those who seek to lead into the deeper heart and soul matter of individuals, congregations, and movements . In the *Soul Care Leader* he brings keen insights with heart and passion both of a leader as well as a shepherd of the soul. His insights into creating a culture are foundational to all who lead others in this quest. It is a necessary read."
—DR MARTIN SANDERS, Founder & President Global Leadership
   Director Doctor of Ministry, Alliance University NYC

One of the many things I love about my friend Rob Reimer is that he doesn't care who gets the credit. He just wants people to get free! This book is tangible evidence of that quality. Some people hoard their best stuff to make sure they are always "in demand." Jesus told us to freely give as we have freely received. Thanks for equipping the saints for the work bud. You're a class act!
—DR. RON WALBORN, VP & Dean, Alliance Theological Seminary and Alliance University

THE
SOUL CARE
LEADER

Healthy Living and Leading

Dr. Rob Reimer

Carpenter's Son Publishing

Published by Carpenter's Son Publishing, Franklin, Tennessee

Published in association with Shane Crabtree of Carpenter's Son Publishing
www.carpenterssonpublishing.com

Edited by Robert Irvin

Cover Design by Darcy Reimer

Interior Design by Suzanne Lawing

Printed in the United States of America

978-1-954437-58-6

DEDICATION

I dedicate this book to those of you who found freedom by processing through *Soul Care*. You didn't read it like a novel; you wore your book out reading it, underlining it, and working it into the fiber of your life. Often in conferences I see people carrying books that look like they have been worn out. The cover is tattered and torn and the book is falling apart because people like you have read and reread it and wrestled deeply with your issues. You have understood that *Soul Care* is not a book to be read, nor a conference to be attended; it is a lifestyle to be lived. And you have lived it! Way to go!

But many of you didn't stop there. You took all you learned and began helping others find freedom in Christ. I cannot tell how many times I talk to someone who has handed out *Soul Care* dozens of times. Some of you have literally bought hundreds of books and given them to others because of your relentless passion to see people experience the freedom you have found in Christ. Again I say: Way to go!

So to those of you who have lived it and sought to help others on the path toward wholeness, I dedicate this book to you. Thank you!

ACKNOWLEDGMENTS

"O Lord that lends me life, lend me a heart
replete with thankfulness."
William Shakespeare, *Henry VI*, Part II, Act I, Scene 1

It is not merely a formality to take time to give thanks; it is a necessity for anyone who wants to walk close to Jesus. It enlarges the heart of both those who give and receive thanks. So to those of you who are listed here, I am truly grateful.

To my family: I love you all and am grateful that God has allowed us to do life together. One of the things I love most about you—Danielle, Courtney, Darcy, and Craig—is how well you get along together. It is a beautiful thing, and I am grateful. Jen, you are a delightful partner in life and ministry. Words cannot express how truly grateful I am for you.

To those of you who have read my books, come to my conferences, shared testimonies of life change, and expressed kind and encouraging words, thank you! The stories never get old. They have strengthened me when I have been weak, encouraged me when I have been discouraged, and often reminded me of why I do what I do.

And to you, Lord Jesus: you alone are worthy. Your kindness, goodness, grace, and love to me have been remarkable. There is nothing I desire more than your presence, to bring you glory, and to represent you well.

ADDITIONAL RESOURCES FOR PROCESSING *SOUL CARE*

Life change is hard. We want to help
support you in this journey.

Visit **www.DrRobReimer.com** to get the resources below!

- Join our *The Soul Care Leader eCourse* for shorter, self-paced video lessons taught by Rob. It contains 40 lessons (over 9 hours of teaching) as well as study notes and questions to help you live and lead others through Soul Care in healthier ways. Our free mini eCourse, *Healthy Living & Leading*, gives you a great look at what the full eCourse is like.

- Join our **Soul Care eCourse** for shorter, self-paced video lessons taught by Rob. It contains 40 lessons (over 9 hours of teaching) as well as study notes and questions to help you process your journey and integrate the Soul Care principles into your daily life. Our free mini eCourse, **Forgiveness**, gives you a great look at what the full eCourse is like.

- Also available - **Soul Care Video Teaching Series (DVD or OnDemand Video)** features Rob teaching through the background of Soul Care and each of the seven principles. Great for individuals, small groups, or church-wide curriculum, the Video Teaching Series will be an invaluable asset to anyone who is going after freedom and fullness in Christ, and to anyone who is leading others along that journey.

CONTENTS

Introduction

THE SOUL CARE LEADER

I didn't receive much practical training for ministry when I was in seminary. They taught me how to study the Bible, how to preach, and how to lead a worship service. That was helpful. There wasn't much practical help, though, for how to work with people who were caught in sinful behaviors, addiction, dysfunction, relational brokenness, grief, or demonization. I didn't get a lot of help with hearing God's voice, learning how to depend upon the Spirit, doing ministry in the power of the Spirit, or developing spiritual authority.

I think the assumption was that if you just taught the Bible and people showed up, they would grow up and become like Jesus. The problem was it didn't work—and not just for the people I was ministering to. It didn't work for me either. We planted a church and the church grew. People came to faith in Christ. But our marriage was in trouble; my wife didn't like me anymore. I was reading my Bible, I was praying like crazy, and I showed up every day. But we weren't making progress. I suddenly found myself wishing seminary would have helped me with life change: my own and others. How do people change? How do you help broken people become healthy? How do you help stuck people find freedom? How could I help others if I didn't know how to help myself?

That dilemma launched me on a life change quest. I knew I had to get healthy, but I didn't know how. God taught me the principles of Soul Care, which changed me and healed our marriage. I wanted to help others with what I discovered, so I started teaching Soul Care in classes, doing conferences, and eventually wrote the book by that name. Many people found freedom, and just like me, they wanted to turn around and help others find the freedom they had discovered. But they needed equipping. I had many people ask, "How do I pass this along? How do I do this with others?"

When I first started doing Soul Care conferences, pastors and leaders would tell me they had experienced life change, but the next time I saw them I asked if they had passed it along to their people. Quite often the answer was no. When I asked why, they almost always said, "I didn't know how."

That's why I wrote this manual. (This material is also available in an e-course format.) It's designed to equip people further in the practice of Soul Care with others. Let me explain what it will and won't cover, and the best way to use it.

First, this is *not* a manual on a topic I cover a good bit: how to do deliverance. One day I will likely write a manual on how to do deliverance, and when I do I'll pass along all the practical tools I can. But I haven't done that here. We will at times touch on deliverance, and some help will be offered. To cover everything I need for that, however, would have made this book too large. (I do have a Deliverance Training Workshop available which is designed to equip people in deliverance. You can go to our website, www.renewalinternational.org, to find out more about that training or to ask to host a Soul Care Conference and/or one of our Deliverance Training workshops.)

Second, I *will* cover quite a bit on the heart and soul of a healthy Soul Care practitioner. I will discuss this because many people are drawn to do Soul Care with others, but some are drawn to this ministry because of their own brokenness. All of us are broken; we are all wounded healers. But we must make sure our souls are reasonably healthy before we venture out to become Soul Care ministers. You teach what you know, and you reproduce who you are. You can't give what you don't have. You only have authority over that which you walk in victory.

I will also focus on the heart and soul of a healthy Soul Care minister, because this ministry is draining. It is hard, and taxing, on our emotional and spiritual resources. I have done Soul Care conferences for more than two decades, and I still say that a three-day Soul Care Conference is the most draining ministry I engage in. It takes a lot out of me; if you don't know how to replenish, how to create healthy practices and rhythms, you will inevitably burn out. There are many people who find it even more draining than I do because of the way they are wired. They listen to people's stories, and they carry the pain with them. I feel compassion for the people, but I don't usually carry the pain with me when the encounter is over. The people who are drawn to this ministry are frequently compassionate, merciful people who find it hard to get out from under the weightiness of people's painful stories. You must learn how to care for your soul or a ministry designed for healing will make you soul sick. So we will talk about intimacy with God and healthy Soul Care practices that can allow you to endure in this ministry for the long haul without burning out.

Third, I will spend a chapter in this book on culture. I think discipleship is about changing culture; as a minister, you are seeking to change from your culture of origin to the culture of the Kingdom of God. Culture is about a set of norms. It is the attitudes, values, beliefs, behaviors, and relational patterns that are normal for a certain group of people. If you are a pastor, or a leader of a small group, and you want Soul Care to take root and produce fruit, then you are attempting to establish it as part of your group's culture. We will spend time talking about how to create a Soul Care culture that allows freedom to flourish.

Fourth, hearing God's voice is essential for Soul Care ministry, so we will spend an entire chapter talking about the prophetic and fine-tuning our capacity to hear and relay revelation from the Lord. Jesus was dependent upon listening to His Father as He did ministry. In the Gospel of John, Jesus said He only did what the Father told Him to do; He only went where the Father told Him to go; He only taught what the Father told Him to say. Listening to His Father's voice was a crucial part of Jesus' ministry approach. And it is a crucial part of doing ministry effectively for the Soul Care practitioner. When we hear God's voice accurately, and convey it compassionately and humbly, God shows up; there is a manifestation of His presence. The presence of God is critical to life change. So many times in ministry I simply don't know what to do, but God does. He isn't confused. He isn't nervous. Hearing God's voice allows His presence to permeate our problems and His peace to prevail in our hearts. Hearing God speak is critically important to helping others to breakthrough.

Fifth, if we are going to be effective Soul Care ministers, we need to develop spiritual authority. I have written an entire book on this subject. I won't repeat what I wrote there, but I will provide some nuance and expand on some of those themes. I highly recommend you read that book along with this one if you want to adventure into the ministry of healing souls. Jesus gave His disciples authority to cast out demons and heal the sick. We cannot heal the brokenhearted, cast out demons, or help people experience breakthroughs without authority. Soul Care ministry isn't about learning a bunch of

> Soul Care ministry isn't about learning a bunch of techniques as much as it is about depending upon the Spirit and becoming people of authentic spiritual authority.

techniques as much as it is about depending upon the Spirit and becoming people of authentic spiritual authority.

Sixth, we have to help people process their issues. Too often people talk about the same issue over and over without getting any breakthrough. They are just talking, not processing. If we are going to experience deep life change, we must shift from talking to processing. We will discuss what it looks like to make the shift and how to do it. Even though I am writing this for you to work with other people on their journeys, I suspect you will find a lot of this material beneficial for your own spiritual journey. Process it for yourself first, and then for working with others.

Finally, if we are going to be effective Soul Care ministers, we need to get to the roots and not just address the fruits. We need to get to the disease and not just manage the symptoms. Too often in ministry we deal with the presenting problems, but we don't know how to get to the root issues that are driving those presenting issues and can help someone get free. We can't just focus on sin management or behavior management; we need to address the issues of the heart and soul. I'll walk through some of the most common root issues and how to address them. Once again, I think it will benefit you to process this for yourself first and then develop it for working with others.

This is an equipping manual. You can read it straight through; in fact, that is how I would approach it on my first read-through. But you will likely need to go back and linger with some chapters for yourself and other chapters for leading others. I do have other equipping resources available on our website other than the Deliverance Training Workshop; there are various three-hour livestreams, many of which are also available on Vimeo on Demand, that can help deepen your wisdom on many of these topics.

Jesus told us to make disciples. Look at how Jesus did it. It wasn't just teaching. Yes, He taught, but He also coached, equipped, modeled, crafted experiences, and demonstrated God's power to make disciples. The church in the West has adopted a largely knowledge-based discipleship approach. It isn't adequate, and it isn't working. We need to learn how to depend upon the Spirit, move in authority, carry the presence of God, and help people experience breakthrough.

Here is the bottom line: We need to make disciples who make disciples. And we need more tools in our tool bag than just teaching. In this manual I hope to help you expand your tool bag so you become more effective as a Soul Care practitioner. So many people are stuck in bondage and living beneath their potential. We need more skilled practitioners who can help people get free. Thanks for joining the ranks!

Chapter 1

FACE TO FACE

I planted a church in New England, and New England has not been kind to church planters. The previous fourteen churches that had been planted in my region all died, but our church plant flourished. People were coming to Christ, lives were being changed. Within a couple of years, we had grown to more than 250 people. The problem was, as I wrote in the Introduction, while the church was growing, my wife didn't like me anymore. That's when I learned about the Soul Care principles that changed my life and saved our marriage. I realized that it took two healthy people to have a healthy relationship. If, on a scale of 1 to 10, you are a 5 in terms of your emotional and spiritual health, the healthiest relationship you can have is a 5! If you want to move from a 5 to a 7, there is only one path to get there: *you must change*. As I learned to live into the Soul Care principles, I began to change, and our marriage started to get healthier.

A few years later I ran into another problem. The church was growing and people were coming to Christ, but I was discontent. The problem arose from the gap between what I was experiencing and what I thought I would experience. When I was 24, I spent a day alone with God, and the Lord laid out his plan for my life. He said to me, "You will plant a church, you will teach at seminary, you will write books, and you will teach leaders internationally. Everything you do, do for revival. That is my call on your life." I had been living with an expectation of experiencing a revival. I thought that if I was faithful and did my job, revival would simply happen. But it didn't. We were growing, and if we compared ourselves with other churches in our region, we were doing well. But I wasn't simply seeking to grow a church. I was fighting for revival, and that wasn't happening.

Around 1970, about 50 percent of the people in New England went to church. But at the time I was experiencing this growing discontent, only about 5 percent of the people in the region did. I had been following church growth principles, and while our church was growing, it was like we were taking a thimble of water out of an ocean of lost humanity. We might have been winning some local skirmishes, but we were losing the war. I didn't just want our local church to do well; I wanted to see the Kingdom thrive in our region. But it wasn't.

At first my discontent was a holy discontent, but after some time I took offense at God. I felt like God wasn't upholding his part of the bargain. Discontent and disappointment are often important stepping-stones in our development. They make us come to the end of ourselves.

I was attending leadership conferences regularly so I could learn how to lead better. I was desperately attempting to close the gap between my experience and my expectation. I attended the Leadership Summit by Willow Creek the first seventeen years it existed! But every time I attended, I felt depressed. My staff attended with me, and they would say, "What happens to you when you come to these things? It's like you disappear on us." I didn't know why it was depressing to me. But eventually I realized I didn't have what it takes to fulfill my calling. It was beginning to dawn on me that no amount of human effort was going to accomplish what I believed God was calling me to do.

God called me to fight for revival, but I was attempting to lead a spiritual movement with human leadership techniques. It couldn't be done; I didn't have what it takes. That realization led to two things: first, it shifted me from an unholy discontent to a holy discontent. It lit a fresh fire under me for revival, but I wasn't blaming God, nor was I trying to figure it out by human effort. Second, it led to revelation from God on what I needed to move forward. Realizing that I couldn't make revival come about by human leadership efforts, I began seeking God for His plan, not merely waiting for God to make something happen. Prior to this shift, my faith was simple, but too passive.

I had a dream one day about a coming revival. I had the same dream three nights in a row; this was in December 2006. In the dream I was in a sports bar, and an older woman named Mrs. McDonald prophesied over me about a coming revival and God's specific role for me in it. She compared me to two revivalists in history, then said, "Pray for him." The scene went pitch black—and I was in a dungeon. There was a giant demonic beast wielding a huge sword against me. I had this little, itty-bitty sword, and I was fighting him off. I kept quoting Scripture as I battled him; of course, I was fighting with the sword of the Spirit, the Word of God. Eventually I thrust the sword through the giant, and he died. The room grew dimly lit and I saw black panthers coming down from a marble staircase to attack me. One by one I fought them off until they were all gone. I climbed the stairs and came out in the mall where the sports bar was located. I saw a Latina woman cleaning, and I knew she was a prophetess. I asked her, "What is the sign of the coming revival?" She said, "The New Orleans Saints are going to win the Super Bowl." That was December 2006, and a little over three years later the sign was fulfilled when the Saints won Super Bowl 44.

When God gave me this dream, I was so excited. I thought the revival would come quickly. Even before the sign came true, I thought it would come right away. But after the Saints won the Super Bowl, I was sure revival was imminent. Waiting for the promises of God to be fulfilled has caused me much pain and helped me die to self like few other things.

I think one of the most difficult things in my walk with God has been taking the promises of God seriously. So often there is a painful gap between the magnitude of God's promises that are found in His Word or through direct revelation and the reality of my experience. We have several options we can choose. First, we can let go of the promises of God, stop pursuing them, and settle for a life that is humanly possible to achieve but well beneath our potential as Christ followers. Many people land here, but for me it is a life not worth living. I have to take God seriously and close the gap between what God says and my actual experience. Second, we can hold onto the promises and live in denial that the gap exists. If we do this, we will become shallow religious people with trite religious phrases and significant gaps in our soul. Third, we can hold onto the promises of God and wrestle with the gaps, the disappointments, the delays, and the partially fulfilled promises—and struggle to develop a deep, authentic faith.

This last one is what I have chosen, and I have to say it has been the harder path. It has set me up for more disappointments and more failures, more sadness and more grief, more heartache and more pain, more wrestling with God and more difficult questions. But I also have to say it has brought me closer to God; I have seen more of what God can do and I've died to self in a greater way because of this path. I have seen more miracles, experienced more of God's power, touched more of God's presence, and witnessed more of God's break-throughs because of this choice. It has left me scarred by grief and marked by the presence of God. If I had to do life over, I would take this path again.

One day after I had this dream I said to the Lord, "What do you want me to do to fight for revival?" The Lord spoke to me clearly and said, "I want you to preach revival until it comes." The Lord said I had been passive about revival, waiting for it to happen, but He wanted me to fight for revival by preaching on revival and praying for revival like never before. I agreed to preach on revival until it came, but I realized that I had no idea what that really meant!

So I went away to the monastery to be alone with God and seek His clarification.

Moses Holds the Key

As I waited on the Lord at the monastery, I sensed the Spirit saying to me, "Study Moses. He holds the key." I tell this story fully in my book *Spiritual Authority*, but here I am going to simply sum up the key lesson.

What I discovered in my study of the life of Moses is that the key to Moses' leadership was his intimacy with God. In Exodus 3, the first time Moses encounters God, he hides his face from God. This is indicative of shame. He had shame because he had committed murder and ran from it. He had shame from his childhood wounds: abandonment by his parents (though for good reasons) and prejudice (he grew up as a Hebrew in a royal Egyptian family; Egyptians detested Hebrews).

But the face of God is the key to Moses' ministry and the development of his spiritual authority. In that very first lesson,

God gives Moses an impossible assignment. He is told he is to lead the people out of Egypt and into the Promised Land. He feels completely inadequate for the task. He responds to God, asking, "Who am I that I should do this?" It is the voice of shame in Moses' soul. Shame is a head-down posture. If you put your head down to your chest, and you are in a room full of people, the only person you will see is yourself. And you will have a limited view of yourself! That's what shame does: it makes life too much about us. The problem with this approach is the more you make it about you, the more you are bound by your own limitations. You can only accomplish what you can accomplish with your abilities, competencies, and resources.

When Moses asked, "Who am I?" God responded, "I will be with you." That's the key lesson in Moses' life. What Moses discovered is essential for everyone who wants to accomplish something beyond human ability. *The one irrepressible need of our lives is for the presence of God.* God has no limits; if we are going to accomplish more than humans can accomplish, we need God. Moses, to his credit, so internalizes this lesson that for the rest of his life he is on a relentless pursuit of the face of God. He is passionately pursuing God's presence. The story of Moses is not a story of prayer; it is a story of intimacy. He sought God's face.

God never gives us an assignment that we can accomplish without Him. If we limit ourselves to what only we can do with our gifts, abilities, resources, and efforts, we will never see what God can do; we will only see what we can do. God gives us assignments that are impossible to accomplish with our abilities so that we will be forced to learn how to develop spiritual authority and rely on His presence.

Listen: the Kingdom of God is the central message of Jesus. It isn't complicated. When Jesus shows up, the Kingdom comes. When we show up, nothing happens. Jesus said, "Apart from me, you can do nothing." That's what happens when I show up: nothing. I need to be so marked by Jesus' presence that when I show up, Jesus shows up and the Kingdom comes. If when I show up the Kingdom doesn't come, it is because I am carrying too little of the presence of Jesus to be a threat to hell.

I can relate to Moses; that was exactly how I felt. God had given me an impossible assignment, and I wasn't able to lead people where God was clearly calling me to take them. And no matter how much leadership competency I acquired, I knew the goal was still going to be beyond me. I too had shame packed away in the suitcase of my soul. There were all kinds of reasons for the shame in my suitcase, just like there were many reasons for Moses' shame. Some early childhood wounding, separation anxiety, mixed with some bullying, and other factors thrown in for good measure.

When shame afflicts the soul, the mind works overtime to compensate, to question, to figure it out. Sometimes our minds are tormented with self-doubt. Other times we move toward grandiosity where we compare ourselves with others and imagine ourselves—or even fantasize about ourselves—in grandiose ways, all the while trying to bolster our identity, which is damaged by shame. We see ourselves in bigger-than-life ways to compensate for our inner sense of inadequacy and shame. Some people resort to power, control, and anger. Others struggle with addiction as they seek to mask the pain of shame in their souls. Sometimes we just withdraw, feel depressed, and give up. *Who am I?* We feel a need to prove ourselves, and if we can't prove ourselves, then we feel depressed. *Do I have what it takes?* This is the fundamental question of a person afflicted with shame. It is the question Moses was immediately drawn to in his conversation with God when faced with his daunting assignment. It was the question I faced as I wrestled with the call on my life to fight for revival.

The Need for God's Presence

That is one of the fundamental problems of leadership in the church today. We are making it way too much about us: too much about our gifts, our talents, our capabilities, our plans, our programs, our strategies, our resources, our competencies, and our opinions. If you are going to accomplish the impossible, you need God. Only God has unlimited resources; only God has infinite wisdom. Only God has unstoppable power; only God can do the impossible. God gives you an assignment bigger than yourself so that you will begin to make it all about Him.

The key to accomplishing the impossible is the presence of God. This is the key that begins to unlock a different leadership that is more biblical, less businesslike, more God-centered, less me-centered, more about His authority, and less about our human ability to make something happen. We need God's presence to accomplish God's assignment. When you have a God-only-possible assignment, the one indispensable need of your life is the presence of God.

If we are going to help other people toward freedom, wholeness, and fullness in the life of Christ, we are going to have to do it by the power and presence of the Spirit. Not on our ability. Not on our capacity. We cannot change the human heart, heal the human soul, or free a human locked in bondage. We need God. Just like Moses. If God shows up, life change will result. If we show up, not much will happen.

Have you ever noticed that at beginning of both great redemptive movements of God, the Lord appears as a fire that doesn't consume anything? Here in the Moses story, God appears in a burning bush, but the bush does not get consumed. In the book of Acts when the Spirit is poured out on Pentecost, God appears as tongues of fire, but nothing is consumed. Why does God appear as a fire that consumes nothing? It is at least in part because He is showing us that He doesn't need any fuel. He is the God who is self-sufficient, self-sustaining. The rest of us have needs; not God. We need Him. We need God's presence to accomplish God's kingdom assignments. This is why coming to the end of ourselves is so important. That unholy discontent, the disappointment and discouragement, led me to realize that I couldn't do it. I needed God. Moses was in that place also.

It is the presence of God that changes and empowers us. It is the presence of God that enables us to change the spiritual atmosphere over a family, a church, a town, a city, a region. It is the presence of God that makes all the difference that we cannot make on our own, even with all our best efforts. *The one irrepressible need of our life is the presence of God.* "I will be with you." In essence, God is saying to Moses: "I know you feel inadequate. I know you feel like you don't have what it takes to accomplish this impossible assignment. But I will be with you. And that is enough."

Face to Face

Moses pursues God's presence; He seeks God's face. Later on, a phrase appears in Exodus that is like an epitaph for Moses' life: "The Lord would speak to Moses face to face, as one speaks to a friend" (Exodus 33:11). This is the man who hid his face from God at his first God-sighting; now he has become a *face-to-face friend of God.* He has learned that he needs God above all things, and he is pressing in and pressing through to that one end.

This is the key to spiritual leadership marked by spiritual authority. We must develop intimacy; we must become face-to-face friends with God. We must be marked by the presence of God so that when we show up, Jesus shows up, and the Kingdom comes.

I had always prayed. I decided early in ministry that I would prioritize my time with God. I was committed to spending time with Him, and I was disciplined about that goal. But much of prayer was about seeking God's hands, not seeking God's face. I prayed for God to give me wisdom, I prayed for help, I prayed for healing for people, I prayed for anointing. I prayed, "God give me this. Help me here. Give me wisdom. Heal this one. Provide for this." Most of my prayers were characterized by seeking God's hands. When I studied Moses, it lit a fire under me to be marked by the presence of God and become a man of intimacy with God, not merely a man of prayer. I pursued God with new vigor and passion; I coveted His presence like never before.

A Hand Upon the Throne

There is a famous scene in Moses' life in Exodus 17. It is the scene in which Joshua is leading the Israelites into battle against the Amalekites. While Joshua is fighting in the valley below, Moses climbs to the top of a hill. "As long as Moses held up his hands, the Israelites were winning, but whenever he lowered his hands, the Amalekites were winning" (Exodus 17:11).

Moses held up his hands, with the help of Aaron and Hur, and the victory came. The Amalekites were focused on Joshua and the army; they had no idea the real battle was being fought in the heavenlies on a hill by an old man in a toga. Sadly, we are too often like them. We often focus our attention on the earthly battles and get distracted from spiritual leadership assignments necessary for victory. At the end of the battle Moses writes down a critical phrase to summarize what happened. The ESV translates it this way: "A hand upon the throne of the Lord" (Exodus 17:16).

A hand upon the throne of the Lord: this is spiritual leadership. It isn't about human capability, human resources, human ingenuity, or our best human effort. This is spiritual authority. *Spiritual authority is the capacity to touch Heaven and change the outcomes of Earth.* It is the capacity to invite the presence of God to intervene into human impossibilities. This isn't mere human vision, strategy, or good execution. All those things are necessary, but in the end they can only produce what humans can produce with their best effort. If we are going to see the things only God can do, if we want to take on God-given assignments and see them through, then we must be spiritual leaders who exercise spiritual authority. We must develop a face-to-face intimacy with God that allows us to touch Heaven and change Earth. We need to press so deeply into His presence that we bring the weight of His presence to bear upon our problems and bring God's victory to our impossibilities.

When we show up in the public place and God shows up with us because we have been marked by His presence in the private place, we will begin to see more of what God can do. We must walk with such sensitivity to God's presence and God's voice that we carry God's presence into our God-given assignments. If we are to become spiritual leaders with spiritual authority, who lead people to authentic life change, we are going to have to become intimate friends with God. Apart from Him we can do nothing.

Don't miss this vital point: the story of Moses isn't a story of prayer; it is a story of intimacy. It isn't a story about seeking God's hands; it is a story about seeking God's face. It isn't a story about maximizing human capacity; it's a story about carrying the presence of God to confront our impossibilities. It isn't a story about human leadership competencies; it is a story about spiritual authority. I prayed, but not often enough like that. Too often I sought His help, not His presence. I pursued

His intervention, not intimacy with Him at the level I needed. I pursued God for results because I really believed I couldn't do anything apart from Him. But spiritual authority is birthed in intimacy with God, not in pursuit of God's power or favor or blessings or answers to our prayers.

When I learned this lesson from Moses, I realized I needed to make the presence of God my number one priority. Not ministry. Not fruit. Not power. Not help. Not wisdom. Not answers to prayer. Not His hands. *His face.* I need God. The one irrepressible need of my life is for the presence of God. If I am ever going to lay a hand upon the throne, if I am going to touch Heaven and change the outcomes on Earth, I must become a face-to-face friend with God. This is the ground upon which spiritual authority emerges.

And like Moses, for many of us the thing that prevents us from this level of intimacy with God is the stuff we are carrying around in the suitcase of our souls. Things like shame. As I read Moses' story and saw his impact of shame, I realized I was still carrying shame in my suitcase as well. It is most frequently our soul issues that keep us from our next level of intimacy with God.

Spiritual authority is rooted in identity, expanded in intimacy, and activated by faith. I take a deep look at that one sentence in my book *Spiritual Authority.* Spiritual authority is developmental, and developing intimacy with God is fundamental to developing authority.

How do we grow deep intimacy with God like Moses? How do we develop a face-to-face friendship with God? I want to touch on a few themes, and we will come back to this theme later in this book.

Let's start with spiritual rhythm.

If we are going to develop a deep intimacy with Jesus, we must develop a healthy spiritual rhythm. Depth cannot happen with haphazard spiritual practices. You cannot cultivate a beautiful garden if you are unwilling to water, weed, and do the necessary work of gardening. It's the same with your soul. If you are going to grow deep with Jesus, you are going to have to spend time with Jesus, and you will have to do the necessary soul work. Your spiritual rhythm consists of the spiritual practices you engage in when you spend time with Jesus: Bible reading, confession, silence, solitude, prayer, fasting, worship, and more. A healthy rhythm is what you need to stay connected to Jesus, like the branch abiding in the vine (John 15). It is the set of spiritual practices you must engage in so that you are growing deeper in intimacy and sustaining a healthy connection to the very source of life.

Here is the key question I have to ask myself about my spiritual rhythm: What do I need to do on a daily, weekly, monthly, and yearly basis to abide in Jesus and continue to grow deeper with Him in intimacy?

One of the problems, of course, is that what you do today will not always work for you tomorrow. We must adjust our rhythm on a regular basis. I am a very disciplined person, and there is an advantage to regular times set apart to be with God. But there is also a danger to our spiritual rhythm: *when our routine becomes a rut, we become religious.* We all tend to fall prey to this trap. For example, we often read the Bible as part of our rhythm. But all of us have experienced this: we have read two chapters in the Word when, suddenly, we realize we have no idea what we have been reading because our mind has been on something else. We are doing the right thing, but we are not abiding. We are going through the motions, but we are not connecting deeply with God. Our practice has become a rut. We have to do the right thing with the right attitude, or we will become more religious and less intimate. It isn't just about the spiritual practices (like Bible reading), it is about the condition of the heart in the practice.

Let's talk about some key principles to a healthy abiding rhythm.

First, we have to develop a consistent practice of meeting alone with God. We need to practice spiritual disciplines that connect us to God in ever deepening ways. When I began developing time alone with God, I started with two disciplines: Bible reading and prayer. Those were the only disciplines I knew or heard people talk about in my church. I started by reading the Bible through in a year—that takes reading three to four chapters every day. That was a good place to start because it helped me develop a consistent time alone with God, and it also familiarized me with the Bible. My prayer time mostly consisted of three things: thanksgiving, intercession (praying for others), and petition (praying for my own needs), with confession as often as I needed. Again, this was a low-level entry point; it couldn't take me very deep, but I did develop the consistent habit of meeting alone with God. And let me be clear: we can't get close to God without that. We must make meeting with the Lord a priority in our calendar.

I realized that if I was going to go deeper with God, I was going to have to expand beyond the disciplines of Bible reading and prayer. This would help me seek God's hands, but it was not going to take me into a face-to-face relationship with God.

We have to discover which disciplines we need to engage in on a regular basis to connect our heart deeply to God. There are many books on spiritual disciplines. I think Richard Foster's book *Celebration of Discipline* is an excellent resource to introduce the different spiritual practices. I read Foster's book in seminary more than thirty years ago as part of the class we had to engage in regarding all of the spiritual disciplines. I learned about and practiced spiritual disciplines I had never been introduced to at that point in my life. It was extremely helpful to me. It expanded my spiritual toolbox.

Having a host of disciplines at our disposal is like tackling a home project with a full toolbox. By contrast, if all you have is a hammer, you aren't going to get too far on home improvement projects! There are different seasons in life that will require you to engage with different spiritual tools to get you to a new level with God.

When I was in seminary, I decided I would meet alone with God on a regular basis. I vowed to make my time with God a nonnegotiable appointment in my daily calendar. When I started out in ministry, as more people sought me for appointments, I realized that sheer busyness threatened to snuff out my spiritual vitality. If I always said yes to people, I would end up saying no to God. So I put God in my appointment book. If someone asked me for an appointment in my God-space, I said, "No. I can't meet then. I already have an appointment." God got top billing, number one priority.

Jesus said, "I am the vine; you are the branches. If you remain in me and I in you, you will bear much fruit; apart from me you can do nothing" (John 15:5). The command is to abide. Fruit-bearing is a by-product. But too often we live our lives as though the command is to bear fruit. We run around and fill our calendars with people appointments, with meetings, and we attempt to make something happen. Often, we do this to meet some inner need to feel significant, important, or needed. But if our ministry is not motivated by His voice and marked by His presence, we will bear little fruit and live spiritually anemic, depleted lives. I realized that if I was going to see deep life change, it would only happen if I was in an intimate, face-to-face, abiding relationship with Jesus that left me marked by His presence. If Jesus shows up, lives are changed. I want to go deep with Jesus so that, when I show up, I am so saturated with Jesus' presence that He appears at the meeting and touches people's lives.

As a young leader, this decision to prioritize my daily meeting with God was the first critical decision I made regarding my ongoing spiritual vitality. *The second key decision I made was to do whatever I needed to maintain that vital union with God.* The reality is that there are many things in life that threaten to rob us of our spiritual health, and if we are not careful to guard our spiritual fervor, our passion for Jesus will wane. I resolved to monitor my relationship with God so that when something was "off" in my soul, I would deal with it immediately, no matter what. I committed to stay connected with Jesus and deal with all obstructions to my spiritual well-being; therefore, I guarded my heart from all the sin, apathy, pain, heartache, disappointment, doubt, offenses, and other soul-robbing issues that threatened my spiritual life in Christ.

This commitment meant that I would change spiritual disciplines as needed to avoid getting caught in a spiritual rut. It meant that I would get up in the middle of the night, if necessary, to do business with God and remove any blocks that were impairing my spiritual vitality. It meant I would say yes to God whatever He asked, whenever He asked. If He wanted to investigate the suitcase of my soul and remove something that was interfering with my intimacy with Him, I would say yes. It meant I would give Him whatever amount of time was needed to stay intimately connected: yes to regular spiritual retreats, yes to middle of the night wake-up calls from God. When I feel there is something amiss in my soul, it has been my lifelong practice to clear a block of time in my schedule, get alone with God, and linger with Him and do whatever it takes to remove that hindrance. If, in fact, I can do nothing apart from Jesus, I must keep the flow of the Spirit unencumbered in my life. I am committed to keeping my heart in alignment with God.

This was the second key decision: do whatever it takes to stay in vital union with Jesus. If you aren't abiding, you are just busy, not fruitful.

My time with God and this intimate connection were like spiritual air to my spiritual life in Christ; if I don't breathe air physically, I will die. If I don't breathe the spiritual air of God's presence, I will be spiritually anemic. My soul will wither. Like a branch disconnected from the vine, I will become a lifeless branch that bears no fruit. These two life-giving decisions have marked me, and I invite you to make the same commitments to God: (1) Make time with God your number one, nonnegotiable priority. Put it on your calendar. (2) Commit to God that you will do whatever you need to stay vitally connected to Jesus. These two decisions have helped ensure that I am doing the right spiritual practices for the right reasons.

This is where you have to begin. Is Jesus your first love? Are you spending adequate time alone with God to abide in Him? Is your time with God a nonnegotiable in your life? Are you saying yes to people so much that it is causing you to say no to God? Are you willing to do whatever it takes to keep vitally connected to Jesus? When you sense some block in your relationship with God, are you committed to carving out as much time as needed to get right with God again? Are you carrying more evidence of His presence in your life today than three years ago? Do you need to make any changes to your current spiritual practices? Take time to reflect and make the changes you need.

Second, our attitude has to be about attending to His presence. When we engage in a spiritual practice, like Bible reading, our heart needs to be set on fully attending to His presence in that activity. Sometimes we do our spiritual disciplines out of a sense of duty. If you are like me, you often form little to-do lists. We have to call Jim, respond to our emails, make various appointments, mow the lawn, vacuum the house, change the sheets, read our Bible, pray . . . . Sometimes the spiritual practices are just another item on our to-do list. These are the practices that "good Christians do." But the Pharisees did those things, and they killed Jesus. It isn't merely about doing these spiritual things; it is about doing these things with the right attitude. We have to attend to His presence. We aren't reading the Bible for information only; we don't want to read the Bible just because we are supposed to. Our motivation must be intimacy with God.

The purpose of reading the Bible isn't to know the Bible; the purpose of reading the Bible is to encounter the Living God. So when I read the Bible, I want to attend to His presence in the Word. This makes the Word a life-giving pathway. Second Timothy 3:16 says, "All Scripture is God-breathed." I don't think Paul meant simply that when the authors of the Bible penned the words of Scripture they were inspired by the Holy Spirit, and it was infallible in its original writing. Don't get me wrong: I believe both those things to be true. But I don't think that is what Paul meant. I think Paul meant that every time we pick up this holy writ called Scripture, we are one Holy Spirit breath away from a fresh encounter with the Living God. When we read Scripture, the Spirit is illuminating certain passages; He is highlighting certain words and phrases. He is making God known to us; He is personalizing that passage to us. He is revealing Himself to us. The Spirit is stirring within us, and God is meeting us in the text. So when I come to Scripture, I want to find those places where the Spirit is breathing on the text for me—where He is making the Scripture real and alive in that moment. I want to meet God in the act of Scripture reading.

The problem is I can get caught in a rut. When I first started reading the Bible, I was young. When I was a young teen, the youth leaders challenged us to read the Bible. I was in junior high school when I first started reading sections of

Scripture. Then when I was 16, our senior pastor challenged our church to read the Bible through in a year. So I read three to four chapters a day to meet that goal. That was a good and useful practice, and I learned a lot. But it wasn't always the best way for me to connect deeply to the heart of the Father through the Word. I often blew past the breath of God in the text because I had to get my three to four chapters done. My goal was to read the Bible through in a year; my goal wasn't to encounter the Living God. The Spirit stirred, but I was too intent on achieving my reading goal. We must have the right goal, and the right attitude, when we sit down to engage in our spiritual practices.

I must keep my time with God fresh and not allow it to become stale. Change often holds the master key; I need to change my approach if I am going to go deeper with God. I can't keep doing the same thing and not have it become a rut. So sometimes I read the Bible, sometimes I study Scripture. When the Lord challenged me to study Moses, saying that he holds the key, I studied the life of Moses. I didn't read it. I *dug in deep* to figure out the key to Moses' life that the Lord wanted to reveal to me. I scoured the pages of the text for the secrets God was trying to show me, and the Spirit breathed on the text. This changed my life. It caused me to seek God's face with new vigor, passion, intentionality, and consistency.

Sometimes I meditate on Scripture. I take a small portion and meditate on it, linger with it, and wait for the Lord to reveal Himself to me. I have meditated on a singular passage for months at a time because the Spirit was still breathing on it for that long. This is where I could find the face of God—in the breath of God. For example, I meditated on Psalm 23 for a year. I was reading it one day and the Spirit breathed on verse 4: "He restores my soul." That phrase stirred deep within me, and I knew the Spirit had some fresh revelation, some fresh encounter for me in those words. I was at the monastery when

I first meditated on it, and I heard the Lord say, "My presence comes in many forms. There is my healing presence, my empowering presence, my loving presence. But what you need is my restorative presence." The Lord went on to show me that His restorative presence was found in silence and solitude. Thus, the pastoral imagery in the Psalm: lying down in green pastures, being led beside quiet waters. The Lord wasn't trying to teach me a lesson and increase my knowledge; the Lord was trying to shepherd my soul into His rest. This is what it looks like to seek God's face. I lingered with Psalm 23 for an entire year and brought myself under the restorative shepherding care of God. I meditated on it, mused over it, reflected upon it, and prayed over it. For many months I sat with that phrase in my mind and on my heart: "He restores my soul." I would wait in silence and His restorative presence came. Day by day. And the Spirit met me and changed me. The purpose of meditating on Psalm 23 wasn't to understand it but to *experience* God's shepherding presence in the text. The Lord became my shepherd in a whole new way because of that year. I had been on the front lines of battle for revival and my soul was tattered and torn, but under His shepherding care, He restored my soul.

Sometimes I pray the Scripture. The easiest place to begin is the Psalms. They are a prayer book, and I frequently pray the Psalms back to the Lord in my own words. I often pray the Psalms according to the day of the week. So, as I write, today is the 15th. Therefore, today, I would pray Psalm 15, 45, 75, 105, and 135. I pray the words that touch my heart, the words that resonate with my life circumstances. I pray back to God in my own words the things that are connecting with my life in the moment. This year I have started praying the letters of Paul over my family every day. I read one chapter in one of the New Testament epistles, and then I pray that over my life and the life of my family. It has been a rich practice, and I have met God in new ways.

Here is the point: We have to attend to His presence in the spiritual practices we engage in, and that means we have to keep it fresh. We have to do new things to stay connected and go deeper, to avoid the ruts of religion.

I do this in worship as well. Worship has been a vital pathway for me to seek the face of God. But I need fresh worship songs that move my soul if I am going to connect with God in worship. There is something known as the heuristic principle. Simply stated: when we sing a song about thirty times, the song no longer moves our hearts, and we can begin to sing the song while we think about something else. Again: the routine can easily become a rut. You have had this happen to you while singing a familiar worship song in church. You're thinking about lunch, about an appointment, about a conversation that needs to happen. The song isn't touching your heart and connecting you to the Father. This is why I have to change music often. When I can't find fresh music that moves my heart, I find new ways to worship because worship is a vital discipline that helps me fix my eyes on Jesus and draw near to Him.

In 2020 I leaned into thanksgiving often. It was a tough year, the year COVID-19 was introduced to us all. I wrote in my book, *Calm in the Storm,* that COVID is not just a killer, it is a thief, and the reality is that it has stolen way more than it has killed. For example, it robbed me of much human connection. I wasn't able to see my mom and dad for nearly a year because my dad is high risk. I couldn't do in-person conferences for seven months because of COVID restrictions. We started doing livestream conferences, but I was literally speaking to the back of my phone; it was a soul-sucking activity! On top of the loss of human connection, there were financial ramifications for us. Most of our income comes from conferences, and as they were all canceled, we had to find new ways of generating revenue to support our family. Plus, with no conferences, book sales were much lower—another large financial impact. Before COVID I was distributing 350 *Soul Care* books per week through local bookstores and Amazon (not counting what I sold at in-person conferences). After COVID hit, the sales dropped to less than 10 percent of that: thirty per week. They have recovered, but not to the level they were.

It also robbed me of much of the joy of ministry: the human touch, the laughter, the tears, the stories of life change, and seeing the power of God visit his people. On top of all of that, during this season there has been a great deal of racial tension, political division, and intensified anger in our country. It has been unsettling. I was sitting with a group of friends one day in my backyard and everyone was talking about all the problems, hostility, and negativity. I left the night feeling depressed. I got alone with the Lord and said, "I can't keep doing this. This negativity is wearing me out. It is weighing me down." I heard the Lord say, "Take Paul literally." Immediately, two passages from Paul came to mind: Ephesians 5 and 1 Thessalonians 5.

In Ephesians 5:15-20, Paul says, "Be very careful, then, how you live—not as unwise but as wise, making the most of every opportunity, because the days are evil. Therefore do not be foolish, but understand what the Lord's will is. Do not get drunk on wine, which leads to debauchery. Instead, be filled with the Spirit, speaking to one another with psalms, hymns and songs from the Spirit. Sing and make music from your heart to the Lord, *always giving thanks to God the Father for everything*, in the name of our Lord Jesus Christ" (emphasis mine).

In 1 Thessalonians 5:16-18, Paul says, "Rejoice always, pray continually, *give thanks in all circumstances*, for this is God's will for you in Christ Jesus" (emphasis mine).

I wrestled with what the Spirit was saying to me: "Take Paul literally." Give thanks for *everything* . . . always. Give thanks *in all circumstances.* So, in 2020, I did what God challenged me to do. I started giving God thanks for everything and in all circumstances: for the political division, for COVID, for the isolation, that racism was being exposed in our country, for Trump, for the elections, for Biden, and on and on. As I gave thanks for everything, and in all circumstances, it shifted something in me. It took my eyes off the circumstances, off of me, off of the negativity, and put my eyes on God. I don't think we can make the most of every opportunity when the days are evil *unless our eyes are on God.* When the days are evil, we must paint God back into the picture or we will lose hope and our light will be dimmed. Our circumstances often cause us to put our eyes on ourselves. When our eyes are on us, we make it too much about ourselves and can't see God's perspective, or His presence, amid all the darkness. Thanksgiving *in* all things and *for* all things allows us to attend to God's presence in the darkness once more. It helps us see the face of God.

No matter what you do as a spiritual discipline—Bible reading, worship, silence, solitude, prayer, or thanksgiving—attend to His presence as you do it. Don't just do the right spiritual practices, do them with the right heart.

Third, when you plateau, adjust your rhythm. As we walk with Jesus there will be hills and valleys and places where we feel weary, stuck, and plateaued. Often when we are plateaued, we need to adjust our spiritual rhythm. Our current mix of daily, weekly, monthly, and yearly practices is no longer working for us, and we need to tweak our rhythm to get unstuck. When I get stuck, I go to the Lord, acknowledge that I am stuck, and ask him what to do. Theology 101: God is smart, and He knows stuff we don't know.

I examine my heart because I want to make sure there is nothing hindering my connection with Jesus. Sometimes we are stuck or plateaued because there are issues that need to be addressed and corrected. But not uncommonly, I discover that the problem is with my spiritual rhythm: it has simply become a tired rhythm. So I seek the Lord for how to adjust it: what should I change? What should I do differently?

Often the Lord calls me to sacrifice. Sacrifice has a way of getting me unstuck like perhaps nothing else. Sometimes He asks me to pray and fast for a few days or a week; that will usually help me to breakthrough. Sometimes He asks me to get up in the middle of the night and pray; He asks me to sacrifice sleep. Sometimes He asks me to get alone with Him for a day, to sacrifice time, to go on a spiritual retreat. These acts of sacrifice are often the very thing I need to get moving again, to lead me into a fresh encounter with Jesus. They help me seek the face of God with renewed passion.

At other times, the Lord just knows that I need to adjust my daily rhythm. My routine has become a rut. Adding thanks for everything and in everything in 2020 helped me navigate through the sadness and weightiness of that season. The Lord always knows. So ask Him what to do when you find yourself at a plateau.

Let me provide an example. Please hear me: this is descriptive, not prescriptive. I am merely describing my rhythm as it exists right now; I am not telling you this is what you should do. You need to figure that out with God. Everyone is different, and everyone has a different calling. You need to live your life, not mine. But I give this as an example so you can apply parallel learning.

Daily: Every day I get alone with God. At least three to four times per week I spend a longer block of time alone with God, at least two hours. Some days, especially when I am doing conferences, I might only spend about half an hour with the Lord. I usually start with some journaling. I have a prayer journal and I record almost everything in that space with God. I write out most of my prayers. I start nearly all my prayer times by talking to the Lord about my to-do list for the day. The reason I do this is because if I don't think about it, process it, and talk to God about it, it can easily distract me from God's presence. I will start thinking about my agenda, conversations I must have, emails I must return, and so on. So I start with praying through my daily agenda, and I bring my day before the Lord.

Nearly every day, I also process my emotions with God: the good and the bad. I process my angst, fear, anger, hurt, sadness: any presenting negative emotions. I also process the good emotions: the joy, victories, peace, love, the things for which I am grateful, and so on. I celebrate the good and process the bad. I want to unpack the negative emotions from the suitcase of my soul. If I don't, they will once again distract me from His presence, and they will occupy space in my soul that limits my capacity for God. Sadly, if I don't process those negative emotions, they will end up accumulating in my soul and become a block between me and God. Unprocessed negative emotions never lead to a healthy soul. Next, I often spend some time reading, meditating, and praying through Scripture. I allow God to move, speak, stir within me as I work through the text. My current plan is to pray through one Psalm, read several chapters in the Bible as I read through it in a year, and meditate on one gospel passage. When this approach becomes stale, I will change it to make it fresh again. I often change translations or read multiple translations at a time as well.

As I write this . . . yesterday we had to put our dog to sleep. She was fourteen years old, had cancer, and her breathing had gotten labored over the last few days. Over the years she was annoying at times, but we all loved her, and we cried together as a family when she died. But I was not able to be there with the family when they took her to the vet to have her put to sleep because I had a livestream training event that had been scheduled months earlier. Everyone else in the family went with Tootsie to say goodbye and stayed with her as the doctor gave her the injection and she passed. Today, as I got up and spent time with Jesus, I processed my emotions. I cried some for the dog, I cried some for my family, and I cried because I didn't get to say goodbye and be there for her last moments. But I cried most for the fact that I miss many of life's important moments because of my calling. There are times when I am traveling and a family event happens, and I cannot be there. I miss key moments in life, and it saddens me deeply to miss them. The Lord brought to my mind this Scripture: "Everyone who has left houses or brothers or sisters or father or mother or wife or children or fields for my sake will receive a hundred times as much and will inherit eternal life" (Matthew 19:29). I processed my sadness and allowed the words of Jesus and the Spirit's presence to comfort me. This is why I process my emotions every day. I don't always have something sad to process, but whatever is there, I process it. I want to travel light; I want to keep my suitcase as empty as possible so there is more room in my soul to experience God's presence and hear God's voice without all the static of unprocessed emotional pain, turmoil, or distraction.

If we are going to carry God's presence into our divine assignments, we must empty the suitcase of our souls. Processing in my prayer time is vital to experiencing the fullness of Christ in my soul.

Weekly: Usually one day per week I fast breakfast and lunch. I do a twenty-four-hour fast. So, for example, I don't eat from dinner on Wednesday night until dinner on Thursday night. Jesus said to his disciples, "When you fast . . . " Not if you fast. As I mentioned in the last section, three to four times per week I try to spend a longer block of time with God.

Monthly: I take one day per month for a spiritual retreat. This is a day I spend alone with God. I used to go to the monastery every other month for a retreat, but when God called me to travel more, I couldn't take any more time away from home, so I had to adjust my retreat practices. I live on a lake, so now, one day per month, I sit on my porch, look over my lake, and spend a day alone with God. It is a rich time for me. I do have to confess: I miss the monastery. There are definitely deep places I cannot get to with God without spiritual retreats. We will talk about this topic more later in the book.

Yearly: I still try to get to the monastery a few days every year. I also spend one month per year writing. Typically, during that month, I fast breakfast and lunch on the days I am writing, then I eat dinner with the family at night. I start each day with an extended block time with God, about three hours. Then I ride my bike 15 to 20 miles before spending the afternoon writing. It is a time of refreshing and deep intake of spiritual nourishment. Evenings I spend with the family. I don't do any people appointments, ministry activities, speaking engagements, or conferences during this month. I know not everyone can do this, but not everyone has my calling. I travel 120 days per year on top of my teaching load. This is a necessary part of my spiritual, emotional, and relational intake that allows me to maintain my schedule for the rest of the year. I couldn't sustain my schedule over the long haul without these yearly breaks. And it allows me to fulfill my calling, which is to contend for revival around the world through writing, speaking, and mentoring leaders.

This rhythm allows me to stay connected with Jesus. It keeps me free and full. I sense His presence and His anointing and I hear His voice. I am growing deeper and loving better. So it is working for now, though I am sure I will need to tweak it again before long. That's just the nature of abiding.

Summary: Seeking God's Face

Let me end this section by talking about seeking the face of God. Let me review some of the key practices that have allowed me to do this. Attending to His presence is vital to seeking His face. I have to remind myself, often, to attend to God's presence; it is easy to fall into the religious rut of "doing devotions." I want to attend to His presence when I am in the Word, when I worship, when I am in silence before the Lord, and when I pray. Whatever spiritual practice I engage in, this is the heart attitude I want to assume.

I have mentioned blocks of times alone with God and spiritual retreats. Nothing has helped me go deeper in intimacy with God like consistent block times alone with Him and the regular practice of going on spiritual retreats. There are places of depth I cannot get to without a longer period of time to dwell in His presence. There are breakthroughs in intimacy I cannot access without retreats. There are places and spaces of spiritual weightiness that I simply cannot get to with my daily devotional practices.

One last thing. If we are going to seek God's face, we must feed our desire for His presence. We will never rise above our level of longing for God. It is our longing for God that motivates us to pursue Him. It is our longing that moves us to pay the price. When my longing wanes, my intimacy stagnates. So I must intentionally feed my spiritual hunger. I read books that trigger desire in my soul for God. I spend time with people who are on fire for Jesus, and being with them stimulates spiritual thirst in my soul for new depths. But probably the thing that is most helpful for me to ignite longing is sacrifice. There are few things that trigger my longing for God like a sacrificial act. My three favorite acts of sacrificial pursuit of God are fasting (sacrifice of food), night watch (sacrifice of sleep), and spiritual retreats (sacrifice of time). When I feel plateaued, apathetic, that my passion is low, or that my desire to pursue God is waning, I turn to sacrifice. I go on a fast, I do a night watch, or I take a spiritual retreat. The result? The fire is reignited. We must keep the fire burning or our pursuit of God's face will surely be severely impaired.

Take some time with God to evaluate your rhythm. Important questions: is your current rhythm working? Are you deeply connected to the heart of God? Are you hearing God's voice regularly in your life? Are you sensing God's love consistently? Are you growing in deeper intimacy with Him? Are you becoming more like Him? Is Jesus your first love? Are you loving others more tenderly and patiently, like Jesus? Are you speaking the truth in love with courage? Does your soul feel peaceful, free, full, and light? Are you running the race these days unhindered? If you can see that you are growing deeper in intimacy and Christlike maturity, and you are representing Jesus well to those around you (full of truth and full of grace), then your rhythm is probably working for you right now. Periodically, you will need to evaluate it and adjust it.

If you aren't in a season of life where your rhythm is working, if you are feeling plateaued, if you aren't growing deeper in intimacy and Christlike maturity, then block out some time with God and ask him: "What do I need to change in my rhythm?" Some of you need to make some changes to get over the hump. Others of you need to reconstruct a healthy rhythm that can allow you to grow. Do whatever you need to stay vitally connected to Jesus. It's worth it!

Chapter 2

A HEALTHY LEADER

It takes two healthy people to have a healthy relationship. If, on a scale of 1 to 10, you are a 5 (in terms of your emotional and spiritual health), the healthiest relationship you can ever have is a 5. Water seeks its own level. You marry to the level of your brokenness. People who are 5s don't marry 8s. If you want to have a healthier relationship with others, there is only one path to get there: you must change. Even if your spouse refuses to change, if you become healthier, you will have healthier interactions with the other person. You won't grow deeper in intimacy with them if they refuse to mature, but you will respond in a healthier way.

When my wife no longer liked me, I couldn't ignore it. There was brokenness in our souls that was keeping us from having a healthy relationship, and unless we confronted it, we were going to be stuck in a very unsatisfying relationship. We might not have made it in the marriage. At best, we would have survived with lots of tension, shallowness, loneliness, and pain. But if we wanted to thrive in our relationship, we had to change and become healthier people.

It wasn't just my marriage that was at stake. It takes a healthy leader to lead a healthy church. Eventually the brokenness would have adversely impacted the church. Too often I have seen churches that were growing because a leader was gifted and could attract a crowd, but the leader had not dealt with the issues of his or her own soul, and the atmosphere became toxic. I've seen churches disintegrate due to the dysfunction of a leader. We have to become healthy people if we are going to create a healthy environment or influence others in a healthy way.

When Jesus sent out the disciples he said to them, "Freely you have received, freely give." You can't give what you don't have. You only have authority over that which you walk in victory. When you have lived into a truth, *then* you have authority over that truth, and when you minister in that area you create an atmosphere of breakthrough for others.

> You only have authority over that which you walk in victory.

If you are going to be a Soul Care practitioner, you have to live in freedom or you can't create an atmosphere where others can get free.

Jen and I often laugh that I am doing Soul Care ministry. It wasn't at all the way I started ministry, nor is it a natural inclination for me. I am not pastoral, nor am I a counselor. I was focused on leadership: becoming a better leader and developing leaders around me. I went to leadership conferences, read leadership books, and sought to equip others in spiritual leadership. I still do a lot of leadership development and mentoring, but when my life changed, I started seeing the authority God had given me in these areas of victory. I was creating atmospheres of breakthrough for those around me.

Let's talk about some key areas we need to work on if we are going to be healthy leaders who can lead others into spiritual and emotional health.

First, we must live into the principles of freedom that I talk about in *Soul Care*. You cannot lead people where you have not been. *Soul Care* isn't a book to be read like a novel, nor is it a conference to be attended over a weekend. These are the principles of freedom that must be lived into and integrated into our daily life. One of the great problems with Western Christianity is that we are a knowledge-based discipleship culture. We even misquote Jesus all the time: "You will know the truth, and the truth will set you free." But that isn't what Jesus taught—at least not in its full and proper context. I have spoken to hundreds of pastors and quoted this and told them it was wrong, and not one of them could tell me the accurate quote. Jesus actually said, "*If* you hold to my teaching, you are really my disciples. *Then* you will know the truth, and the truth will set you free" (John 8:31, 32). Jesus didn't teach knowledge-based discipleship. Jesus taught *obedience*-based discipleship. Jesus was interested in integration; He wanted us to live out the truth.

At the end of the Sermon on the Mount Jesus said, "Therefore everyone who hears these words of mine and puts them into practice is like a wise man who built his house on the rock. The rain came down, the streams rose, and the winds blew and beat against that house; yet it did not fall, because it had its foundation on the rock. But everyone who hears these words of mine and does not put them into practice is like a foolish man who built his house on sand. The rain came down, the streams rose, and the winds blew and beat against that house, and it fell with a great crash" (Matthew 7:24-27). We cannot just know the truth; we cannot simply declare the truth. *Knowledge without obedience results in a diseased soul.* Declaration without integration leads to disintegration in the soul.

When I started doing Soul Care Conferences, pastors would often approach me and say, "Can I have the PowerPoints? I want to go home and teach it this weekend." My answer: No. You will just be passing on knowledge, and you may end up inoculating them to the authentic. If you teach it without living into it, you will pass on knowledge that won't lead people to victorious living. We have far too much of that in the church already.

In 1 John 1:6 the Apostle John writes, "If we claim to have fellowship with him and yet walk in the darkness, we lie and do not live out the truth." John isn't saying we don't know the truth. He isn't saying you couldn't pass a theology test. He isn't saying that you don't know the right answers about who God is, about what God wants. He is saying that you aren't living it out in your life. This lack of integration leads to darkness in your soul and a powerless life. You cannot live in darkness without disease in your soul.

The principles I teach in *Soul Care* are principles of freedom in Scripture that we need to integrate into our daily lives. If you obey Jesus' teaching, your life will work out better and you will have more freedom. The principles in *Soul Care* are like the inviolable principles of the soul; they are like the laws of nature. If you violate the law of gravity, there will be a consequence. You jump off a twenty-story building, you are going to have a bad outcome. And yet these inviolable laws of the soul are as real as the laws of gravity. The commands of God are laws of the universe that guide our soul into a healthy state of being. If you violate them, they will do damage to your soul. Paul says we reap what we sow (Galatians 6).

Too often we focus on behavioral change and sin management, but true life change begins with the heart. In *Soul Care*, I wrote, "Growing up is a hard business, and it is a heart business." And: "You cannot fix the problems of the soul by a change of behavior only." As we live out these principles of freedom, our lives change. Sure, behaviors are cleaned up along the way, but it isn't a case of external change only. Our heart is coming into alignment with God as we surrender to Him. Jesus said to the Pharisees: "You Pharisees clean the outside of the cup and dish, but inside you are full of greed and wickedness. You foolish people! Did not the one who made the outside make the inside also? But now as for what is inside you—be generous to the poor, and everything will be clean for you. Woe to you Pharisees, because you give God a tenth of your mint, rue, and all other kinds of garden herbs, but you neglect justice and the love of God. You should have practiced the latter without leaving the former undone" (Luke 11:39-42).

The first principle of Soul Care is about our identity. We have to overcome the lies we believe about ourselves. We will never live to our potential if we believe things about ourselves that the Father does not believe about us. Lots of people know who they are in Christ; they can quote the verses and make declarations about their identity, but they are still living like unloved people. James 2:17 says, "Faith by itself, if it is not accompanied by action, is dead." Unless we integrate our identity so that we live like deeply loved children of God, we are just holding onto knowledge without transformation.

Recently I had a week where I took five hits on public spaces. People wrote against me. I was hurt. I long to get to the place where public attacks don't bother me at all, but they still do at times. I have been praying through a chapter of an epistle for much of this year. On this particular day, when the third attack came, I happened to be in 1 Peter 2. Peter talked about how Jesus dealt with insults: he didn't retaliate, he didn't threaten. "Instead, he entrusted himself to him who judges justly" (1 Peter 2:23). That really resonated with me because I suffered a public criticism and there were things said about me that were not true. I processed the hurt with the Lord. And I told Him that I long to get to the place where I no longer feel hurt, when I stop making life so much about me. I long to get to the place where I don't feel insecure or defensive.

The good news is that I did not retaliate. I didn't threaten. I didn't even respond. But I also don't have the level of grace or security in my soul that Jesus manifested. Jesus didn't defend himself, retaliate, or threaten because He had entrusted himself, completely, to Him who judges justly. He had accepted the Father's opinion of Him: "This is my Son, whom I love, with Him I am well pleased." Because Jesus had accepted the Father's opinion of Him, people's opinions didn't sway Him, dissuade Him, or discourage Him. He had fully integrated what the Father said about Him, and He lived as the deeply loved Son of God. That's integration, not merely knowledge. I still have more integration to do. I have been working on it for almost thirty years, but a week like this stirs my emotions and reminds me that I have

> He had fully integrated what the Father said about Him, and He lived as the deeply loved Son of God. That's integration, not merely knowledge.

more work to do. So I asked Jesus to continue to form His love in me so I could love my enemies like He does. It was rich. Deep. Meaningful. And I met Jesus in a powerful way. I gave thanks for criticism and the shaping influence it has on my life when I process it well with Jesus.

Thankfully, I have made progress. Years ago, I would have been hurt; I likely wouldn't have retaliated, but I would have thought about it for days. It would have occupied emotional space in my heart and soul; it would have preoccupied my mind with thoughts, imaginary conversations, and rumblings of anxiety. However, years of integrating my identity in Christ, years of holding onto the Father's opinion about me, allowed me to process and walk through this series of attacks within an hour or so. I would love to be completely free, but I am still in the process of holding to the truth (John 8:31). I am still integrating and learning to act on what the Father says about me. I am learning to live like a deeply loved son of God in all my interactions. I am not there yet, but I am much farther down the road then I used to be.

The second principle of Soul Care is about repentance. Again, it doesn't do me any good to know about living in the light with God and others if I am actually living in the darkness and hanging onto secrets. All the knowledge in the world cannot produce life change. I need to continue to live in the light. Repentance isn't just something I need to do once while at a conference. Repentance is something I need to live into every time I sin. The problem is that so often we are running so fast through life that we miss the conviction of the Holy Spirit. We say something that is insensitive or do something that is selfish, and we fail to confess the offense that God reveals to us. And we now carry unconfessed sin in the suitcase of our soul. So we have to set aside time regularly just to allow the Lord to shine light and get back into alignment with Him. Again, knowledge without integration leads to disintegration.

There have been times when the Lord felt distant to me. When I feel that distance, my regular practice is to set aside a block of time alone with God and go after it. I give God space to shine light into my heart and see if there is anything unconfessed that is hindering me. I mentioned last chapter that the Lord told me to take Paul literally and give thanks in all things and for all things. I was struggling with grumbling. This has been a tough season around the globe because of COVID and its implications. I was spending too much time focused on the negative things: talking about them, thinking about them, grumbling about them. They had hindered the flow of the Spirit in my life, and I needed to repent to experience the fresh flow of the Spirit.

> Knowledge without integration leads to disintegration.

In 1 Corinthians 10, Paul talks about lessons from Israel's history. The Israelites wrestled with idolatry, sexual immorality, testing the Lord (rebellion), and grumbling (1 Corinthians 10:6-10). Grumbling? Really? Everyone grumbles. That doesn't seem to be in the same category as the other three. Idolatry: that violates the number one commandment. Rebellion, the Old Testament says, is as the sin of witchcraft (1 Samuel 15:23). Sexual immorality destroys families, reflects poorly on the Father's faithfulness, and was often intermingled with idolatrous practices as those guilty of this sin strayed morally with people from the surrounding nations that worshiped other gods. These are three really big sins! But grumbling? Why is that such a big deal? Every complaint we utter is ultimately an accusation against the goodness of God. So God called me to repent of grumbling and replace it with thanksgiving. It lifted me out of the spiritual lull I was in. Repentance isn't simply something we have to do occasionally; we need to practice repentance every time we sin, and often we blow past the convictions of the Holy Spirit because we are running too fast in life.

I am not going to go through all the principles of Soul Care to illustrate them for you. The point is clear. We can't just know these things; we must integrate these truths into our daily existence. Are you living them out? I teach a lot of pastors. They know the Bible. They know these truths, but often when I sit down and talk to them, they talk to me about the symptoms of disintegration in their soul, in their relationships, and in their leadership. This is because they haven't really integrated these truths. Too often we listen to someone teach about identity or repentance or forgiveness and we think, *Yes. I'm with you. I know that.* Sure you do. But are you living like a deeply loved child of God in all your interactions? Obedience is the only way to become a person of depth and authority.

When I was in my doctoral work, one day Haddon Robinson, my professor, opened class with a stunning statement: "Gentlemen [there were all men in my class], there are only about fifteen themes in Scripture." Everyone asked the same question: "What are the fifteen themes?" Except me. I had a different question blooming in my heart: "How do you preach to the same church for many years on only fifteen themes?" As I silently asked the Lord that question, I heard His still, small voice deep in my inner being. He said: "There is infinite depth in those fifteen themes. You have to go deep." Depth is about integration, not declaration. It is about obedience, not knowledge. Depth is about living out the truth, not knowing the truth.

Before I move on, let me say one last thing. Don't move past this section and think: *I'm living all of this out. I'm good.* I have been living out these principles for more than thirty years, and I still need to go deeper. Don't stop in the shallow waters of religion. Press in to the deeper things of God. There is always more.

> Don't stop in the shallow waters of religion. Press in to the deeper things of God. There is always more.

Second, we have to have healthy boundaries. We can't have healthy boundaries with others if we don't have a healthy identity. Think of your identity like a fence around a yard. It has unique and distinct boundaries. Everything inside the fence is yours; everything outside the fence belongs to someone else. Codependency occurs when our boundaries get confused. Either someone jumps over our fence and puts some responsibility on us for something that is their obligation, or someone jumps our fence and tries to take responsibility for something that is in our yard. Imagine if your neighbor started throwing his or her garbage over the fence into your yard. They are responsible for that garbage! But when we don't have a healthy identity, when we haven't integrated the love of God deeply into our lives, we allow people to throw stuff into our yard and we take responsibility for it. Or we cross the fence and put something we are responsible for into our neighbor's yard. We throw our garbage over their fence. You are the only one responsible for you. But often when people get abused or bullied, or grow up in a highly controlling home, they have a sense of powerlessness; they feel and act like a victim. You may have been victimized, but you are not a victim—not in Christ you aren't. You are more than a conqueror. You can do all things through Christ who strengthens you. But if you still feel powerless and are looking to someone else to rescue you, you are still acting like a victim. You may know that you are loved, but you are still acting like an unloved, powerless person. You are still living off of the lie, and boundaries will become an issue for you.

This is particularly vital for people who are trying to help others in Soul Care ministries. People will burn out in this ministry if they don't have healthy boundaries. Soul Care ministry and other helping ministries draw a lot of people with tendencies toward codependency, people who are desperate to see others around them change. They have this compelling need to help others, but it is often driven by unhealthy identity issues. They get their significance from helping others. Codependents are often rescuers who want someone to change more than the person wants to change. We have to break that before we can do this ministry in a healthy way.

Let me give another image for codependency. In a codependent relationship there is often a person who is needy and a person who needs to be needed. The person who is needy always looks like the weak link in the chain. But the reality is the person who needs to be needed is attracted to this codependent relationship because they get their significance from being a rescuer; that is what makes them feel valuable. Sometimes I talk to people in helping ministries who are getting burned out, and they feel resentful that people "always demand so much of me." Or they can't understand why everyone around them is so needy. The reality is there is something broken and unaddressed inside of *them* that draws them to needy people like a magnet. They need to be needed. They gain a sense of importance from being needed by others, by being a rescuer. But it is unhealthy and unsustainable.

Please hear me: I'm not saying this to be mean. I recognize this comes from a person's painful story. But I also have seen so many people engage in helping ministries with unhealthy boundaries. Take time to heal and strengthen your identity so you can engage in helping others in healthy ways.

The key to breaking free from codependency is to secure a healthy identity. We have to understand where we begin, and where someone else ends, and where they begin and where we end. What are we responsible for, what are they responsible for? We have to have enough security to say no when people start to throw their trash into our yard. We must honor the fences and not climb over and take responsibility for other people's lives. We must learn to not take on too much, not to feel guilty for saying no, and not to feel like every need is a divine assignment.

We have to take responsibility for our own life. We are the ones responsible to create healthy boundaries that come from a healthy identity. As we develop a healthy identity, internalizing the love of God, we can start to act like deeply loved children of God.

Let me talk about the difference between boundaries and shields. A shield is an act of self-protection that allows the lowest level of dysfunction to rule the relationship. We pick up the shield of anger, for example, to protect ourselves from someone who is emotionally unsafe. The problem with shields is they are indiscriminate. Not only do they block out this person from hurting me, they also block God from healing me. They are self-protections, and they preserve our unhealthy identity and our dysfunctional interactions; they preserve the self-life. A shield preserves dishonor in the relationship. But a boundary calls people to a higher level of functionality and preserves everyone's dignity and honor.

Let me give an example. Let's say someone comes to me and yells at me and calls me names. If I get defensive and yell back or counterattack, or become passive-aggressive, I am putting up a shield to protect myself. I am stooping to the lowest level of dysfunction in the room. But let's say I take this approach instead. I say to the person: "I am sure what you are saying is important. I want to listen to you. But I feel attacked right now by the way you are saying it. If you can rephrase it in a way that is honorable, I would be happy to listen. And I will be sure to treat you with dignity and respect as well." This attempts to put up a boundary that doesn't allow me to be mistreated, and I am trying to elevate their level of health and preserve honor in our interactions. I am raising the water level, so to speak, of relational health by putting up this boundary. I am acting like a deeply loved person—not defending or retaliating, just like Jesus before his accusers, because of His security. I don't resort to yelling or name-calling, but neither am I being so weak that I do not speak up. I am giving the other person an opportunity to reframe the relational interaction in a healthier way.

In John 1:14 John says of Jesus, "The Word became flesh and made his dwelling among us. We have seen his glory, the glory of the one and only Son, who came from the Father, full of grace and truth." In every relational interaction Jesus was full of grace and full of truth. He didn't have a tension between grace and truth. He didn't have a balance between grace and truth. He was full of grace, and He was full of truth. This should be our goal in every relational interaction. We cannot be relationally mature until we learn how to act full of grace and full of truth—or as close as we can approximate that reality. But how did Jesus interact in this fullness of grace and truth? He knew who He was. He had a completely secure identity. In his opening words, John writes, "In the beginning was the Word, and the Word was with God, and the Word was God. He was with God in the beginning." How did John know this about Jesus? Because Jesus knew it about Himself and made it known to John and the disciples.

In John 13, Jesus takes the low road; that is, He lowers Himself to wash His disciples' feet—something unthinkable for a royal to do. But John says, "Jesus knew that the hour had come for him to leave this world and go to the Father. Having loved his own who were in the world, he loved them to the end . . . Jesus knew that the Father had put all things under his power, and that he had come from God and was returning to God; so he got up from the meal, took off his outer clothing, and wrapped a towel around his waist. After that, he poured water into a basin and began to wash his disciples' feet" (John

13:1, 3-5). Jesus had integrated His Father's opinion of Him, so He was able to serve with appropriate boundaries. He knew when to say yes and when to say no. He knew when to speak and when to be silent. He knew when to correct and when to encourage. He knew how to perfectly and fully speak and interact in every situation with grace and truth because He knew who He was, that He was fully loved by the Father. He could be full of grace to those who attacked Him. He was so secure in the Father's love; He could be full of truth without fearing any repercussions of disapproval.

This is the beauty of deepening your identity. It enables you to act in relationally mature ways: full of grace and full of truth. We can be responsible for ourselves because we are secured by love and not powerless, and we can avoid taking responsibility for others because we don't need to be needed: our value is not dependent on that.

In the end, we only have four tools in our toolbox to help someone else change. First, we can have a conversation. If it is a mature, Jesus-like conversation, it will be full of grace and full of truth. After we have said what needs to be said in the fullness of grace and truth, and the person has understood but has chosen not to change, we need to put that tool away. If we continue to try to talk them into changing, we become manipulative, controlling, and coercive. After putting that tool away, I only have three tools left in my toolbox to help someone change: love, wait, and pray. That's it. I need to love, wait, and pray until their hearts open again to further conversations.

> This is the beauty of deepening your identity. It enables you to act in relationally mature ways: full of grace and full of truth.

When we want someone to change more than they want to change, we feel frustrated, and they feel manipulated. We need to stop acting fearful and trying to force people to change. We need to stop being codependent and trying to take responsibility for someone else's life. We need to entrust them to God; codependency reveals a lack of trust in God. We need to love and accept them where they are. We need to wait for them to be ready to change. We need to pray for them, that they will change and trust God to work in their hearts. It is hard, but it is healthy.

Jesus demonstrates this with the rich young ruler. He called the man to leave everything and come follow Him because wealth was this man's all-consuming priority. But the man would not walk away from his wealth. Mark says that Jesus looked at the man and loved him when He spoke this hard truth into his life. But then he watched him walk away. He didn't feel a compelling need to chase the guy down and convince him to change.

In the Image of God

You are created in the image of God. God is sovereign; that means you were created with a degree of sovereignty. This has at least two implications. First, you were created with authority. God is a sovereign ruler, the ultimate King. You were created in His image for rulership. Adam and Eve were given dominion; that's rulership. Jesus entrusted us with the keys of the Kingdom of God. You have a degree of rulership. You have authority by God's grace to enact God's rule over the enemy, evil, and the effects of evil in the world. Second, being created with a degree of sovereignty means you have choice. God has ultimate choice; He can do anything that is not inconsistent with His character. We have limited choice; we cannot choose to become, say, a bird for today if we want. But we do have choice; we can choose our actions and attitudes. We are not victims—not to our circumstances, nor to the enemy of our soul. In Christ we have choice. We need to exercise our choice to get into alignment with God. But we cannot choose to get our children or our spouse in alignment with God. That is their choice, not our choice. God respects His image-bearing sovereignty in them, and so must we. We cannot trump their will; God will not. He honors the sovereign image He has put in them, just like Jesus honored the sovereign choice of the rich young ruler.

I cannot tell you how many times people ask me if they can cast demons out of someone who isn't looking present at a conference and doesn't really want to change. No. No. No. That is a codependent question; that is a rescuer mentality. That is dishonoring the sovereign image-bearing will of another. Have a conversation, and make it full of grace and full of truth. Make sure you have said everything you need to say, but say it with the graciousness of Jesus. And then love, wait, and pray. *That person has to want to change.*

Overly caring people are also often overly responsible people. They take on too much. This is part of not having healthy boundaries. Listen: not every need is your responsibility. Not every opportunity is your assignment. There are always more needs than you have capacity to meet.

How did Jesus decide which assignments to take? In Mark 1 Jesus is preaching the Good News of the Kingdom, healing the sick, and casting out demons. He gets up early in the morning, while it is still dark, to pray. The crowds gather at the doorstep while He is out praying and the disciples come to get Him. They say, "Everyone is looking for you!" Jesus says, "Let us go somewhere else, to the nearby villages, so I can preach there also. That is why I have come" (Mark 1:35-38). Jesus left people in need to go to the next village. While Jesus was on the planet, He was limited to one place at a time. He was really human, and He had very real human limitations. He had limited resources, limited time, limited energy. He needed food, He needed sleep, He got tired. He couldn't meet everyone's needs. So how did Jesus decide what to do?

Jesus only did what the Father told Him to do. In John 4:32-34, Jesus said, "I have food to eat that you know nothing about . . . My food is to do the will of him who sent me and to finish his work." As long as Jesus was doing what the Father told Him, the Father supplied the strength and resources to do it. This was the key to Jesus' ministry. Jesus simply sought to do the will of the Father. In every situation Jesus asked Himself: What is the Father doing? Then He simply joined the Father in what He was doing. Fulfilling the Father's assignment was food to Jesus' soul. It gave Him pleasure and was replenishing. When we try to generate spiritual activity out of our ability without the empowerment of the Spirit, it drains us quickly.

In John 5:19, Jesus said, "Very truly I tell you, the Son can do nothing by himself; he can do only what he sees his Father doing, because whatever the Father does the Son also does. For the Father loves the Son and shows him all he does." In John 5:30, Jesus adds, "By myself I can do nothing; I judge only as I hear, and my judgment is just, for I seek not to please myself but him who sent me." Jesus testifies that He can do nothing by Himself. He is in complete submission and complete dependence on His Father. While Jesus was on the earth, He did not do His ministry out of His divinity. Rather, He did His ministry out of His Spirit-empowered, Spirit-anointed humanity—and that is how we must do it. Jesus had to do ministry in dependence on the Father.

Jesus also taught that He said nothing on his own. John 7:16: "My teaching is not my own. It comes from the one who sent me." John 8:28: "When you have lifted up the Son of Man, then you will know that I am he and that I do nothing on my own but speak just what the Father has taught me." John

12:49, 50: "For I did not speak on my own, but the Father who sent me commanded me to say all that I have spoken. I know that his command leads to eternal life. So whatever I say is just what the Father told me to say." John 14:10: "The words I say to you I do not speak on my own authority. Rather, it is the Father, living in me, who is doing his work." John 14:24: "These words you hear are not my own; they belong to the Father who sent me." Jesus spoke with ancient, weighty, and piercing wisdom because He only said what the Father told Him to say.

One of the things that hinders effective ministry is when we talk too much. We make it too much about us. We share opinions without wisdom, words without weightiness. If we are going to be effective in ministering to others, we need to attempt to hear God's wisdom and relay what we hear as accurately as we can. If you tend to be a "talker," seek to intentionally limit your words when you are ministering with others. Listen to the person and to the Spirit, weigh your words carefully, and try to limit yourself to what is truly from God. You won't get it perfectly right, but being intentional about it will make you more effective.

> One of the things that hinders effective ministry is when we talk too much. We make it too much about us. We share opinions without wisdom, words without weightiness.

Jesus lived in complete submission and dependence on the Father. He only did what the Father told Him to do. He only said what the Father told Him to say. He only went where the Father told Him to go. This was the key to Jesus' powerful ministry. Jesus didn't do ministry because He was driven by His compassion (though, of course, He was the most compassionate person who ever lived). Jesus did ministry in response to the Father. Jesus didn't do ministry because He was moved by human need. Jesus did ministry in obedience to His Father's directives. People did not determine Jesus' agenda. Jesus did not determine His own agenda. Jesus simply aligned himself with the Father's agenda. This is vital to being a healthy Soul Care practitioner.

The secret to success in ministry is to find what God wants and do it. Only do what the Father tells you to do. You will often feel compassion for things you should not engage in. I have written a book, *Soul Care*, that has sold more than 80,000 copies at the time of this writing. I have taught tens of thousands of people in conference settings. I am a public figure: people friend me on FaceBook, Twitter, Instagram, and LinkedIn. They find my email, or they write private messages on social media about their desperate situations. But I simply cannot respond to every social media message or email. I cannot respond to every cry of desperation. I cannot meet every need, and I cannot do every deliverance. It is impossible. My heart goes out to these people in need, but I simply cannot do it. I have to honor my limits. I have to decide what I should say yes to and what I should say no to. Here is my simple approach: Find what God wants and do it.

I've developed a grid in my life that helps me make decisions. I know my calling. God has called me to fight for revival. Everything I do must be about that goal. I write, teach, and mentor leaders for revival. I feel particularly called to help pastors, leaders, and larger churches who can influence others so they can reproduce these things. If someone calls me and asks me to do a marriage conference, the answer is no. I have learned things about marriage; I have things to teach about marriage. But I am called to revival. Other people are called to help marriages; that is not my assignment. Every need is not your assignment. Every difficulty is not your battle. What is God's assignment for you? Find what God wants and do it.

Everyone is worthy of love, but not everyone is worthy of an investment. Jesus invested in the three, the twelve, the seventy, and the one hundred and twenty. Then he invested in the crowds. Not everyone got invited into the inner circles. Many were jealous and many were hurt because of Jesus' choices. But Jesus was secure in the Father's love; He wasn't responsible for people's responses. He was responsible simply to do what the Father told Him. So He spent a night in prayer and choose twelve men to be His disciples. Many others were disappointed that they were not in the inner circle. But His Father was pleased. If we continue to please people, we will displease the Father. If we say yes to people, we will end up saying no to the Father. Find what God wants and do it, then rest secure in His love. This is how you develop healthy boundaries that allow you to be a healthy Soul Care practitioner.

Third, we have to process our negative emotions. We cannot allow negative emotions to accumulate in the suitcase of our souls without them resulting in spiritual, emotional, or even physical problems. John Sarno was a medical doctor in New York. He wrote a book called *Healing Back Pain*. Dr. Sarno discovered that many people who were undergoing back surgery didn't need it. The root of the back pain was unprocessed negative emotions. Unprocessed emotional pain doesn't just cause us physical problems (back pain only being one example), it can cause us spiritual and emotional problems and even relational problems. We want to travel light through life, and that means we need to unpack our suitcase regularly by processing our negative emotions.

In 2013 I found myself in one of the darkest places of my spiritual journey. I was wrestling with this question: Does God lie? It wasn't a theological question. It was an emotional question. I had four promises that God had given in my life, and none of them had come to reality. One had come with the audible voice of God, but there was little to no progress. One was a promise of revival and God's specific role for me in this move of the Spirit. God gave me a dream about this coming revival; in the dream he gave me a sign (the dream about the New Orleans Saints winning the Super Bowl). The dream came three nights in a row in December 2006. The Saints won the Super Bowl in 2010. The dream was clear. The sign had come true. And it was 2013 and things were going in the wrong direction. I was pastor of a church and I had been praying for revival, preaching toward revival, and fighting for revival, but things were only getting worse. People were attacking me, and it felt like the church was unstable for the first time since I had planted it. Why? I had battled for a long time and was taking many hits, and yet all the promises were far from coming true. This is why I was wrestling with the question: Does God lie?

I was processing the pain of disappointment and heartache. Every day I was spending time trying to unpack the negative emotions that had accumulated in the suitcase of my soul, but I wasn't making much progress. Finally, one day in September 2013, I said to my wife Jen, "If I can't get past this, I am going to have to quit. I can't keep preaching when I am struggling so deeply with this question in my soul."

Shortly afterward I called my friend Ron Walborn. I said, "I need a day in your life." He said, "Anytime. When do you need it?" I love Ron for many reasons, but I will never forget that gesture. I knew how busy he was and what a gift his time would be to me. I told him I was wrestling with the question: Does God lie? I said I needed to process my grief and disappointment with a safe person. One reason I went to Ron was because Ron had wrestled with this question and spent some time processing this with me some years earlier. I said, "I'll make it a little bit of fun for us. I'll buy us tickets to the Pirates playoff game, and we can process in the car on the way down to the game. Then we can root for the Pirates and process in the car on the way back." Ron was a Pirates fan, and the Pirates hadn't made the playoffs in quite some time, so that part was fun for him. On the way down I unpacked the disappointment, sadness, heartache, hurt, and anger that had accumulated in my heart. I was unfiltered. He grieved with me. It is often hard to find someone who can listen to your unfiltered emotional pain without trying to fix you with religious slogans and truisms. I didn't need to be fixed; I knew the truth and didn't need anyone to quote Scripture at me. I needed to unpack, and unpacking is often messy.

> I didn't need to be fixed; I knew the truth and didn't need anyone to quote Scripture at me.

Ron said two things that were helpful. First, he said, "Bud, you believe this stuff about the Kingdom and revival to your toes. Just keep preaching. We preach God's Word, not our experience." True.

Second, Ron said, "You are an intense guy, and this has been an intense season, as you know. You need to have more fun." I confess this didn't sound like very spiritual advice, but I took on fun as a spiritual discipline. I started engaging in fun, replenishing activities with a grateful heart.

In Psalm 34:8 David wrote, "Taste and see that the Lord is good." But how do you taste and see that God is good? I think one of the ways you taste and see that God is good is by participating in fun, replenishing things in life and giving God thanks. James said that "Every good and perfect gift is from above, coming down from the Father of heavenly lights, who does not change like shifting shadows" (James 1:17). The problem is that when the shadows are shifting, we often no longer see the light of God's goodness. Hardship diminishes our perception of the goodness of God at the center of our souls. But when we participate in good things with a grateful heart, it restores our understanding of the goodness of God.

All this advice turned out to be incredibly helpful for getting out of the dark, but it took time, and it was only one piece of the puzzle.

Dark Night of the Soul

Sadly, not only was I wrestling with disappointment during this time, the presence of God was nowhere to be found. I was going through a dark night of the soul that lasted many months. John of the Cross talked about the dark night of the soul; when he did, he was not referring to emotional pain or hardship. John was referring to a time in our lives when we are no longer aware of God's presence or voice. God hides Himself from us. John of the Cross tells us that the purpose of the dark night of the soul is purgation; God is purging us. The problem is we often don't know what God is up to because we have no sense of His presence or His voice or His guidance in these dark nights. We must simply keep our eyes on Jesus and persevere.

Hardship diminishes our perception of the goodness of God at the center of our souls. But when we participate in good things with a grateful heart, it restores our understanding of the goodness of God.

The Lord had prepared me for this dark night of the soul. One day I was at the monastery and reading Thomas Ashbrook's book, *Mansions of the Heart*. Ashbrook unpacks some of the concepts that Teresa of Avilla illuminates in her book, *The Interior Castle*. Ashbrook talked about the fifth mansion, which describes this deep, intimate connection with

Jesus, and as he described it, he spoke of things that I had been experiencing but had never heard anyone talk about before. I was so excited to see what was in the next chapter, so I read on. And the next chapter, the sixth mansion, was the dark night of the soul. I read the chapter and went out for a walk with the Lord. I said to the Lord, "I have cultivated your presence my whole life. I don't want to be without your presence or your voice." I heard the Lord say, "Even if you cannot sense me or hear me, am I not still with you?" I said, "Yes, Lord, of course." He said, "If you look for me, you will learn how to spot me in the dark." I knew it was coming. And I knew I had to learn how to spot God in the darkness.

One day in the midst of this season of heartache and darkness I picked up my Bible and read Hebrews 11. I was reading the passage to inspire myself to push on through the dark. This chapter is about the Hall of Faith. These are the people who had promises from God, just like me, and they held on, and God delivered! We love these stories. Of course, in some cases they sum the story up in a paragraph, as with Abraham and Sarah. They believed God for the promised child in their old age and God delivered, but it was twenty-five years later that God delivered! That's easy to read in a paragraph, but there is a lot of untold pain and tears when it is your twenty-five years of waiting!

I was reading through the chapter and the pattern continued: God promised, they held on, God delivered. And then I read these words beginning at verse 32: "And what more shall I say? I do not have time to tell about Gideon, Barak, Samson, and Jephthah, about David and Samuel and the prophets, who through faith conquered kingdoms, administered justice, and gained what was promised; who shut the mouths of lions, quenched the fury of the flames, and escaped the edge of the sword; whose weakness was turned to strength; and who became powerful in battle and routed foreign armies. Women

> That's easy to read in a paragraph, but there is a lot of untold pain and tears when it is your twenty-five years of waiting!

received back their dead, raised to life again." Aren't these great stories? Don't we love them? God promised, they held on, and God delivered.

But that isn't where it ends.

The author goes on to say: "There were others who were tortured, refusing to be released so that they might gain an even better resurrection. Some faced jeers and flogging, and even chains and imprisonment. They were put to death by stoning; they were sawed in two; they were killed by the sword. They went about in sheepskins and goatskins, destitute, persecuted and mistreated—the world was not worthy of them. They wandered in deserts and mountains, and in caves and holes in the ground. These were all commended for their faith, yet none of them received what had been promised" (Hebrews 11:35-39). Wait. *What?* Did you read that last sentence? These people all received a promise from God like everyone else. They held on like everyone else, but they didn't receive the reality of the promise. I read that passage that day and my heart sank. I thought: You *do* lie! You gave them promises you didn't deliver on, and they were commended for their faithfulness!

Then I read the last verse in the chapter.

"God had planned something better for us so that only together with us would they be made perfect" (Hebrews 11:40). And then I got it. There are times when God gives someone a promise and they think it is for them; they hold onto it and battle for it like it is for them. But God never intended it for them. He gave it to them so they would battle for it for a future generation. God entrusted it to them because He believed they would be faithful and selfless enough to fight for a future generation. They would live for an eternal purpose, one bigger than themselves. And I knew, all at once, what God wanted to know from me: Would I battle for revival with my dying breath even if I never saw it? Would I battle for that promise like it was for me even if it was for another generation? I laid on the floor that day before the Lord and I surrendered. I promised the Lord I would battle for revival with my dying breath even if I never saw it in my lifetime. It was an important purging moment.

Even so, the dark night didn't lift for quite some time, but at least there were moments in which I was learning to spot Him in the dark.

One day I was sitting in my living room weeping and Jen came in. She said, "What's wrong?" I said, "I just miss Him." I missed His presence. About two weeks later she came back in the living room while I was sitting in my rocking chair weeping again. She said, "What's wrong?" I said, "He's back!" His presence was intermittent for a long time after that, but the fruit of the dark night was remarkable. I immediately began to see a dramatic increase in the power of God in my ministry. I saw more of the power of God in the next year of my life than all my previous years put together. And it has continued—though not without some necessary, temporary interruptions along the way.

Almost every day when I am alone with God, I process my emotions. I try to process my positive and negative emotions. I don't want disappointment or sadness or hurt or grief accumulating in my soul. Unprocessed emotion often results in offense against God and causes our hearts to become hard. It diseases our soul and becomes an impediment on our spiritual journey. Unprocessed negative emotions will hinder our relationships with God and others. So every day I unpack. I process the emotions that are in my heart. I start with the surface emotions and dig to the deeper emotions that are not always presenting. The Psalms have been a very helpful guide along the way.

Americans are not very good at processing negative emotions in a healthy way. We tend to medicate pain in a comfort-based society. We don't deal with pain at the root; we try to alleviate the symptoms. But the Hebrews are a long-suffering people. They have suffered much, and they are masters at grieving and processing their negative emotions. Nearly half the Psalms are lament Psalms: they work through sadness, grief, anger, and other negative emotions. They express them honestly, and then the author turns to God in faith and surrender. As I said previously, I often just read through a handful of Psalms until I come across one that resonates with my emotional state, and then I pray it back to God in my own words.

> Americans are not very good at processing negative emotions in a healthy way. We tend to medicate pain in a comfort-based society.

We put our souls at great risk when we fail to process these negative emotions. I think most midlife crises are merely unprocessed accumulated disappointments. I don't know anyone over 50 who isn't disappointed with life at some level. When you're in your twenties you have all kinds of ideals about what your life is going to be like. You have a vision, or at least expectations, for your career, finances, marriage, family, and meaningful contributions to the cause of Christ. You work hard on those things during your twenties and thirties. You are advancing your career, creating family life, trying to establish a sense of financial stability, security, or wealth, and working to make a difference. But somewhere along the way you start to realize everything isn't going to work out like you had hoped. Your marriage is good, but there are some things that are a little disappointing. Your kids are good, but there are some areas that haven't gone the way you expected. Your finances may be good, but not like you had hoped. You have made some contributions to the cause of Christ, but not everything has looked like you thought it would. And you start to accumulate disappointments. Life isn't working out like you dreamed it would. And no matter how good it is, it is never all that you long for in a fallen world.

The problem is that our passions run toward our visions and goals. And now that the vision feels diminished and the goals unachievable, our passion leaks. We are susceptible to misplaced passions. Many people turn to illicit things, immoral things to try to light the fire that once fueled their life, to make them feel alive again. Others become disappointed, disenchanted, cynical, and even embittered. Still others settle for the good life. They don't rebel against God, but Jesus is no longer their first love, and the Kingdom is no longer their motivating passion. They settle for trying to be decent people and become focused on the temporal pleasures that can sooth their disappointed hearts rather than looking to the eternal.

I think this is what happened to David. God had promised David victory over his enemies. David was fighting and battling for the land that God promised His people. He had battled throughout his twenties and thirties and forties, and here he is middle-aged and disappointed. He had fought his enemies, but the victories were still not complete. The enemies were still surrounding him. And then we come to this sentence in 2 Samuel 11:1: "In the spring, at the time when kings go off to war, David sent Joab out with the king's men and the whole Israelite army . . . But David remained in Jerusalem." He failed to process his disappointments. They had accumulated over years, and now they filled the suitcase of his soul. They robbed him of his joy, his spark, his passion. And they

> Here is the challenge. Process your emotions on a regular basis. Make this part of your daily routine. Travel light.

set him up for an affair that led to disastrous consequences over his life, family, and kingdom for the rest of his days.

Here is the challenge. Process your emotions on a regular basis. Make this part of your daily routine. Travel light. You won't be able to resolve all your emotional pain every day. Sometimes you will carry sadness or grief with you into your daily prayer time for months on end. But don't ignore it; go after it. Process it with God and others.

We Must Practice Self-Care

Fourth, we need to practice self-care. We have to monitor our well-being physically, emotionally, and spiritually. Think of your soul like a car's dashboard. You have a gauge that tells you how full your tank is. If you ignore your gas tank, you will end up on the side of the road out of gas. Too many people have ignored their physical, emotional, and spiritual tanks and ended up in significant trouble that could have been prevented.

Picture three gauges that make up the dashboard of your soul. The gauges read from empty to full. The three gauges on your dashboard measure your physical, emotional, and spiritual well-being. You may want to draw the gauges on a piece of paper and place a line to show how full, or how empty, your three tanks are. Be honest. Denial will only lead to more heartache.

How would you rate your **physical tank** right now? Are you taking care of yourself? Are you eating right and exercising? Do you have a high level of physical energy? Just like a gas tank, where are you between empty and full? I try to ride my bike at least a few times each week. Probably 15 years ago or more, I went on a three-week fast. I dropped 20 pounds, and I really wanted to keep the weight off. The only problem was I started to eat again. I decided the only way I was going to keep the weight off was if I learned how to eat healthy and start exercising. I downloaded an app that helped me count calories. I entered everything I ate, and I learned to eat healthy. I also started riding my bike. I have been able to keep the weight off and I feel better. When I eat right and exercise, I have more energy. I feel better physically and emotionally. It also helps me better manage the stresses of life. I want to lose about five additional pounds at the time of this writing, and I have a few aches and pains that come with getting older, but I would say I am about three-fourths full on my physical tank.

I went through one tough season in ministry where I was under many attacks and much criticism. I would go out on a bike ride in nice weather, and the exercise and outdoors helped lower my stress and replenish my energy levels. If you already don't feel great and you go through a high-stress season, it will drain your energy levels and you will be gasping for air emotionally. In high-stress seasons, I often taken a walk outside through the woods or in a field and soak in the sunshine and beauty of creation. Just the exercise and being outdoors helps replenish me.

Think about your **emotional tank.** Where would you rate yourself between empty and full? Are you feeling joyful, peaceful, loved, and fulfilled? Or are you feeling stressed, empty, tired, angry, bored, anxious, depressed, or weary? Sometimes Christians, especially people in ministry, monitor only their spiritual tank. If they are reading their Bible, praying, serving, giving, and doing the spiritual things they are supposed to be doing, they think this should be sufficient to keep them healthy. But you can do all the right things spiritually and still find that your physical and emotional tanks are on empty. If we ignore this state of being for too long, we will burn out or possibly even blow up our lives.

During one dark season of my life when I was under a great deal of stress in ministry, my wife Jen said to me, "You should read novels again. You were an English major in school. You liked novels. But now you only read professional journals and leadership books and books that relate to ministry. But then you never take your mind off work." It was solid advice. I started reading for pleasure again. It was emotionally replenishing to me. Then I started listening to audio books while riding my bike. I was able to enjoy the outdoors, get exercise, and take in a book that replenished my emotional tank. That has been a great practice for me.

I mentioned earlier that my friend Ron Walborn told me I needed to have more fun. I am an intense individual with a lot of passion. The great thing about being a passionate person is you get a lot done in life; you make things happen. The bad thing is you suffer more disappointments. The more passionate you are, the more you expect from life. And things don't always turn out the way you planned. So if you're not careful to process your disappointments, they will accumulate in your soul and begin to rob you of joy. I had to learn to both process my negative emotions and fill my soul with things that were fun. I had to taste and see that the Lord is good by participating in the good gifts from God with a grateful heart. I can't tell you how many times I talk to ministers and see this weighty, stressful gloom that hangs over them. I say to them, "You need to have more fun in your life. What do you do for fun?" Too often they look at me blankly, and after a long pause they say, "Not too much." Taste and see that the Lord is good. Do you need to address your emotional tank? Do you need to process negative emotions? Do you need to fill your emotional tank with more replenishing activities and fun?

During COVID I often found my emotional tank low. COVID was a thief. It robbed me of traveling, doing in-person conferences where I see life change, and human interaction. I was doing livestream conferences to make a living, but most of the time I was talking to the back of my phone. Jen and I realized we were both feeling sad, down emotionally, so we added more fun to our lives. We visited several national parks during COVID. There were fewer people there, so there were no lines. You had to pack in your own food, which was a little inconvenient, but we had a great time, and it helped replenish our emotional tanks.

Consider your **spiritual tank**. Where does your line fall between empty and full? Are you feeling deeply connected to God: hearing His voice, sensing His presence, and experiencing His love? Are you living free and full in Christ? Is Jesus your first love? Are you preoccupied with Jesus? We think about the things we value most; what most preoccupies your heart and mind? We can be doing all the right things—reading our Bible, praying, serving, giving—and doing them for all the wrong reasons. Just like the older son in the parable of the lost son. All too often we become become duty-bound elder sons. But this isn't Jesus' plan for our lives.

One of the keys to thriving spiritually is to recapture our passion for Jesus when it wanes. Think about the church of Ephesus. In Revelation Jesus says to this church, "I know your deeds, your hard work and your perseverance. I know that you cannot tolerate wicked people, that you have tested those who claim to be apostles but are not, and have found them false. You have persevered and have endured hardships for my name, and have not grown weary. Yet I hold this against you: You have forsaken the love you had at first. Consider how far you have fallen! Repent and do the things you did at first" (Revelation 2:2-5). Sometimes people say, "Love for God is not emotional. You just have to obey." Listen: faithful-

> Are you preoccupied with Jesus? We think about the things we value most; what most preoccupies your heart and mind?

ness matters, and it matters a lot. But God is not looking for a duty-bound, passionless bride. Look at the church in Ephesus. All Jesus does is commend them for their good deeds, hard work, perseverance, solid doctrine, and long-suffering. But they did all of that and still lost their first love. Jesus wants them to recapture their passion!

Jesus calls this church to repent and do the things they did at first. When my passion for Jesus starts to wane and I feel stalled spiritually, I set aside a block of time to be alone with God. I first ask the Holy Spirit to show me if there is any sin hindering my relationship with Him. Sometimes I'm feeling disconnected from God because I have done something to grieve the Spirit, and I blew past the stop sign of conviction. If there is no sin impeding my connection, I begin to talk to the Lord about my lack of spiritual passion, and I ask Him what to do about it. Let me give you my three most common pathways out of spiritual lethargy.

First, God often calls me to sacrifice. As I've written, one of my most common sacrificial acts that leads me out of spiritual lethargy is to take a spiritual retreat for a day or two. Often this larger block of time alone with God will reveal something that helps me get unstuck. Sometimes God shows me some unprocessed emotion that has robbed me of my passion for Jesus. Sometimes just the day alone with God will recapture my passion as I encounter the beauty of Jesus. There wasn't any big block; I just needed some dedicated space alone with God. I needed a fresh encounter with His presence. My best moments with God have most often occurred in block times alone with God; it is hard to create quality time with God without setting aside some quantity time. There are times in my marriage when we both need to renew our love for one another. Often we will get alone together for a day, set aside everything else, and just reconnect. We slow down and pay closer attention to one another. This long, slow day in Jen's presence is often the very thing I need to rekindle my love for her. It is the same in my relationship with God.

There are other times God calls me to sacrifice food; He calls me to go on a fast. There are a lot of things about the spiritual life I do not understand, but I still know them to be true. I am not sure I always understand why fasting helps me rekindle my fire for the Lord, but it does. Some of it, I suspect, is because at times we use eating when we feel empty inside, but the emptiness is not physical hunger. Think about this scenario. You finish dinner and clean up. Then you go into the other room and you are reading, or watching a show, or looking at social media, and all of a sudden you start to feel this little empty feeling. And you wander into the kitchen and rummage through the kitchen cabinets looking for something to satisfy the empty place. Now, here is the reality: you aren't hungry; you just ate. What is that empty feeling? I think many times it is actually spiritual hunger that we misdiagnose and try to satisfy with a physical solution. But when we take away all of our props and lean hard into God with fasting, it awakens our spiritual appetite for God, and we start to long for His presence. It's the very thing we need.

There are other times the Lord calls me to sacrifice a night's sleep or a few hours of sleep. I feel the Lord is calling me to be alone with Him through "the watches of the night." David practiced this (see Psalm 63:6). God's people have done night watches throughout history. It has been a place where God has spoken to me and I have encountered Him. It has often been a path that has awakened my love for God. When we meet Him, when we encounter Him, love is awakened. Sacrifice is often the path to awakening love.

Second, when I am feeling spiritually plateaued and need to awaken my passion, I will often change my spiritual rhythm. When routine becomes a rut, we become religious. Change is usually the key to getting out of the rut. I ask the Lord what He wants me to do differently, and an idea will come to me as I persist in asking and waiting. This insight often happens on a retreat day. At one time in my life I was going to the monastery just once per year. I was feeling a bit weary one June as I made my way to the monastery for my annual retreat, and as I drove up the driveway I heard the Lord say to me, "You need to come to the monastery every other month." That started many years of bimonthly retreats. When I began going to the monastery every other month it was like I was undergoing a spiritual revival. I entered a new level of loving intimacy with the Lord. He knew what I needed. Another time I was in a spiritual funk. I sought the Lord and heard Him say, "You need to spend more time in silence." I had been practicing silence some in my life, but not consistently. I sensed Him calling me to spend time in silence daily. It awakened love in my heart for the Lord. I would sit in silence and long for His presence.

Third, sometimes what I need to awaken my love for the Lord is for my heart to be pierced. The one thing God wants most is access. The key for our hearts to be accessible to God is brokenness. We need a broken, humble, contrite heart before the Lord. Sometimes our hearts grow spiritually dull, and even a little hard, before the Lord. Hardship can harden the heart if we don't process it well. Our hearts can also become hard because of our self-life; we make things too much about us. We are focused on our needs, our wants, and our desires, and our hearts are desensitized to the Lord because of our self-focus. (This is one of the reasons I think sacrifice is important: it breaks our self-focus.) What we need to reawaken our sensitivity to the Lord's presence is a tender heart. We need the Lord to pierce the hardened places in the soil of our soul.

I don't garden much, but Jen likes to garden, and occasionally I give her some assistance. Unfortunately, our property has lots of clay, and the soil is often hard and unwelcoming to the plants and seeds. Before we can plant something in our yard we have to break up the hardened ground. I usually bring out my pickaxe and pierce the clay-hardened soil and begin to break it up. We replace the hardened soil with soft topsoil that is welcoming to the tender shoots.

So it is with our hearts.

When my heart is no longer moved by the things that move God, I pray for a fresh piercing of the heart. When my heart seems a little dull and insensitive to the things of the Lord, I pray for that fresh piercing of the heart. When I am no longer moved by the pain of others, no longer pained by my own sin, no longer brokenhearted over the lostness of humanity, I pray for a fresh piercing. I often couple this with a retreat day or fasting or both.

I don't just pray and passively wait for God to do it all. I actively engage in the process. I read books I know will move my heart and begin to soften the soil of my soul. I read books of great saints who have lived all in for Jesus and finished well, books that challenge my heart to be broken and humble before the Lord. I read them slowly and prayerfully and ask God to make my heart soft and tender before Him.

There are two books I have read more than any other book except the Bible. They are books that move my heart toward humility, and that is why I have read them so often. The one I have read the most is a book by Fenelon, *Let Go*. In my opinion no one in the history of the church has ever understood death to self like Fenelon. I cannot read Fenelon slowly and prayerfully without it piercing my heart. I have read this book nearly forty times. Sadly, I have read it that often because I often feel the pull of my self-life. My self-life cries for me to make life too much about me, and if I listen to its cry my heart hardens and I need a fresh piercing. Fenelon is a master with a spade and a pickaxe. He is a master gardener and has helped me cultivate the soil of my soul more times than I can possibly count. I have come to realize that every time I feel miserable in my life it is because I am making it too much about me. If I don't reverse that trend, my heart will harden and the flame of my first love for Jesus will begin to die out. So I pick up the old book again and slowly and prayerfully let the Lord have access.

The other book I have read many times is Corrie Ten Boom's *Tramp for the Lord*. It may be the best book I know to illustrate what a revived life looks like. As I read it, my heart longs for God. I feel the piercing every time. It is the very thing I need.

> I have come to realize that every time I feel miserable in my life it is because I am making it too much about me.

I love when my heart is tender before the Lord. Even sitting here thinking about it I can feel the heat behind my eyes. When my heart is tender, I feel alive. I feel compassion; I sense His presence. I hear His voice and I experience His love. I know His pleasure and I feel the tender affections of the Father when I am with others in pain. I am quick to apologize for hurtful words and actions. I am slow to defend and quick to own my part. When my heart is broken, humble and contrite before the Lord, I am living in step with the Spirit. I am sensitive to God and others. I am becoming the man I want to be. This is why the Proverb writer said, "Above all things, guard your heart, for it is the wellspring of life" (Proverbs 4:23).

Be careful to monitor the condition of your heart. Let me go back to the image of the dashboard on a car, but let's use it a different way. Most cars usually have a dashboard with some gauges on it that indicate the health of your car. There is a gas gauge and an oil gauge and a heat gauge. You can't ignore these gauges without having some problems. I think all of us have similar indicators in our life that show us when we need a spiritual checkup. They flash at us and indicate to us that our hearts are growing hard.

Dashboard for the Soul

I've created a dashboard for my soul to do a quick check on my spiritual well-being. I have noticed there are a few signs that my heart is starting to harden, that I am getting out of alignment with God. I will share my indicators as an example. I encourage you to create your own dashboard with your own indicators.

The first gauge I need to pay attention to on the dashboard of my soul is my *compassion gauge.* When I am in right alignment with Jesus and my heart is soft, I feel compassion for others. I am not the most naturally compassionate person. But when my heart is soft before the Lord and I am in step with the Spirit, I feel the tenderness of God for those around me. When I lose that and people become merely an interruption, I'm in need of a spiritual checkup. My compassion dashboard light is blinking, and I need to get alone with the Lord and look under the hood.

The second gauge I must monitor is my *brokenness gauge.* When my heart is tender before the Lord, I'm quick to own my sin and slow to defend myself. If I am in alignment with God and Jen comes to me and says, "When you said that, it hurt my feelings," I will feel the piercing of the Spirit. My eyes will tear up and I'll say, "Oh, sweetie, I am so sorry." If I am out of step with the Spirit, I will defend, blame, or even coun-terattack. When my response is defensive, my heart needs a fresh piercing. I need to get alone with God and deal with the condition of my heart.

The third gauge I need to attend to is my *peace gauge*. When my heart is right before the Lord, peace rules my heart. It is the peace of Christ. Jesus is never nervous. He is the Prince of Peace. He has promised that He will give His peace to us. When I am in alignment with God, His peace is imparted to my inner being. When I lose His peace, I am out of alignment. How do I know this? Because He hasn't lost His! So if fear and anxiety start to ripple through my inner being, it is time to get alone with God and deal with my inner being. Why have I lost the peace of Christ? What's underneath that? My emotions are often an early indicator that something is off in my soul. When I sense something out of alignment, I block out time alone with God to go after it.

The fourth gauge is my *passion gauge*. When my heart is tender before the Lord, Jesus is my first love. When my heart hardens, I often become self-focused, and something other than Jesus occupies my heart and pre-occupies my mind. Too many earthly attachments can rob me of my first love. Disappointment with God can disrupt my passion for Jesus. I have to get alone with God and, with the help of the Spirit, diagnose the root of the problem. Jesus is the most im-portant person, and He alone is worthy of my first love.

> When my response is defensive, my heart needs a fresh piercing. I need to get alone with God and deal with the condition of my heart.

The fifth gauge I have to keep an eye on is my *listening gauge*. If my heart is soft before the Lord, I am usually sensitive to His presence and His voice. When the voice of God is seldom and distant in my life, it is often because there is something wrong with my heart. I am preoccupied with something else. I have to get alone with God and make an adjustment.

Take time to develop a dashboard for your soul. Ask the Lord for insight. Talk to those closest to you and get their input. What are the indicator lights that flash on your dashboard to show that you are out of alignment with God? What are the symptoms that begin to express themselves when your heart begins to harden? If you can identify those things, then every time you see those symptoms in your life you will know it's time to pull over and look under the hood.

Summary: The Healthy Leader

We've looked at four areas of a healthy leader: (1) we have to integrate Soul Care principles into our daily life; (2) we have to create healthy boundaries; (3) we have to process our negative emotions in a positive way; (4) we must practice self-care. Take time to journal, pray, and reflect. Are there areas where you need to make changes?

John Maxwell once said that the key to your long-term success is found in your daily routine. This is a brilliant concept. So in my life I have created daily or near daily routines around these areas that keep me on target. For example, in my time alone with God every day I make sure my soul is in alignment with Him. If I have angst in my soul, or if I am carrying too much anger, I take time, not just to process the emotion, but to find the root. My negative emotions are often my first indicator that something is out of alignment with God. Why am I angry? Why am I feeling angst? Often it is a Soul Care principle (like identity) that is causing me the disturbance. I find the root, make an adjustment, integrate the principle into my soul, and get back in alignment with

> My negative emotions are often my first indicator that something is out of alignment with God.

God. Often I start with the presenting problem (like anger or anxiety) and chase it back to the root. These Soul Care principles often reveal the root of my symptomatic issues.

For example, let's say I notice my anger levels are spiking. Often I can catch this before I even act out on it because I spend daily time processing my emotions in my time with God. I start talking to God about the anger. I ask Him to help me understand why I am angry. What's underneath that? I may be angry because I'm hurt by something someone said to me. Then I have to apply the Soul Care principle of forgiveness. I may be angry because I am fearful. Unfortunately, when I experience weak emotions (fear, shame, sadness, and things of a similar nature), my presenting feeling is often anger. So I have to peel back the layers, unpack the surface emotion, and figure out what is really driving the anger. If I discover fear is the driving reason for my anger, I need to appropriate the Soul Care principles for overcoming fear. Sometimes I am angry because of grief: I've experienced some loss in my life, and I have to process the sadness, loss, or disappointment that is motivating my anger. Sometimes I'm angry because I am wrestling with an identity issue. The issue of my value has become dependent upon whether people like me or whether I am in control. My anger reflects the fact that I can't control an outcome, and that makes me feel less important. I have to integrate the Soul Care principle of my identity, that the issue of my value was settled at the cross. I have to hold to the truth that I am deeply loved by God and get off that shaky platform to overcome the anger. Sometimes I'm angry because I have said yes to too many requests. I have too many balls in the air I am attempting to juggle, and I am feeling stressed. In reality, if that is the case, it is only because I have taken on assignments the Lord has not given me. If that is true, why am I doing this? Why do I have unhealthy boundaries? Is it my identity issues? Is it people pleasing? I need to wrestle with that question, surrender it, and get healthy boundaries back into my life.

The fact that I have a daily practice of processing these presenting problems with God keeps the suitcase of my soul relatively free and light. If you want a healthy soul, you have to build daily practices into your routine. I am not spending hours every day doing this. I spend a few minutes every day. Usually that is enough to keep me healthy. But we can easily miss things—and that is where awareness of the dashboard gauges becomes most helpful, when these symptoms start to present themselves. Then we need to spend whatever time is necessary to get to the root, settle the issue, and get back in alignment with God.

Let me mention two things that have been extremely important to my journey toward wholeness. First, I am aware of the presenting symptoms of soul disease. When I feel anger, or angst, I am out of alignment with God. Something is off in my soul. When I feel lethargy, I know something is off in my soul. When I feel anything other than free and full in Christ, I go after it. Second, I have connected these presenting symptoms to various root issues in my life. I only made those connections through doing the hard work of processing. I have spent a lot of time reflecting, praying, journaling, reading, and wrestling with the symptoms to figure out what was underneath. I started noticing patterns, and thus the presenting symptoms helped me. When I felt the symptom, I knew something was off in my soul, and I got alone with God and figured it out.

Let me end with a final example. Anxiety has become a gift to me. I know that might sound shocking; this is not the way most people think about anxiety! But I have come to realize that whenever I feel anxiety something is off in my soul. Anxiety is there to show me that something is out of alignment in my life. Therefore, when I feel anxiety I get alone with God and go after it. I wrestle, journal, and pray until I figure out why I am anxious. Then I deal with the roots, not the symptoms—and the peace of Christ returns.

Do you have daily or near daily practices that allow you to integrate Soul Care principles? Do you have daily or weekly practices in place that ensure you are living with healthy boundaries? Do you have a daily or weekly practice to process your negative emotions in a positive way? I do the latter in my daily prayer journal. You don't have to do it that way, but you do have to find a way to keep your suitcase light. Do you have daily practices of self-care? I monitor my three tanks— physical, emotional, and spiritual—and when I start to feel the emptiness, I make an adjustment. I pay attention to the dashboard of my soul, and when I see one of these indicator lights flashing, I deal with it.

Look at these four areas of healthy leaders. What changes do you need to make? What daily practices can you add that will help you continue to grow and sustain the practices of a healthy leader?

Don't ignore them. Put your head down and keep ministering. Go after it.

Chapter 3

CREATING A SOUL CARE CULTURE

One time I was in Ocean City, Maryland and I went for a bike ride. I had been riding my bike 15 to 20 miles most days for many years, so I was in pretty good shape. Sometimes when I go for a bike ride I feel exceptionally strong that day and make really good time. I'm not sure why that is. At any rate, on this day I felt really strong. I rode in one direction for about 10 miles and then turned around to head back to our rental house. I suddenly realized why I felt so strong that morning. I was riding the entire time with the wind at my back! I hadn't realized it. I now had to ride back 10 miles against a strong wind. The way home was exhausting.

When we get the culture of our organization in alignment with our vision, we feel like we are leading with the wind at our back. It feels much easier to lead and accomplish our goals, and we feel empowered. If you are a pastor or a small group leader and are trying to implement Soul Care into your local context, you have to understand how to create a Soul Care culture. What are the cultural components that produce an atmosphere where we feel like we are leading a Soul Care environment with the wind of God at our backs?

Deep Life Change Culture

To create a culture that is hospitable to Soul Care, we have to create a deep life change culture. There are three aspects of a deep life change culture we need to explore: anointed teaching, true community, and the presence and power of God.

First, to create a deep life change culture there must be **anointed teaching**. When I say anointed teaching, I probably don't mean what most people think I mean. Most people think about a gifted teacher; I will assume the communicator is a gifted teacher. By anointed teaching, I mean the teacher has *lived into the teaching*. They lead people down paths of wisdom they have traveled. They have integrated this truth into their lives, and they embody the concept. When you live into a teaching you have authority over that area, and you create an atmosphere of breakthrough for other people. A gifted teacher can communicate concepts, but without the anointing of the Spirit the teaching will be interesting but the life change factor will be low. However, when the teacher lives out the truth they communicate, and they communicate it even more effectively because of the wisdom they have developed while living it out, there is a Spirit-saturated atmosphere that is conducive to life change. There is a weightiness to the words they convey because they have been marked by the presence of the Spirit in their lives.

In Matthew 10 Jesus sent out the twelve and gave them authority to drive out demons, heal the sick, and preach the gospel of the Kingdom. Jesus said to them, "Freely you have received, freely give" (Matthew 10:8). You cannot give what you do not have. But what you have deeply assimilated into your life, you can impart to others who are earnestly seeking freedom.

As I mentioned, I never expected to do this kind of ministry. I started my ministry focused on growing as a leader, reproducing leaders, and creating a leadership environment. The church was growing and people were coming to Christ, but when Jen and I hit a marriage snag, I was forced to deal with my brokenness. As the Lord taught me these principles of life change and I started implementing them, I began to develop spiritual authority in these areas. I found I had the wind at my back when it came to helping people gain freedom in Christ. Leadership is necessary. Good leadership can gather a crowd and mobilize them on mission. But authority creates breakthrough atmospheres. I started teaching Soul Care, and people started having breakthroughs. Life change was happening everywhere I taught these things—at seminary, in my local church, in conferences. And it became very apparent that God had anointed me to communicate these principles of freedom in such a way that people experienced deep life change. That's what happens with anointed teaching. You only have authority over that which you walk in victory.

The second key component of a deep life change culture is **true community**. You were created in the image of God. God is community: Father, Son, and Holy Spirit. They have lived in perfect community for all eternity. There has never been any darkness or division between them; there has never been any deception, hiding, tension, animosity, or dissension. They have lived in perfect harmony for all eternity. Since you were created in God's image, you were created for true community. But sin has disrupted community and causes darkness, rifts, and divisions between us. Sin makes us want to hide.

Think about Adam and Eve. They were regularly walking in the garden with God, naked and unashamed. But as soon as they sinned, they felt shame and covered their nakedness. They weren't just covering up physically, they were covering their sin. They blame, excuse, justify, rationalize, and deny their sin. They start moving toward the darkness for cover. But there is no freedom in the darkness.

If we are going to experience the freedom Jesus has purchased for us with His blood, we are going to have to move into the light. We must walk in the light as He is in the light. In 1 John 1:5-7, John says, "God is light; in him there is no darkness at all. If we claim to have fellowship with him and yet walk in the darkness, we lie and do not live out the truth. But if we walk in the light, as he is in the light, we have fellowship with one another, and the blood of Jesus, his Son, purifies us from all sin." If you follow John's logic in the passage, you realize that John made an illogical statement. He said *God* is light. In *Him* there is no darkness. And if we walk in the light as *He* is in the light, we will have fellowship with . . . one another. He should have said we will have fellowship with *Him*. That would have made logical sense. Whenever someone in the Bible seems to jump logic tracks, you have to realize they have a presupposition we don't yet understand that allows them to leap to that conclusion. So the question is: what is the presupposition John holds as he makes this statement?

John understands the biblical truth that God opposes the proud but gives grace to the humble. If we are truly walking in humility, we will be honest with others; we won't try to manage our image or attempt to look better than we are. If I am trying to look better in your eyes than I really am, that's pride. If I walk in pride with you, I am not really walking in the light with God, because God opposes the proud. So, John concludes, if we are really in the light with God, because we are walking in humility, we will be in the light with others.

Humble people won't have any secrets and won't pretend to be something they are not. Light is the way of God's Kingdom. Darkness is the way of Satan's kingdom.

You are a spiritual being in a spiritual world; you are always giving away spiritual access. You do not get to choose *if* you give away access; you only get to choose *to whom* you give away access. When you pick up the tools of the kingdom of darkness, you give access to the evil one. When you pick up the tools of the kingdom of light, you give access to God. If we pick up secrecy to cover our sinfulness, we are giving Satan access. We cannot walk in freedom in the kingdom of light by using the tools of the kingdom of darkness. We must walk in the light as He is in the light. We must walk in the light with God and others. This is the only path to victory.

This is why I always do small groups as part of Soul Care. Sadly, people are often tempted to skip the small groups. They just want to experience the teaching—they do this because we have a Western, knowledge-based approach to discipleship. People come to the conference for the information, and they mistakenly assume the information will lead to transformation. But the Pharisees knew the truth. They read their Bible and memorized large portions of it, but they killed Jesus. All their knowledge didn't help them. They were still living in pride and walking in darkness.

Everybody needs a few people in their life with whom they walk in the light. You don't need to wear your heart on your sleeve and tell everybody everything. But you should have a few people with whom you are living in open, honest, confessional community. I have a few people in my life who know everything about me. No one can ever come to me and say, "You did such and such" except that I would be able to say, "Yes, but Jen knows that. Martin knows that. Heck, I wrote that one in a book!" It is incredibly freeing to live without secrets. Every day when I get up, the guy I look at in the mirror is the person I am presenting to those closest to me. That light-living lifestyle causes us to feel loved and free; it breaks the enemy's grip of shame and condemnation over our souls.

Some of you—and many of the people we minister to—have been deeply wounded in community, and thus many people are reluctant to be vulnerable. But if you have been wounded in community, you can only be healed by community. God will only take you so far on your healing journey before He calls you back into community to finalize the healing process. You have to choose to slowly make your way back to community. Don't grab the first person you meet off the street and say, "Let me tell you everything I ever did." You'll likely get burned again. Instead, find someone to open up to bit by bit. If they are faithful to your sacred trust, open up a little more. If they are faithful again, open up still more. As you build trust, it heals your wounds, you trust more and share more, and you find more freedom.

I have been doing Soul Care conferences around the world for a long time. People join triads and often end up with people they do not know. At first, often, they are reluctant to open up and share. But as they start to become vulnerable and receive compassion, they open up more, and I have seen many deep friendships established in a three-day conference. Many times relationships are established in a conference that last for years, and sometimes they continue to meet together once a month and stay in the light with each other because they found so much freedom and healing from the triad experience.

Third, if we are going to create a deep life change culture, we need to **access the presence and power of God**. Only God can change the heart. We don't just need a theology about God's presence and power, we need an authentic experiential knowledge of His presence and power.

There is no authentic proclamation of the gospel of the Kingdom in the New Testament without a demonstration of power. The central message of Jesus is about the Good News (gospel) of the Kingdom of God. The Kingdom of God is the reversal of everything that went wrong with the world when sin entered the world. Sadly, too often, we have reduced it to this: you're a sinner; Jesus came to earth and lived a sinless life; He died and rose again; when you put your faith in Jesus your sins are forgiven; and when you die you go to Heaven. That is one part of the gospel of the Kingdom, but only one part. But there is more to the Kingdom than that: it is the reversal of everything that went wrong when sin entered the world. It is the restoration of the way things were intended to be. So when Jesus comes and preaches the gospel of the Kingdom, He casts out demons. He heals the sick. He feeds the hungry. He reverses all the effects of sin. Jesus' victory over sin gives Him power over the effects of sin.

The proof that Jesus has overcome sin is the fact that Jesus has the power to dismantle the effects of sin. When Jesus sent out the twelve disciples, He gave them authority to drive out evil spirits and heal sickness (Matthew 10:1). He did the same thing with the seventy-two whom He sent out in Luke 10. They come back and declared, "Lord, even the demons submit to us in your name!" (Luke 10:17). They have success, but in Matthew 17 they run into a problem. They can't cast out a demon from a young boy. Jesus was on the Mount of Transfiguration, and when He arrives on the scene He says to His disciples, "You unbelieving and perverse generation, how long shall I stay with you? How long shall I put up with you?" (Matthew 17:17). The word in Greek translated *perverse* is a word that means to distort the truth. They were proclaiming the gospel of the Kingdom, but they were perverting the message they proclaimed by not being able to demonstrate the message by casting out demons. If Jesus has overcome sin, then, by necessary implication Jesus can overcome the effects of sin. There is no authentic proclamation of the gospel of the

Kingdom in the New Testament without a demonstration of power.

Paul said to the church at Corinth, "When I came to you, I did not come with eloquence or human wisdom as I proclaimed to you the testimony about God. For I resolved to know nothing while I was with you except Jesus Christ and him crucified. I came to you in weakness with great fear and trembling. My message and my preaching were not with wise and persuasive words, but with a demonstration of the Spirit's power, so that your faith might not rest on human wisdom, but on God's power" (1 Corinthians 2:1-5). Paul came in weakness; it wasn't about his power. But Paul also came proclaiming the message of the Kingdom, and he demonstrated that with power. The power of God proved the message that Jesus was King and had conquered sin, the devil, and all the effects of evil.

Jesus didn't just come to save us from sin. He came to save us from all of the effects of sin. 1 John 3:8 says, "The reason the Son of God appeared was to destroy the devil's works." Gary Thomas writes, "Jesus chased out ignorance, defeated the demonic, and released the ill and oppressed. In other words, as Jesus walked, hell broke apart at his feet. Jesus and hell could not occupy the same spot, so wherever Jesus went, hell was dismantled. Together, His life and teaching provide a clear goal—seeing hell break apart at our feet and the coming forth of the kingdom of God" (Gary Thomas, *Seeking the Face of God: Strengthen Your Walk with God By Exploring the Faith of Our Spiritual Ancestors*, p. 19). Exactly. If we carry the presence of God, we should see the things Jesus saw.

I know many of you are not seeing the level of God's power you would like to see. Neither am I, but I am experiencing much more than before. Let me give just a few thoughts about increasing God's presence and power in your life and ministry. First, faith really matters; we have to develop our faith. I wrote the book *Deep Faith* because the development of my faith was so critical to the release of more Kingdom activity in my life and ministry. It is important to understand the message of the Kingdom and know that the demonstration of power is normal in the Kingdom. Second, perseverance is crucial to experiencing Kingdom power. At first, I read my Bible, and I believed Jesus was the same today as He was when He walked the earth, but I wasn't seeing the things I read about in the Bible. However, I would not allow my lack of experience to define my ministry. I persevered in pursuing God, preaching the truth of the gospel of the Kingdom, and praying for the Kingdom to come on earth as it does in Heaven. And over time, with perseverance and much suffering, there were more demonstrations of power. Third, prophecy is often the gateway gift to the acts of the Kingdom, so we need to learn how to hear God's voice. I cannot tell you how many times in my ministry a supernatural act of God was preceded by a prompting of the Spirit; this is the reason I will spend an entire chapter on the prophetic. And fourth, if we are going to experience more of God's power, we need to carry a greater sensitivity to God's presence in our lives. I'll talk more about that below.

Creating the Culture

As leaders, how do we create this culture of deep life change? What must we do to create a Soul Care-thriving culture?

First, if we are going to create this culture, **we need to dismantle the parts of our current culture that interfere with establishing a deep life change culture**. John's disciples came to Jesus one day and asked Him why His disciples didn't fast. Jesus said the time would come for them to fast, but not while the bridegroom was with them. Then he said, "No one sews a patch of unshrunk cloth on an old garment, for the patch will pull away from the garment, making the tear worse. Neither do people pour new wine into old wineskins. If they do, the skins will burst; the wine will run out, and the wineskins will be ruined. No, they pour new wine into new wineskins, and both are preserved" (Matthew 9:16, 17). Jesus was saying that for a new culture to be created, some of the old ways of doing things have to be done away with.

For example, many people try to implement Soul Care over an already existing religious culture. Religion often has a checklist mentality. There are certain things you have to do to belong. You have to read your Bible, pray, tithe, serve, evangelize, go to church, and probably more things in each culture. And there are certain things you can't do if you are going to belong. You can't lust, you can't steal, you can't be angry, and so on. If you check off the items on the lists, you are accepted. If this religious mentality isn't dismantled, then people just learn a new set of items to be checked off in order to belong. For example: to belong, you must be honest. So people are honest enough to be accepted in the religious community, but they aren't completely honest. They are honest about some safe things, but they hide the really dark parts; they remain in bondage and shame, but they check the honesty box in their minds so they can belong. This old culture keeps them from experiencing the culture of the Kingdom. So we have to confront some of these old manners of being before we can create a new normal set of patterns.

Let's consider the intersection between culture and discipleship. Culture is what we consider "normal." It is a set of expectations, attitudes, and behaviors that most of a people group consider normal. Discipleship is ultimately about changing cultures. We are trying to help people shift from the culture of their family and region of origin to the culture of the Kingdom of God. People are deciding to come under the rule of King Jesus and follow His cultural norms; they are submitting to His values, His ways of living, behaving, and relating. When Kingdom culture clashes with our American culture, our Korean culture, our Canadian culture, or our family of origin culture, if we don't choose Kingdom culture, we are not followers. This is what Jesus meant when He told us we need to hate our mother and father and follow Him. He doesn't hate your mom; His point is that our loyalty and allegiance to Him now must take precedence over all other loyalties. Kingdom culture needs to become our new normal.

As leaders, we have to be intentional about confronting the aspects of our current culture that come in conflict with the culture of the Kingdom of God. All human cultures are fallen. Yet not all aspects of culture need to be changed. We have to discern what particular aspects of our current culture will inhibit Kingdom culture from being established. Those are the things we need to intentionally dismantle. This is what Jesus did. This takes real reflection, thought, and wisdom.

Let me provide an example. Many people in evangelical religious environments are afraid of the Holy Spirit. They are particularly afraid of the manifestations of the Holy Spirit. So before we can create an atmosphere where the presence and power of God can freely flow (which is normal in the culture of the Kingdom), we have to tear down this fear of the Holy Spirit. This must be addressed. Often in these environments, I say, "Jesus isn't afraid of the Holy Spirit. Fear of the Holy Spirit is demonic. Fear of the Spirit is a tool of the enemy to keep you from freedom and fullness in Christ." Literally, you can see these words land on people with revelatory impact. In Pentecostal or charismatic environments, you have to fight against learned behaviors. The manifestation becomes the normal—even when it isn't authentic. A holy man prays for you, and you know, in some Pentecostal environments, that you are supposed to fall over. So people don't fall because the Spirit comes upon them in power, as happens to the prophet

Ezekiel or the Apostle John in the book of Revelation, they fall because they are supposed to—it is a learned behavior, a cultural expectation. But these kinds of learned behaviors often keep us from authentic movements of the Spirit. We aren't to imitate certain learned behaviors or resist certain things that are authentically from the Spirit. We must simply give the Holy Spirit true access and let Him do what He wishes to do—without fear, without control, and without faking it or manufacturing it.

Second, if we are going to create an atmosphere where Soul Care thrives, **we have to create cultures of grace**. We are calling people to share openly and honestly. We are asking people to be confessional, to walk in the light with God and others, to live free in Christ. Therefore, we must create a safe environment for them to take these emotional risks.

We have to create an environment where sharing honestly is the norm and is safe. This means we will have to love and accept people where they are, just as Jesus did. We want them to be honest; we cannot judge them for their sin. We have to recreate an atmosphere where confession is welcomed, where judgmental attitudes are unacceptable. When hiding is normal, judgment flourishes. People who have secrets live with shame. Shame leaves us with a lack of self-acceptance and often results in judging others. You can't give what you don't have.

Creating a culture of grace also means we are going to have to lead with vulnerability. This is my rule for sharing: I will share anything that will help you, but nothing that will cause you to stumble. If I am struggling with something I think would cause you to stumble, I will share that with my inner circle of trusted confidants who can handle that and help me gain victory. I am not going to conceal that issue, but I am not going to share it recklessly in a way that could shipwreck someone's faith.

In Psalm 73, Asaph, the worship leader, shares vulnerably that his "feet had almost slipped; I had nearly lost my foothold." He nearly lost his faith because of the prosperity of the wicked. He couldn't understand why God let the wicked prosper. But he also says, in verse 15, "If I had spoken out like that, I would have betrayed your children." In other words, he didn't share this publicly when he was in the throes of defeat lest he cause someone else to stumble. But once he gets to a place of victory, he writes it in a psalm for all eternity. You can share nearly anything from the place of victory, but you have to be careful what you share publicly as a leader from the throes of defeat. The rule of thumb is to do what is best for others, not for yourself.

For example, as I mentioned in chapter 2, in the summer of 2013 I was struggling with the question: Does God lie? I had four promises that the Lord had given me, but none of them were making any headway. It felt as though God had lied to me. I couldn't share that struggle from the pulpit when I was in the middle of it because it could have caused some people in my congregation to stumble. So I processed it with some close friends. But once I reached the other side of the struggle, then, from the place of victory, I shared it in a sermon with my congregation. It was a powerful sermon when delivered from a place of victory. But it could have devastated some if I had shared it while still in the throes of defeat. Be wise with whom you share, but don't go underground and struggle alone. This will help you create a culture of grace.

Third, if we are going to create a culture of deep life change where Soul Care excels, **we have to create an equipping culture.** In Ephesians 4 Paul says, "Christ himself gave the apostles, the prophets, the evangelists, the pastors and teachers, to equip his people for works of service, so that the body of Christ may be built up until we all reach unity in the faith and in the knowledge of the Son of God and become mature, attaining to the whole measure of the fullness of God" (Ephesians 4:11-13). The leader's job is not merely to do the work of ministry, but to equip the saints to do the work of ministry. No one in the family of God gets a junior Holy Spirit. The same Spirit that lives in Christ lives in each of us.

When I was a pastor I noticed that a lot of people could give good answers about who the Holy Spirit was and what the Holy Spirit did, but they weren't walking in the things of the Spirit with power like the disciples. Jesus said, "Apart from me, you can do nothing." We need the presence and power of the Spirit to mark our lives if we are going to make an eternal impact. My job as a pastor is to equip the saints for the work of ministry, so I thought about how I could do that. Most churches simply teach on the Holy Spirit. But teaching isn't equipping. And just because people can pass a theology test, that doesn't mean they can move in the ways of the Spirit. So I decided to do a Holy Spirit weekend. We taught on things of the Spirit and then created a lab time where we created space to practice living it. For example, we taught how to hear God's voice, and then we broke people into groups of three where they would listen for a word from the Lord for each other. This gave people practical experience time to move in the things of the Spirit. We taught people how to pray for the sick, and then we had sick people stand and they all prayed for one another. They were learning how to minister in the Spirit, and then they had an opportunity to do it right there, in a safe environment, where they could receive coaching. That's equipping. Too often in churches we do teaching without equipping and people are left with knowledge devoid of experience. That's not what Jesus did. A huge part of creating culture is creating experiences where people live into the ways of the Kingdom.

I do not want to simply teach what to do, but how to do it. I seek to create experiences where people can begin to practice those things. That is vital to equipping. In my book *River*

Dwellers I teach how to walk in the things of the Spirit. In my book *Soul Care* I teach how to live out the freedom and fullness of Christ. In *Deep Faith* I teach how to develop faith and move in the things of the Spirit. In *Spiritual Authority* I teach how to develop authority. Most of the time in church we tell people what to do but fail to equip people how to do it. We need to provide solid teaching and experiences to help people master the things of the Spirit.

When I do Soul Care conferences, I always equip people at the host church to do deliverance. Saturday is deliverance day, and everyone wants to get in my line to experience deliverance because I am the "expert." But here is the reality: first, I didn't start off as an "expert." When I started, I had little training, no experience, and no idea what I was doing. I had to learn by doing. Second, if I do deliverance for the rest of my life, I could help tens of thousands of people get free. But if I train and equip people to do deliverance, we could see hundreds of thousands of people set free. It is far better that I equip people. Jesus could do deliverance far quicker and better than the disciples, but He didn't just do deliverance. He equipped and empowered them to do deliverance, then coached them. This was, and is, a much better plan for advancing the Kingdom.

As I wrote in the last chapter, this type of ministry sometimes attracts people who are codependent. They need to be needed; helping others gives them a sense of significance. They aren't healthy yet and need to take some time to get healthy before they get deeply involved with Soul Care ministry. We want to help people get healthy. We want to empower people to do ministry, but we don't want to appoint people as leaders of ministries unless they are reasonably healthy people. So we have to choose people wisely. Paul cautions Timothy, "Do not be hasty in the laying on of hands" (1 Timothy 5:22). Paul is warning Timothy not to promote people into ministry positions before they are spiritually mature enough to handle it.

So how do we know who to entrust ministry to? An old acronym for choosing leaders is helpful. We should choose people who are FAT: faithful, available, and teachable. We should choose people who are growing. They are not just learning the concepts; they have a track record for implementing these principles in their lives. They are not just hearers of the word, but doers (James 1:22). These are people who complete their assignments and put what they learn into practice. They are also available. They are courageous people willing to take risks. They make time for God's Kingdom activity in their lives. They prioritize the things of God. And they are teachable. They display humility and are open to you as a leader. They grow through criticism and handle negative feedback responsibly.

I want leaders who display a heart for God. I look more to the heart than to the competencies. It is nice to have gifted people, but if I have to choose between gifting and a heart for God that displays character and humility, I will choose heart every time. I want people who have a heart for God and heart for people. They are characterized by love because, according to Jesus, love is the most important thing.

Everyone is worthy of love; not everyone is worthy of your investment. Those are two separate things. I have a limited amount of time and energy to invest. So I want to invest wisely. I want to invest in people who will turn around and produce Kingdom fruit. I want to invest in people the Lord calls me to invest in. I always pray and ask God if I should make an investment in someone, because I can't invest in everyone. There are more people out there who want mentoring than I can possibly mentor, more people who need ministry than I can possibly minister to. So I seek the Lord for His direction.

Finally, if we are going to create an environment where Soul Care can flourish, **we need to carry His presence**. Good teaching and programs alone will not produce deep life change.

Only God can change the human heart. We need to learn to become Spirit people. When Jesus shows up, Kingdom stuff happens. Jesus said, "I am the vine; you are the branches. If you remain in me and I in you, you will bear much fruit; apart from me you can do nothing" (John 15:5). The truth is that too many believers aren't carrying enough of God's presence to be any threat to hell. We need to learn how to abide in such a way that the presence of Jesus is saturating our lives so that when we show up, Jesus shows up, and the Kingdom happens around us because Jesus is there. This demands that we move from religious activity to authentic intimacy with God.

In Luke 11:13, Jesus said, "If you then, though you are evil, know how to give good gifts to your children, how much more will your Father in heaven give the Holy Spirit to those who ask him!" There is always more of God; He is infinite. You can always experience more of His presence, more of His voice, more of His love. But you have to pursue. The context of this statement in Luke 11:13 is, "Ask and it will be given to you; seek and you will find; knock and the door will be opened to you. For everyone who asks receives; those who seek find; and to those who knock, the door will be opened" (Luke 11:9, 10). You can have as much of God as you want, but no more than you are willing to pay the price for.

A Needed Filling of the Spirit

In a later chapter I will talk about how to increase our capacity for more of His Spirit. But in this chapter let me talk about another crucial concept: the filling of the Spirit. We need to be baptized, or filled, with the Holy Spirit. It isn't about having a past experience with the Spirit. The key question is: are we currently walking in the filling of the Spirit? Is the Spirit's presence and power marking our lives? If not, then regardless of past experiences, we need a fresh filling.

How do you know if you are walking in the fullness of the Spirit? There certainly should be the fruit of the Spirit (Galatians 5). We ought to manifest the character of Christ in increasing measure when we are walking in step with the Spirit.

Our lives ought to be marked by love. Jesus said that the most important thing is to love God and the second is to love people. We can have great insight, but if we lack love, we represent Jesus poorly. We can be party to great miracles, but if we lack love, we simply represent Jesus poorly.

There also ought to be power. When Jesus shows up, the Kingdom comes, and the devil's works are destroyed. In Acts chapters 1 and 2 there are clear signs of what it looks like when men and women walk in the fullness of the Spirit. There are a series of when/then statements. When we are walking in the current fullness of the Spirit, then this ought to occur. Let's look at these a little closer.

Acts 1:8: "You will receive power when the Holy Spirit comes on you." First, when we are walking in the fullness of the Spirit, there ought to be power. This isn't my idea; this is Jesus' idea. The presence of Christ is in us, and when Jesus shows up He demonstrates power that reverses the effects of the fall. When Jesus preached the gospel of the Kingdom, He cast out demons and healed the sick. In the book of Acts, after the Spirit is poured out on the day of Pentecost, the disciples move in power. There is healing and deliverance. The presence of God in them manifests the power of God around them. Jesus told them they would be baptized with the Spirit (Acts 1:5). To that point, all they knew was their experience of baptism: they were taken into the water and completely soaked and immersed in water. Jesus promised them some coming of the Spirit where they would be soaked, drenched, and immersed in the presence of God.

This is not their regenerative experience with the Spirit. That occurred in John 20:22: "And with that Jesus breathed on them and said, 'Receive the Holy Spirit.'" The John 20 experience was their regeneration, their born-again, or born-from-above, experience. The baptism of the Spirit was a new and different experience. It was an empowerment of the Spirit.

This baptism (Acts 1:5) or filling (Acts 2:4) of the Spirit was not a one-time occurrence. The same disciples were filled again with the Spirit in Acts 4:31. If we are going to walk in the current fullness of the Spirit, we need fresh encounters, fresh fillings, fresh baptisms. I was filled with the Spirit when I was 19. I surrendered my life to Christ and had an encounter with the manifest presence of God and deep love of Jesus. I didn't even know what the experience was called, but it changed me. I was filled again with the Spirit at various points and in various encounters with God along the way.

In many ways, the one that produced the most results was the least dramatic. I had gone through a dark night of the soul, where I had no sense of God's presence or His voice. This went on for some months. When the Spirit revealed Himself to me again it was very gentle—just a gentle re-entry of His presence. But after that fresh encounter with the Spirit, I saw a dramatic increase in supernatural power. The first conference I went to after that experience almost everybody I prayed for had a significant encounter with God's presence and power. Pursue *His presence*, not specific manifestations. It is the presence of God we want to pursue and carry to others.

Notice that after the disciples were filled again with His Spirit in Acts 4:31, there was an increase in power. Verse 33: "With great power the apostles continued to testify to the resurrection of the Lord Jesus." Acts 5, beginning in verse 12: "The apostles performed many signs and wonders among the people. . . As a result, people brought the sick into the streets and laid them on beds and mats so that at least Peter's shadow might fall on some of them as he passed by. Crowds gathered also from the towns around Jerusalem, bringing their sick and those tormented by evil spirits, and all of them were healed." You only get to do shadow healings after your second filling of the Spirit! With the fresh filling there is more of God's presence, and with the increase in His presence often comes an increase in God's power.

Next, when we are walking in the current fullness of the Spirit, we will witness to who Jesus is and what Jesus does. Again, let's look at Acts 1:8: "You will receive power when the Holy Spirit comes on you; and you will be my witnesses." When the Spirit comes on you, there will be power. And when the Spirit comes on you, you will be a witness. You see this throughout the book of Acts. The believers are bold witnesses. When they are filled again with the Spirit in Acts 4:31, Scripture says, "And they were all filled with the Holy Spirit and spoke the word of God boldly." When the Spirit comes with power, we are secured in the Father's love. With security comes boldness. I had never shared my faith with anyone before I was filled with the Spirit. After that encounter with the Spirit I started making appointments with my friends to tell them about Jesus. No one told me I was supposed to. I didn't have any classes in evangelism. I simply did it because I had experienced the reality of Jesus' love and didn't want anyone to miss out on the fullness I had received.

A witness simply tells what she or he has seen, heard, and experienced. Think about being an eyewitness to a car accident; all you do is tell what you have seen, heard, and experienced. When we are walking in the fullness of the Spirit, Jesus is active in our lives, and we experience His transforming presence and influence. We have a story to tell about who Jesus is and what Jesus does because we are experiencing His life-changing power. This life-changing work of the Spirit gives us both the desire and the ability to witness.

One of the easiest and most effective ways to witness is to look for the divine intersection point—that is, the point where Jesus' life-changing work in us intersects with what another person needs Jesus to do for them. For example, Jesus has helped me in my marriage. The marriage crisis we experienced early on became the impetus for Jesus' life-changing work in me that led to deep healing in our marriage. So when I am talking to someone with relational pain, this is often an open door for a witness. Jesus has helped me overcome anxiety, so when I am talking to someone who struggles with anxiety or another emotional malady, this is often an intersection point of witness.

When we are walking in the current fullness of the Spirit, we are constantly creating new avenues for witness because of Jesus' ongoing transformational work in us. And when we are walking in the fullness of the Spirit, we have the desire to be near people who don't know Jesus and help them know Him. This is a mark of the Spirit's fullness in our lives. When we lack power or witness, we need a fresh filling.

Lastly, when we are walking in the fullness of the Spirit, we will prophesy. That is the third when/then statement about walking in the fullness of the Spirit that we see in Acts. In Acts 2, after the disciples are filled with the Spirit, Peter preaches on the day of Pentecost and quotes from the Old Testament prophet Joel. He says, "In the last days, God says, 'I will pour out my Spirit on all people. Your sons and daughters will prophesy, your young men will see visions, your old men will dream dreams. Even on my servants, both men and women, I will pour out my Spirit in those days, and they will prophesy'" (Acts 2:17, 18). When our lives are marked by God's presence, we hear God's voice. Prophecy simply means that we hear God's voice; He often speaks to us so that we will relay a message to someone else for their benefit. We will talk about this more in the next chapter. But for now, simply note that when we are walking in the fullness of the Spirit, we should hear God's voice.

When we are no longer seeing God's power, hearing God's voice, or craving opportunities to witness out of fresh experiences with Jesus in our lives, we need a fresh filling. It isn't enough to know that we were once filled with the Spirit. The key question is: are we currently walking in the fullness of the Spirit? Just be honest with yourself. If not, then pray and fast and seek God for another fresh filling, a new awakening of God's presence and work in your soul.

I've learned a lot from people who were part of significant moves of the Spirit. Charles Finney was the key player in the Second Great Awakening. There were times when Finney came to a town and preached and the power of God was so readily available that nearly the entire town was converted. Brothels and prisons would shut down because the spiritual atmosphere over a town had completely changed. It was such a powerful revival that, five years later, 80 percent of the new converts were still walking with God.

But Finney also noticed that sometimes the power would dry up. The waves of the Spirit would cease. There was an ebb and flow to the presence and power of God being manifest. When the power of God dried up, Finney would lock himself away and pray and fast with Father Nash, his prayer partner. They would pray and fast until they experienced a fresh filling, a new visitation from the Holy Spirit. Then the revival would start again with a new wave of power.

I have seen this principle in my own life as well. There was a time in my ministry when I didn't see much of the power of God. I believed it. I preached it. But I didn't see much demonstration of God's power. So I kept believing, but I also pursued God's presence. At first I saw a little increase in God's power, but it wasn't like I had hoped for, expected, or read about in the Bible, so I kept pursuing more of God's presence.

There were many ups and downs in the journey. There were great moments with God in intimacy and there were great disappointments. There were attacks along the way from the enemy and from people. It is nearly impossible to experience more of God's power without embracing the fellowship of Jesus' sufferings (Phil 3:10, 11). So through it all, I kept pursuing God. Then there was the dark night of the soul, when all tangible signs of God's presence disappeared. I couldn't hear His voice or feel His presence. But I kept coming to be with Him day after day. I knew that the purpose of the dark night of the soul was purgation. Ultimately, to experience more of God's fullness, there needs to be less of us. The biggest problem with the church around the world today is that we are making it too much about us and not enough about Jesus. I'll say it again: the Kingdom really isn't complicated. When Jesus shows up, the Kingdom comes. When we show up, not much happens.

After the dark night of the soul ended and the Spirit gently appeared again, there was an immediate and tremendous increase in power. For the next year, every conference I did, I saw God move in power. People were healed; lives were changed. Deliverances flowed freely; people encountered God's presence and love. As I taught on baptism of the Spirit and prayed for people, large numbers of people were filled with the Spirit with clear demonstrations of God's power. It was unlike anything I had ever seen. But after a year of the Spirit's tangible power, I noticed it started to dry up. Thanks to Finney's testimony, I knew what to do. I took some time off to pray and fast and seek God for a fresh filling. After doing so, the presence and power of God returned in full force. Since then I have seen that pattern continue: when the power of God dries up, I pray and fast and pursue until the presence and power of God return.

I think God is simply trying to remind us that it isn't about us. It is all about Him. Apart from Him we can do nothing. Every time I show up, I come with empty hands. I can't do anything to change a human heart, free a human soul, or heal a human body. I can't do anything to help someone experience God's presence or love. I must be marked by Jesus' presence and His power. I need to walk in the fullness of the Spirit. If we are going to create atmospheres of deep life change, we must be people of the presence.

Communicating Cultural Change

Partnering with God is often a strange combination of the supernatural and the natural. I have just been talking about the supernatural: walking in the current fullness of the Spirit, hearing God's voice, and seeing God's power. We need that. But if we are going to create a culture of life change where Soul Care thrives, we also need to talk about some really practical human things. We have to communicate this new culture to people. If we don't communicate it effectively, people will not pick it up mysteriously. This is part of the job of a leader.

We cannot create a new culture or change an old one without effective communication. Too often when pastors want to change a culture in a church, they assume they should start by teaching in the pulpit. But this is not the most effective way to create cultural change. There is a simple sociological reason for this.

Vision is best cast dialogically. Let's say I am trying to cast a vision to a group of people, and Jose and Jane are sitting in the audience. They listen to my presentation, but they have questions. They are good people. They are on board with me and the church. But they aren't sure about this new direction, and they have questions. They are wondering: What about this? What about that? If they do not have an atmosphere to express those questions, they will not buy into the vision. It is not that they are bad people or resistant; they simply need to understand, and that requires dialogue. If they have an atmosphere to raise their questions and I can interact with them—I can say, "I've thought about that, and here is a solution"; or, "I haven't thought about that, that's a great question; let's consider that together"—well, *now they are engaged in the process*, and they are working the vision out in their own mind.

This is what it takes to create vision carriers. A culture cannot be changed across a group of people without vision carriers. We need key influencers to model and articulate the vision to others. If I am the only vision carrier, the vision hasn't made its way into the cultural norms. If there is no opportunity to express concerns, questions, and objections, listeners will likely still come to the church, but they won't buy into the vision because of their unspoken questions and objections. I can't change the culture unless other leaders start to live out these new values.

Let me walk through the process of how I sought to create cultural change as a leader. I attempted to create change in concentric circles of influence. I started with the smallest inner circle. When I was a pastor, that was my staff. When I had a new idea, I would gather the staff around the boardroom table and say, "I have a new idea. I want to float the idea balloon across the room. Feel free to shoot it down." Then I would present the idea and we would dialogue about it. People would weigh in—sometimes in favor of the new idea, sometimes in opposition. We would talk it through from many angles. Sometimes they would raise a question I hadn't thought of, and as soon as they raised the question, I realized this was not going to work (bad idea or wrong timing). Other times they would raise questions I had thought about, and I had some answers for, and they would be persuaded. And still other times they would raise questions I hadn't thought of, and together we would come up with a solution, and all parties would be convinced that this was a good way to go.

If the idea balloon was shot down by the staff, it never went further. But if the idea balloon made it through the first gauntlet, I would then take it to the next circle of leaders—board members and small group leaders. I would go through the same exercise. I would say, "The staff and I have been praying and thinking and we have a new idea. We think God might be in it. But we want to float the idea balloon past you. Feel free to shoot it down." And the process would begin again. They would ask questions, raise objections, seek clarifications, think about ramifications, and we would hash the idea around. Sometimes they thought of questions that the staff and I hadn't thought of, and the idea would be shot down. Other times they sharpened our thinking with new thoughts, perspectives, and questions.

If the idea balloon made it across that second group of leaders, I would bring it to the congregation. This is when I might talk about it on a Sunday morning. But now when people raised objections, they would discuss it with their small group leaders (we were a church of small groups, not a church with small groups), and those leaders had already thought through it, prayed through it, and had buy-in. They were vision carriers. They were helping shift the culture. A new norm was being created.

This process took much longer than if I just made a decision and communicated it. Ideas formed much slower. It often took several rounds of conversations at each level: with the staff, board, and small group leaders. But it was also smoother, more peaceful, and more effective at creating culture. Ideas were more carefully shaped, molded, and adopted by the community over time. Vision is best cast dialogically. Yet too many leaders treat vision as a monological event, not a dialogical process. Too often leaders think they are to go up the mountain, hear from God, come back down from the mountain, cast the vision, and then the people of God are going to buy in. That isn't the way it works, and it won't shift a culture.

To create a Soul Care culture in a church, you must get the senior leadership team on board. If you are not the senior leader, you have to begin with the point leader. They have to buy in. Often at conferences I have people ask me how to create a Soul Care culture, but they are not the senior leader, and the senior leader hasn't bought in. This is what I tell them. First, if you're not the senior leader, the best you can do is create a subculture. If you want to create a Soul Care culture throughout the church, you must get the senior leader fully on board. They have to adopt Soul Care as a lifestyle, and they have to model it for the people, or it won't become part of the culture. So give the senior leader the book, tell them how it impacted you, and ask them to read it. Second, if the senior leader buys in fully, they can begin working the process to create culture. If the senior leader does not want to implement it across the culture, but they don't oppose it and are willing to bless it, you can create a subculture. You ask for their blessing, and you start doing a Soul Care group. Sometimes a senior leader will begin to see this subculture of Soul Care taking root, they will see lives being changed, and they will then get on board and want to work it into the entire culture.

If the senior leader opposes using Soul Care in the church (which usually happens because of the teaching on deliverance), then you have two options left. (You could, of course, be divisive or rebellious. But I don't include that as a real option because it isn't in alignment with Jesus.) First, you can serve as a prophetic voice to the culture. You pray and wait for the senior leader or senior leadership team to be open to the concept. You love, serve, and try to speak into the culture with patience and wisdom as God leads, doing all without being divisive or a nag. Second, you move on to another context where they embrace the concepts of Soul Care and want to implement those principles of freedom in their context.

Let me talk about how we implemented Soul Care at the church I pastored, South Shore Community Church (SSCC). I was the founding pastor, but I did not implement Soul Care from the beginning because I didn't know these principles when I started the church. A year or two into the church plant, Jen and I started having marriage problems, and that led me down this journey. I read all sorts of books, had countless conversations with Jen, and processed all of these learnings with God in prayer. I was learning the key principles of freedom and wholeness and working them into my life.

Eventually I got healthier, our marriage got healthier, our relationships on staff got healthier, and I started forming the lessons I learned into principles I could communicate to others. As I started discovering tools to get healthier, I invited my staff into the process. I handed them the best books I had read. We went to a Leanne Payne inner healing conference. We were journeying together into the path of wholeness. It was the first concentric circle. We didn't just learn about this cognitively; we were living it out in community. Unless the leadership team lives out these principles, you cannot create a Soul Care culture.

After the staff worked it out, I took all of our small group leaders through the teaching, triads, and experiences. We bought them all the key books (*Soul Care* wasn't written at this point), and I taught them all of the principles of Soul Care. There was teaching, discussion, and experience. We formed the leaders into triads, and we created an atmosphere where the presence and power of God was accessible. We brought them through the principles, and we equipped them to minister to others. We were integrating these concepts into the leaders' lives, and this took many months. I had worked through it on my own for many months, the staff and I had worked through it together for many months, and now we worked through it with leaders for months. I had not preached on the principles yet. We were moving the culture into the leadership of the church, creating a new normal among the leaders.

Finally, I brought it to the congregation. We got all of our small groups together on Wednesday nights and I taught through all of the Soul Care principles. The small groups broke into triads and worked these principles out in community. We met every week for four months.

After we had taken all of our people through the Soul Care material, we worked on creating a Soul Care ministry. All of our small group leaders had been trained in the material. However, we realized they were volunteers, and many times people needed more help than they could give, so we developed a Soul Care ministry. We had people who were equipped to do this ministry. They usually had passion and gifting that would allow them to thrive in this area. We brought them through a seminary level course (literally the same course I was teaching at seminary). We had them read the books, do the assignments, and we equipped them. We had two levels of leaders in the ministry. There were people who led small groups of people through Soul Care. They would play the *Soul Care* teaching DVDs, have the people read *Soul Care*, and lead the people through the process of implementing the principles in their life. Then we had people who teamed up to do some one-on-one ministry with those who needed something beyond the small group experience.

We tried to get every person who attended SSCC to go through this Soul Care experience. The first time we brought it to the congregation we took hundreds of people through it. That created common language and common experiences. It helped set the culture. When new people joined us from that point on, we had the Soul Care ministry set up and they went through Soul Care as part of their assimilation into the church. Whether they had transferred from another church or they came to Christ at our church, we wanted everyone to go through Soul Care. Soul Care became the new normal.

We have talked about the kind of culture we have to create. A deep life change culture has anointed teaching, true community, and accesses the presence and power of God. Most churches are Word and program cultures. They teach the Word and they create programs—for children, youth, and adults; and programs for discipleship, evangelism, freedom, recovery, serving the poor, and so on. But for a church to create an atmosphere where the kingdom thrives, and renewal can occur, we have to move beyond Word and program cultures. A Word and program culture cannot sustain renewal.

A culture that sustains renewal needs to be a soul and Spirit culture, rooted in the Word and mobilized on mission. We have to deal with the issues in the soul or they block the flow of the Spirit and impede freedom and fullness in Christ. We have to create a culture where we access the presence and power of God, because only God can change the human heart. All of this has to be rooted in the Word. It has to be solidly biblical or we can get off course and lack depth. And then we have to mobilize people on mission. If we don't mobilize people on mission, healing churches can become sick places that are ingrown.

Final Principles

Let me end this chapter with a few more key principles for creating culture.

First, to create culture we have to communicate the values and the vision. Again, we have to integrate that into the normal behaviors, attitudes, and expectations of the people over time through concentric circles; we must do this if we are going to get it to stick. But then we have to continue to clearly articulate the preferred future. Vision leaks. We must continually communicate the vision and lift the values, finding fresh ways to say things. We can communicate with words, stories, testimonies, videos, sermons, conversations, and more. Stories and testimonies are a vital way to create culture. We often had leaders share testimonies about their Soul Care journey. As they told stories about inner healing, deliverance, and forgiving those who sinned against them, their vulnerability reinforced the value that this was a safe place where you could work on your issues. This was a place where people could change in the presence and power of God.

Second, to create a Soul Care culture in our context, the senior leaders of the community must model it for others. We have to integrate these principles into our lives so that others can see them. The principles of Soul Care need to be more than principles we can articulate; they need to be a lifestyle that can be observed. Remember: you only have authority over that which you walk in victory. If as leaders we want to create an atmosphere of breakthrough for others, we have to live out these principles so others can get free. Vision and values are more effectively caught than taught. John Maxwell says, "People do what people see."

Third, we need to enculturate the leadership team. We have to work it into our culture by reproducing leaders who live this out at every level of the church or organization. This is what Jesus did. He lived it, and He created inner circles of leaders who He discipled, mentored, and coached so they could live it and reproduce it. He had the inner circle of three: Peter, James, and John. He also had the twelve, the seventy-two, and the 120. These leadership teams became the foundation of the early church. This is why I worked through concentric circles at South Shore—the staff, the board and small group leaders, and eventually the congregation. We were working these values into the lives of people so we could create a culture of deep life change. We need leaders who live it, model it, articulate it, and reproduce it.

Fourth, we have to tell stories. Stories help culture become reality; they make it real and sticky. For example, when I wanted to make deliverance part of our culture, I taught on deliverance from the Gospels, and I had people tell their testimony of being set free. In the beginning I asked people who were respected leaders to share their testimony on Sunday morning. They were credible; their stories were compelling and believable. As the stories were told, they became normal, and culture is what is normal to us. When deliverance isn't normal, the church is abnormal to the King and his Kingdom, because deliverance was normal for Jesus. So I had to normalize it for our church. I had a lot of medical doctors in the church. Several of them came to me one day and said, "When you talk about deliverance, you make it sound so normal." I said, "It is." They said, "Well, it isn't normal to most people." I said, "It is normal to Jesus." They said, "Yes, well, to *you* and *Jesus* it is normal. But when you teach it, you make it sound like it is just supposed to be normal . . . for everybody." Exactly. And they learned how to talk to their patients whose presenting problems were demonic in such a way that they normalized the spiritual world, led many people to Jesus, brought them to church, and helped them find freedom in Christ. That's Kingdom normal! And that's the power of creating culture.

Fifth, to create a culture, you have to celebrate the right things. As the old leadership adage goes, "That which gets celebrated gets done." So celebrate when people start to live out the new culture. For example, when we planted the church we wanted to mobilize everyone on mission.

Therefore, whenever we caught people doing mission-oriented things, we celebrated it. We had them come up front and share their story, and we prayed over them and honored them. That reinforces the values you want to see enculturated, and it inspires others to follow this lead.

Sixth, to make a culture stick, use sticky phrases. Culture is always about reshaping language. Common language is critical to cultural creation. Therefore, using sticky phrases that are memorable and reproducible is a powerful aide to making culture stick. My friend Martin Sanders, head of the doctoral program at Alliance Theological Seminary where I teach, says that one of the most powerful things about Soul Care is that it helps create culture. Martin explains that one of the reasons is because I use a lot of sticky phrases that redefine many concepts that have lost meaning over time in the church. For example, I talk about repentance as "getting back into right alignment with God." When your soul is out of alignment with God, life doesn't work right. I use analogies, like the suitcase of your soul. God shines light into the suitcase of your soul. He never shines light to make you feel bad. He shines light to get you free. I have hundreds of sticky phrases I use and word pictures that communicate key concepts, like "the issue of your value was settled at the cross." When I left South Shore Community, at my farewell banquet the people had dozens of these sticky phrases on signs they hung up all around the room. They were memorable, reproducible phrases that helped create culture.

Finally, if you want to create a Soul Care culture, you have to create experiences that reinforce the culture and develop people. Jesus does this; He doesn't just teach. He creates experiences. He casts out demons and heals the sick and then He equips and trains the disciples to do the same Kingdom ministry. He releases and empowers them to do the works of the Kingdom. They come back and report to Him what they have done and He coaches them. This experiential equipping environment is essential for culture crafting. It helps create vision carriers. This is what we did at SSCC with the staff, then the leaders, and eventually the congregation. We created a Soul Care atmosphere where they could experience life change and then be equipped, empowered, and released to minister to others. This is what I seek to do in class environments or Soul Care conferences. I attempt to create a culture where people can begin to experience this new atmosphere. It has worked for hundreds of thousands of people across the world. It is a reproducible atmosphere.

We cannot create culture if we are the only ones doing the ministry. Jesus was clearly the best at deliverance and healing, but He wasn't the only one who did this ministry; He passed it on. We have to create an atmosphere where we can equip people to do these supernatural things—like hearing God's voice, and ministering healing and deliverance—and we make it accessible to everyday people. My wife said to me, "You are the best person I know at taking supernatural things and making them accessible to everyday people. You help people do the things that Jesus did." That's equipping. That is critical to creating a Soul Care culture. I teach a methodology on deliverance, and I do deliverance training workshops because this is reproducible, and if you are going to change the culture of a church you have to develop spiritual leaders who do the works of the Kingdom. If you just teach it, without equipping, most people will not reproduce it.

Soul Care Conferences, Holy Spirit Weekends, and Deliverance Training Workshops were all tools I created to equip and train people in soul and Spirit activities essential for a deep life change culture. They have been reproduced across the globe to great effect. They help create an atmosphere for the Kingdom to come.

Peter Drucker was one of the forerunners in the modern leadership movement in the business world. Drucker understood the importance of vision, strategy, and culture. Drucker said, "Culture eats strategy for breakfast." We must develop culture.

Chapter 4

HEARING GOD'S VOICE

One day I was doing a deliverance on a woman at a conference. I sensed that she had experienced a wound through some sort of trauma that occurred to her mother when she was in the womb. I have done thousands of deliverances; I had only had this thought a handful of times. I asked if she was aware of any trauma that occurred to her mother when she was in the womb. She said no. I had never met the woman before; I didn't know her story. But I as prayed for healing she sobbed; this unlocked some deep pain.

The next day a woman approached me and told me she was the mother of the woman I had prayed for the day before. She went on to say that she had been physically abused by her husband while her daughter was in the womb, but that she never told anyone, including her daughter. As she told me this she wept. She said she and her daughter ended up talking about all this the night before, and they experienced healing in their relationship. She hugged me and thanked me as she said, "No one knew. It had to be God." That's what the Bible calls *prophecy*. Prophecy is simply hearing God's voice. This example is a word of knowledge, which is one of the gifts that falls under the umbrella of the prophetic.

Prophecy is a gateway gift to activity of the Kingdom. When we hear God's voice accurately and relay his words humbly, Jesus shows up, and Kingdom things happen. This is why it is so important we learn how to hear God's voice. I said in the previous chapter that if we are going to minister effectively in Soul Care, we are going to have to access the presence and power of God, and one of the best ways to do that is through the prophetic. I cannot tell you how many times I have been able to help someone get free or encounter God in a deep, transformational way simply because God told me something that led to the divine appointment. Prophecy is often precursor to the power of God being released.

> When we hear God's voice accurately and relay his words humbly, Jesus shows up, and Kingdom things happen.

The baptism, or filling, of the Spirit often leads people to hear God's voice. Let's look at Peter's teaching on the day of Pentecost. He quotes Joel's prophecy: "This is what was spoken by the prophet Joel: 'In the last days, God says, "I will pour out my Spirit on all people. Your sons and daughters will prophesy, your young men will see visions, your old men will dream dreams. Even on my servants, both men and women, I will pour out my Spirit in those days, and they will prophesy"'" (Acts 2:16-18). After I was filled with the Spirit at 19, I started hearing God's voice regularly. I didn't receive any teachings on the prophetic; it was simply an overflow of the Spirit's presence.

In the Old Testament there were a few people who were set apart to be prophets—to hear God speak and relay His messages. But Joel, one of God's prophets, foresaw a time where God would pour out His Spirit on all His people, and all of His people would prophesy. It no longer would be just a select few, but there would be a community of people soaked in the Spirit, and they would be prophesy. They would hear from God directly for themselves and others. This was part of God's plan to make all of His people into a nation of priests who could bring His presence, His message, and His Kingdom to the world.

I have heard people argue that prophecy no longer exists today because of 1 Corinthians 13:8: "Where there are prophecies, they will cease." But the context clearly explains when they will cease:

> *For we know in part and we prophesy in part, but when completeness comes, what is in part disappears. When I was a child, I talked like a child, I thought like a child, I reasoned like a child. When I became a man, I put the ways of childhood behind me. For now we see only a reflection as in a mirror; then we shall see face to face. Now I know in part; then I shall know fully, even as I am fully known* (1 Corinthians 13:9-12).

Prophecy will cease when we get to Heaven and see Jesus face to face. In Heaven, we won't need prophesy because we will have direct communication and direct access to God. Now we only see dimly. We only hear some of what is to be revealed. We know in part. The plain meaning of the text is prophecy shall continue until we see Jesus face to face in Heaven, and

> Now we only see dimly. We only hear some of what is to be revealed. We know in part.

then the imperfect shall disappear. We shall know fully even as we are fully known.

In some church settings prophecy is dismissed out of hand. And I have been in other church settings where it has been done poorly, even recklessly. I think it is a dangerous thing to disregard or explain away a biblical truth because some people have misused it or even abused it. John Wimber once said: "The answer to abuse is not disuse but right use."

Fortunately, there is quite a bit of solid biblical instruction to help us navigate our way through wise use of prophecy. Let's look at some of those passages as we examine the three parts to prophecy: receiving a word from the Lord, interpreting the word, and delivering the word.

Receiving a Word

Paul wrote, "Do not put out the Spirit's fire. Do not treat prophecies with contempt but test them all; hold on to what is good" (1 Thessalonians 5:19-21).

When we receive a word from the Lord, it ignites the Spirit's fire in our hearts. It stirs our spiritual passion for Jesus as we hear His voice, sense His presence, and see His Kingdom activity. Hearing from God revitalizes our spiritual passion; this is why Paul tells us not to put out the Spirit's fire and not to treat prophecy with contempt. If we treat prophecy with contempt, we risk extinguishing the flames of the Spirit. We treat prophecy with contempt when we ignore God's promptings or claim He does not speak at all.

If we are going to receive a word from the Lord, we must believe that God speaks through direct revelation. We must come in simple faith, quiet our hearts, and learn to hear His voice. God said that He will speak to us through the Spirit, and we must take Him at His word. We must not treat prophecy with contempt. Rather, we must learn how to hear the promptings of the Spirit.

This is critically important for us as leaders. 1 Corinthians 12-14 is the largest New Testament teaching on the prophetic. Paul says, "Now to each one the manifestation of the Spirit is given for the common good." When the Spirit gives us a prophetic word for someone else, there is a manifestation of God's presence as we deliver that word. Jesus shows up, and when Jesus shows up, Kingdom stuff happens. Think about the story I told to open this chapter. The daughter was healed and delivered; the mother and daughter had a healing in their relationship. And everyone knew that God had revealed this knowledge supernaturally and drew near to the Lord. Prophecy really is a gateway gift to things of the Kingdom. It is crucial to hear God's voice if we are going to minister in God's power to help heal people's souls. Jesus heard His Father's voice. The apostles heard the Spirit speak. This was critical to the presence and power of God being manifest in their midst so life change could take place. Jesus said, "Apart from me you can do nothing" (John 15:5). Prophecy is one of the key ways that we cooperate with Jesus' presence to do His Kingdom work.

Obviously, God speaks through the Bible, and we need to be grounded and rooted in the Scriptures. All of these prophetic promptings, these forms of direct revelation, need to be tested by what God has already said through His Word. If they are not in accordance with His written Word, then it is not God speaking. The Word of God is inspired by the Spirit, and it is our rule of faith and life. The Spirit of God will not tell us something by direct revelation that contradicts His Word. I also believe there are certain depths with God that can only be found through deep reflection on and understanding of Scripture. We need to be people of the Word. But we also need to be people of the Spirit. It is not either/or, it is both/and.

Let's explore six ways that God speaks directly to us through His Holy Spirit. I am not going to include here that God speaks to us through Scripture. God does speak that way, but here we are exploring how God speaks to us through direct revelation. These are not necessarily the only ways God speaks, but they are listed here to help us develop sensitivity to the Spirit's voice. These are common ways God speaks to His children.

Whispers of the Spirit

First, the Spirit speaks through whispers; this is also often referred to as a prompting or leading of the Holy Spirit. Essentially, God directs our thoughts. It is certainly easier for God to direct our thoughts if we are giving Him an opportunity to speak by quieting our hearts and attuning ourselves to His presence and voice.

Often when I am on a retreat day, people will "randomly" come to mind as I linger in God's presence. When someone comes to my mind, I always pause and ask the Lord if there is anything He wants me to pray for or say to that person. Not infrequently a thought will come to mind. I text the person, tell them they came to mind in prayer, and that this phrase for them came to my mind. I ask them if it means anything to them, and most of the time it is precisely what they needed.

We must practice listening to God in our private time with Him before we start trying to master this in the public place. Effective prophetic ministry flows out of personal private intimacy with God. The more I draw near, the more I cultivate His presence and become sensitive to His voice personally, the more likely I will hear His voice in the ministry contexts God calls me to.

Many of the ancient writers referred to this as "the still small voice of God," referencing Elijah's encounter with the whisper of God in 1 Kings 19. God appeared to Elijah not in the wind, nor in the earthquake, nor in the fire, but in a gentle whisper. These promptings are easy to miss because they are a gentle whisper, and we are a busy people.

We are going to have to take some risks with the whispers. We cannot expect to operate in certainty. The problem for many of us is that when the Spirit whispers to us like this, we don't act on faith because of our uneasiness with risk. We analyze the thoughts that come: *Is that God? Is that me? I'm not sure. How can I tell?* And we talk ourselves out of faith. Lean into these whispers and test them humbly.

When someone comes to me with a presenting need they want me to pray for, I always begin the prayer time by listening for the Spirit's voice. I simply take a risk and tell the person exactly what came to mind and nothing more. I was at a conference recently, and I was talking with someone who told me that they never sleep through the night. There could be a million reasons why someone can't sleep through the night, but the thought that immediately came to my mind was sexual abuse. I said to the person, "Were you sexually abused?" He said, "No." I said, "To your knowledge, was your mom, dad, or any of your grandparents sexually abused?" Again, he said no. But I know that lots of families don't talk about those things openly, so I asked a follow-up question (based on my experience with sexual abuse spirits): "What was your earliest erotic sexual thought? Was it before puberty?" He looked puzzled and said, "Yes. It was really young." I asked another series of questions that are symptoms of demonic spirits of sexual abuse, and every one of them hit the mark. I said, "You have sexual abuse demons. That's why you can't sleep well through the night. They often trouble people in the night. We will do your deliverance at the end of the conference, and you should sleep better." We did, and he has. Again, this is the power of a prompting, but you have to take a risk.

We have to pay attention to the thoughts the Holy Spirit brings to mind. We often fight against symptoms, but God knows what the root of our presenting problem is, and He can often bring that to mind and help people get free. Not everyone who can't sleep through the night has sexual abuse spirits, but the Holy Spirit knows why everyone can't sleep through the night. And He might just be willing to tell us and help a person get free.

I was teaching this principle in the early days of South Shore Community Church, which I planted in October 1995 in a town south of Boston. We only had a handful of people at the time. One night I received some devastating news; it was one of the worst nights of my life. Right after receiving this devastating news, I took a phone call from the newest member of our small group, Jan.

At the time, Jan was a brand-new believer. She was coming home from work, and she was praying. She got a whisper of the Holy Spirit to call me. It was about midnight. It was an incredibly risky phone call to make. She risked the hour, she risked looking like a fool, she risked being wrong, and she risked calling her pastor on a potential prompting of the Spirit. She stepped out in faith and made the call. It was one of the most memorable, timely phone calls I've ever received. I knew God knew the devastating situation and cared about what was happening in my life. The presence of God was revealed to me in the prompting Jan received. And Jan learned God does speak, even to new believers. But she had to take a risk and obey the whisper she received.

The Audible Voice

Sometimes God speaks in an audible voice. Jesus heard the audible voice of His Father at His baptism and at His transfiguration. Paul heard the audible voice of God at his conversion. Whenever I speak to an audience about prophecy, I ask how many have heard the audible voice of God, and it is not uncommon to see one quarter of the hands go up.

A number of years ago a woman sent me an email. She attended our church occasionally, when she was in the area visiting family. She was from a very traditional Congregational Church with no charismatic leanings whatsoever. She wrote me an apologetic email with a word from God she had received for me. She told me she knew how busy I was, and she felt really bad about writing to me, but she had been out on a walk in the woods when she heard the audible voice of God. He said, "Tell Rob to write a book." She argued with God respectfully. She told him how busy I was leading a church, teaching at seminary, raising a family, and she didn't want to tell me to write a book. She got home and told her husband, who was even more reserved and traditional than she was. He told her she had to write the email to me because God spoke to her out loud. She reluctantly did.

What she didn't know was when I was 24, as a seminary student, God spoke to me about some of the things in my future. He told me I would plant a church, one day I would teach at seminary, I would travel and speak to other pastors and church leaders, and I would write books. I told the Lord I would do whatever He wanted me to do, but He had to open the doors. I wasn't going to open any of my own doors; I would respond to His direction. By the time I received the email from the woman, all of those things had come true—except for writing books.

I planted South Shore Community Church when I was 30, and I pastored SSCC for almost 22 years until I left at the end of June 2017. Martin Sanders taught the last class I took as a seminary student, and I stayed in touch with him periodically over the first few years after graduating. When I was in my early thirties he invited me to teach a class with him at seminary. I had never inquired about teaching opportunities. When he asked me, I said yes without hesitation. He said, "Do you want to pray about it?" I told him I didn't need to because God had told me this day was coming. I was just waiting for Him to open the door in His timing.

One Christmas break I was spending time alone with the Lord and he said, "It's time to travel." I said, "Lord, if that's you, confirm it and open the door." In the next month, four people came to me with dreams, visions, or words about me traveling, and suddenly I began to get invitations to speak to pastors around the world. I never sought any of these opportunities; I just prayed and waited for God to open doors. I committed to God I would never open a door that advanced my own cause, but I would walk through any Kingdom door He opened to me for His honor. I was waiting for this door to open to write a book.

I had a file on my computer full of ideas for books I wanted to write one day, and I had been adding to it over the years. Just before this dear woman wrote to me, I was on vacation over Christmas, and as I prayed, I sensed the Lord saying to me that it was time to write. I prayed for confirmation that He was speaking to me, and that is when I received her email.

I responded and thanked her with great joy, and I explained that writing a book was something I felt God wanted me to do, but that I was waiting for confirmation and her email was just what I needed. She replied with great relief and said, "Now I will tell you the rest of what God told me." She went on to say some things about my writing that are just between me and

God, and they are precious to me. They are promises that God has given me about my writing that I pray over on a regular basis. Immediately after she wrote that email, I started writing my first book, *Pathways to the King*.

God speaks in an audible voice. We see it throughout Scripture, and it's not uncommon for people today to hear the audible voice of God. I have heard the audible voice of God once in my life. God woke me up in the middle of the night by calling me by name. I sat bolt upright, and God told me He was going to teach me about spiritual authority.

Pictures: Dreams and Visions

God also speaks through pictures. Peter, quoting from Joel in Acts 2:17, said, "'In the last days,' God says, 'I will pour out my Spirit on all people. Your sons and daughters will prophesy, your young men will see visions, your old men will dream dreams.'"

Dreams are pictures that come to us when we are asleep, and visions are pictures that come to us when we are awake.

Not all dreams and visions are from God, but some are, and we need discernment. Again, it is vitally important that we move with humility, and that we test everything with Scripture.

It saddens me that so many Bible-believing people scoff when I speak about dreams or visions. Yet the Bible, which they highly regard, is full of people having dreams and visions from God. Nowhere in the Bible does it say those dreams and visions will cease. In fact, in this passage in Acts 2, it actually indicates dreams and visions are part of the outpouring of the Spirit "in the last days." The last days, biblically speaking, is the time period from when Christ rose until Christ returns—which means we are now in the last days, and dreams and visions are here to stay until Christ returns.

In the birth narrative of Jesus, God directs people through dreams five times. In Acts, God spoke to Ananias about Paul's conversion in a vision (Acts 9:10). Paul had a vision in the same passage about a man named Ananias coming to pray for him (Acts 9:12). Peter receives a vision from the Lord to prepare him for Cornelius's conversion (Acts 10). God needed to break Peter's prejudice against Gentiles, and God uses a vision which Peter has while he is in a trance (Acts 10:10). These aren't the only times God speaks in dreams and visions; these are just a few examples.

In the Old Testament some prophets were called seers because they had a propensity to "hear" from God visually. They were given pictures, visions, and dreams from God. For some people today, this is the dominant way they receive from the Spirit. I am not a "seer"; I probably only receive pictures 10 percent of the time I receive a word from the Lord. My wife Jen, on the other hand, receives most of what she hears from God through pictures.

Because I do not receive pictures with regularity, over the years this has been an area in which I have had to learn to trust. In the beginning when I received a picture, I would wonder, "Is that God? Is that me?" My pictures were never elaborate when I received them. I am not much of an artist, so my pictures were rudimentary—like stick figures! But I learned to test these images humbly. If I am praying for someone and I get an image I simply say, "I see this. Does that mean anything to you?" What's the worst that can happen? You're wrong; it won't be the last time today! Just be humble, take a risk, and test it.

The times I am most likely to receive a picture is when I am praying for someone for inner healing. I was praying for a young lady one day. I knew she had an abusive upbringing, but I didn't know the extent of the trauma. As I went to pray for her, I waited on the Lord, and I saw a quick image of her as a little girl, sitting in a basket in her closet. This, of course, meant nothing to me, and it didn't seem to have any significance at all, but I took a risk. I simply said, "I don't know if this means anything to you, but I see an image of you as a little girl. You are sitting in a basket in a closet." She started weeping, and I knew then that this meant something. I waited for her tears to subside, and then she told me the story.

When she was a little girl, she said, after she was abused she would go to her room and sit in a basket in her closet and imagine the arms of the basket were the arms of God wrapped around her. By the time she was 16 the abuse got so bad she couldn't take it anymore emotionally; she had a breakdown and ended up in a mental hospital. She was there for a year, and she gave up on the idea that it was God comforting her in her childhood abuse. Until I had that picture. When I shared that image, she knew it was God with her, comforting her through it all. Every time I share that story, I get chills and think to myself: What if I didn't take the risk? What if I dismissed that little image that flitted through my mind? Imagine what she (and I) would have missed out on.

It seems that in healing wounded memories God often uses the sanctified imagination. He gives us pictures. I think this is because our traumatic memories are seared into our brains. This is why a rape victim can walk through a mall, years after experiencing rape, and walk past someone who is wearing the same cologne as her rapist and be triggered to panic—even though she has no idea why. The memory gets locked in because our senses are heightened during the tragic event.

I have talked to people who have done research on the connection between inner healing and neurology. They say that when God's presence comes and touches a painful memory it unlocks the person, and they can literally show how the brain operates differently after God's presence brings healing. His presence restores the brain function back toward normal.

Let's talk about dreams. Not all dreams are from God, as I said, but some are. How can you tell? I think there are three types of dreams. First, there are just your average, everyday dreams. These are normal and have no significance. They make us laugh or smile or scratch our heads in bafflement, but they aren't particularly useful for our journey.

Second, there are some dreams which come from our souls; they arise out of areas of our concerns, or they come from unprocessed issues. Our soul is screaming out to us, "Hey! Pay attention to me down here! I am troubled, and you aren't noticing." Our subconscious pushes through to our conscious mind and brings self-awareness about an issue that is troubling us.

The dominant factor in these dreams is the emotion. For example, if you keep having a dream or dreams that are terrifying to you, you may want to take a moment and pause and ask God, "Is there something I am afraid of that I am not paying sufficient attention to right now?" These dreams are important clues to self-awareness. But they are not prophetic; they are soulish.

> Some dreams are from the Spirit. These are prophetic dreams where God is speaking to us. He is visiting us or revealing something to us.

Finally, some dreams are from the Spirit. These are prophetic dreams where God is speaking to us. He is visiting us or revealing something to us.

In both the Old and New Testaments God communicates to people in dreams. In the Old Testament, God even communicates to two pagan rulers through dreams—Pharaoh and Nebuchadnezzar—and men of God, Joseph and Daniel, interpret the dreams for them. (See the books of Genesis and Daniel.)

One of the most powerful dreams I ever received from the Lord was healing to my soul. I was about forty, and I began to realize that I connected with two out of the three members of the Trinity. I had a deep connection with Jesus. On my very first encounter with God, I encountered the love and forgiveness of Jesus that radically changed me. I have adored Jesus ever since. I connected with the Spirit; I heard His voice and sensed His presence. But the Father felt distant to me. I could have given you all the right theological phrases to describe the Father: He is good, powerful, sovereign. But I also felt as though He is distant, aloof, even a little scary. When I realized there was something wrong in my connection with the Father, that I didn't relate to Him the way Jesus did, I started praying to Jesus: "Show me the Father. I don't know the Father like you describe Him." I had some strong illuminating moments with the Lord across the next few months that were helpful, but I kept praying because I knew there was more.

One night I had a dream. In the dream I was speaking at a men's retreat. Dreams are very symbolic and, to properly interpret them, you have to wrestle with the symbols humbly. I was speaking at a men's retreat because I had a masculine wound from multiple sources in my life—separation anxiety, my Dad's anger when I young, and some bullying. I didn't know anyone at this retreat except for one person. The dream started as I finished speaking. I was stepping from the pulpit and leaving the sanctuary to head to my car. As I went all of these men were hugging me and thanking me. But they were giving me "man hugs"—three pats and you're done. Anything more than that is definitely suspicious!

I finally made my way outside, and there was the man I knew. This guy was being very critical of me at that time. Again, dreams are symbolic; one of the great mistakes people make with prophetic dreams is that they take the people in the dreams too literally and don't understand the prophetic symbolism behind an individual who appears in the dream. This man who was being critical of me did not represent himself, but the critic within. Part of having an identity wound—in my case, a masculine wound—is that it leaves you with shame. Shame blames. It blames God, it blames others, it blames ourselves. I was my own worst critic; no one was harder on me than I was. This man was the only guy in the dream I didn't hug; that's because you can't make peace with shame. You have to put it to death. After I walked past him there was one more man in the parking lot before I got to my car. He gave me a hug just like all the rest. The only problem was that nobody taught him the man hug rules! He held me uncomfortably close for an uncomfortably long time. My skin crawled. Finally he let go of the embrace but held onto my shoulders, looked me in the eyes, and said, "I am your Father in Heaven, and I love you." I lost it.

I woke up sobbing under an incredible supernatural outpouring of the tender affections of the Father. It lasted a long time, and it changed me forever. Never again was the Father distant, aloof, or scary. After that dream, if you asked me to do a word association about the Father in Heaven, without exception the first phrase I would use to describe Him would be "tender affections." I don't just say it; I know it because I have experienced it.

God uses dreams and visions to help heal people's souls. Often during Soul Care conferences God will give people dreams—healing dreams, informative dreams, dreams that bring back and restore repressed memories. God has healed many through these encounters. It happens so frequently that I have now come to expect it as a normal part of the Soul Care journey. So when you are working with people to help them experience healing, ask God to release dreams and visions that bring healing to the soul.

One last note: sometimes God gives someone what can be called an "open vision." This is when someone sees with their physical eyes into the spiritual realm. They still see the material world, but they also see the spiritual realities in it. Again, as with all prophetic revelation, these things need to be tested.

God Speaks to Our Emotions or Body

At times God speaks through our emotions or bodies. Think about conviction, for example. Jesus said the Holy Spirit would convict the world (John 16:8). When the Holy Spirit convicts us there is often an accompanying emotional reaction. We may feel unsettled, or uneasy, or our inner peace may be disturbed. The Holy Spirit doesn't convict us this way to make us feel bad; He does it to get us back into proper alignment with Him. The discomfort is there to make us realize something is out of alignment between us and God. And to help us repent and get back in alignment with Him.

The Holy Spirit also gives us peace. I'm sure there have been times in your life, like mine, when your circumstances dictated you should be fearful or anxious, but instead you had a supernatural peace. This is a work of the Spirit of God within us. Jesus isn't nervous. No matter what you are facing, He isn't wringing His hands in Heaven trying to think about what He is going to do to help you. Jesus promised that He would give us His peace (John 14:27), and it is a peace that passes understanding, a peace not of this world.

Jesus isn't nervous. No matter what you are facing, He isn't wringing His hands in Heaven trying to think about what He is going to do to help you.

Sometimes God gives us peace about a decision we have to make, and we interpret the peace of God as God's yes to this new direction in our life. There are other times when we are going to decide, and we lose our peace; we feel uneasy about it, and we take this as direction from God to avoid this idea. We often accept peace, or the lack of peace, as a way the Spirit communicates to us. It is a way He communicates through our emotions.

Sometimes the Spirit speaks through compassion. Since having the dream where the Father appeared to me, I started experiencing the Father's compassion for people. It was very uniquely and distinctly the Father's compassion. Not infrequently I walk into a room full of people and feel the Father's compassion for someone. Often, in the beginning, I would go up to them and tell them, "I feel the Father's compassion for you," and the person would cry. The Lord usually gave me a word for the person that would be helpful and healing. He was speaking to me first through my emotions and then with a whisper. It was the communication of His compassion that opened me to His leading in a situation.

I discovered that I feel the Father's compassion for someone when they are carrying pain. Many times the person is not even aware they are carrying pain in their soul until I tell them that I feel the Father's compassion for them. I cannot tell you how many times this has happened, and the person said, "I don't know why I am crying." And usually the Lord will give me a word that gives them insight into the pain He is accessing.

As Soul Care practitioners it is important to note that God often uses us in the very places He has healed us. Paul said, "Praise be to the God and Father of our Lord Jesus Christ, the Father of compassion and the God of all comfort, who comforts us in all our troubles, so that we can comfort those in any trouble with the comfort we ourselves receive from God" (2 Corinthians 1:3, 4). When we receive comfort from the Lord, we often have sensitivity to others in the area of our wounding. And when we have experienced the Lord's healing touch in those areas we often carry authority to help others. It is not uncommon for us, also, to carry prophetic sensitivity in those healed areas. We become wounded healers.

In 2 Corinthians 12 Paul is wrestling with the "thorn in the flesh." He asks the Lord to take it away from him. Three times he asked, and three times the Lord refused. The Lord said to him, "My grace is sufficient for you, for my power is made perfect in weakness" (12:9). It is in our area of weakness where we often meet God in His power, and we then carry that healing power to others afflicted with a similar weakness. For example, I have experienced healing for separation anxiety in my life. I always carried a low-level angst in my soul due to separation anxiety, but I received healing at a Leanne Payne Conference. As a result, often when I pray for people I sense if they are struggling with anxiety. They may come for prayer because of a physical ailment, but when I go to pray for them, I will suddenly feel anxiety. I wasn't feeling anxiety before I started praying for them. When this began to happen, I realized this wasn't *my* anxiety. I was feeling *their* anxiety. I've learned to simply ask, "Are you struggling with anxiety?" Every time the answer is yes, and most often the Lord will give me insight into the roots of anxiety, and I pray for the person and they experience freedom. This has happened to me hundreds of times because I am a wounded healer in that area. God has met me in my weakness with His power, and it has brought me comfort. Now He uses me to comfort others with the comfort I have received—even supernaturally and prophetically.

The more I understood this was happening, the more courageous I became with these ministry opportunities. I feel the Lord's compassion and I know I am talking to someone who has pain beneath the surface. I don't wait or hesitate, I jump in: "I feel the Lord's compassion for you." I know the Lord will show up. When I am praying for someone and I suddenly feel anxiety, I don't hesitate. I forge ahead boldly and ask if they are struggling with anxiety. God has showed up over and over in these areas. So now I am alert and look for them. It will be the same with you in your areas of divine intervention. Comfort those with the comfort you have received, but rely less on human words. Talk less. Carry more of His presence and minister more in the prophetic. You will experience far greater life-changing results.

> Comfort those with the comfort you have received, but rely less on human words. Talk less. Carry more of His presence.

One day I experienced the Lord's compassion for a young lady, and I knew the Lord was going to give me a word for her. I was so confident He would that I said to her, "I have a word from the Lord for you." She said, "Tell me." I said, "It isn't here yet, but I can tell it is coming, because I feel the Father's compassion for you." I said this to her for months! Every time I saw her I felt the Father's compassion and would say to her, "I still feel the Father's compassion for you. A word is coming. I can tell." She would say, "Lay it on me!" I would say, "I can't. It's not here yet. But it's coming."

Finally, one day I went up to her with this familiar sense of the Father's compassion, and the word became clear. I said to her, "For months now the Father has given me His compassion for you because you are about to find out something painful. He wanted you to know that He knows, He has known about this all along, and He deeply cares for you. He is with you." Later that week she found out her husband had an affair. God had prepared her for this tragic blow. The Lord was speaking to me through my emotions, as He so often has when He ministers His healing touch to others.

Now, I have to end this section with a word of caution. Please hear me: not every emotion, not every dream, and not every thought we experience is from God. They all must be tested, and they must never contradict what God has plainly said in His Word. Emotions in particular must be carefully tested for two reasons. First, this kind of ministry draws "overly caring" people. It attracts people with big hearts, but sometimes they have big hearts because they carry big hurts in life. Once again, this can lead to codependent tendencies, and when our identity gets lopsided, our prophetic insight gets fuzzy. We must be careful, and we must test everything. Second, we can get "bent" toward our desires and then "hear God" through the idol of our desire. Both things will feel very compelling, as if from God, but they are not. So we must untangle our unhealthy emotions before we can rely on these as indicators of God's voice.

I've spent a lot of time talking about how God can speak through our emotions, but God can also speak to us through our bodies. When I was a pastor our church regularly held healing services where we taught about healing and then invited sick people to receive prayer. On several occasions members of our prayer team experienced pain in their bodies. For example, a shoulder would begin to ache. When this happened, we asked if anyone was experiencing shoulder pain, and usually someone came forward for prayer. We saw many healings as a result of these types of promptings. God speaks to us through our bodies, revealing His agenda for healing.

A Word in Our Mind's Eye

Sometimes the Spirit speaks by giving us a word in our mind's eye. We can see the word in our mind and read it like it is written on a blackboard or whiteboard. This hasn't happened to me often, but on occasion the Lord has spoken to me this way.

I was praying for a man one day who had back pain, and as I waited on the Lord, I saw the word "bitterness." I said, "I see the word bitterness. Does that mean anything to you?" He wept as he talked about his son, who had hurt him deeply. I asked if he was willing to forgive his son. The man prayed a beautiful prayer of forgiveness through many tears; it was obviously sincere and from the heart. By the time he finished praying, the back pain was gone. The man could bend over without any pain at all, and he was jumping for joy.

I will also mention that when doing deliverance, demons will also speak to people in these same ways: with pictures, whispers, audible voices, through what they feel emotionally or physically, and they will spell out a word in a person's mind. Often when the demons spell out a word the letters will be moving around or jumbled as a display of confusion. I often command them to straighten out the letters and spell the word correctly, and they will. It has been a helpful tool in deliverance.

"The Knower"

Finally, sometimes God speaks to us directly through our "knower." As near as I can tell, this is when the Holy Spirit speaks to our spirit, and we know something we would not otherwise have known. We don't see anything or hear anything or feel anything or sense anything. Suddenly, we just know something.

One Sunday, a woman came forward for prayer for some physical pain. She brought a little entourage with her. I had not met her or her family before, so I knew nothing about them. They simply asked if I would pray for physical healing which, of course, I was willing to do. As always, whenever I pray for someone, the first thing I do is wait on God and listen. I paused to see if the Lord had anything to share, and suddenly I just knew this woman was a witch. I didn't hear anything, see anything, or sense anything. I just knew it.

Now you have to be careful the way you deliver a prophetic word! You call some unsuspecting lady a witch and you might get slapped! I waited a little longer as I prayed for a wise way to approach this conversation. After some time the wisdom came and I asked, "Can I ask you a question? Have you ever practiced any other religious practices?" She said, "I was a witch for thirteen years." I said, "That would definitely count."

I asked, "Have you ever wondered if your physical symptoms could have spiritual roots?" I helped her understand she had demonic issues, and we did deliverance, and God brought her some physical healing as well.

Humbly Test

We've examined the various ways God speaks, and I've emphasized many times that we must humbly test what we're hearing. 1 Thessalonians 5:19-21 says, "Do not put out the Spirit's fire. Do not treat prophecies with contempt but test them all; hold on to what is good." Is this thought or image or feeling really a prompting from the Lord? How do you test it? First, we must test it with Scripture. If what you heard disagrees with Scripture, then it is not from God. Period.

For example, I have had people tell me the Lord was leading them into a relationship with someone other than their spouse. No. That's not God. He already covered that one, and He hasn't changed his mind about it.

> Is this thought or image or feeling really a prompting from the Lord? How do you test it?

There are plenty of words we receive that do not contradict Scripture, but that still doesn't mean that they are necessarily from the Lord. For example, let's say you are praying for someone for emotional healing, and you get an image of a child being sexually abused. You aren't going to find a place in Scripture that is going to tell you clearly that this specific image is from the Lord. But I am going to proceed very carefully with an image like that. I most likely will ask the person if they were sexually abused. If they say yes, then that is why God gave me the image, and I will likely begin to talk to them about deliverance. If they have already been through Soul Care and really did the work, then that would be the next needed step. If they haven't done Soul Care, I would move them in that direction first.

If I test this image with the person, however, and they say they were not abused, then what do I do? First, I am not going to insist this is from the Lord and that they have some sort of repressed memory. I don't ever want to suggest that with people, even if I think it, because I might be wrong. I have said to people, "Have you ever wondered if you were sexually abused?" And quite often the response has been yes. And then I ask them why they think they were abused, but I don't suggest that they were. Second, the image may mean something completely different than you think. Maybe they weren't abused sexually, but their mother was, and they have inherited sexual abuse spirits. In that case, that is what needs to be explored.

Second, we need to test the words we receive with other mature believers who honor prophecy and have displayed a consistent track record of hearing God's voice accurately and delivering prophetic words with maturity. I won't test words with someone who treats prophecy with contempt, but I will test words with someone who honors prophecy, walks in humility, and has displayed discernment. Most of the time I test the words with the person they are intended for because they are most likely to know if the word has meaning for them. So when I am praying for someone at a conference, if I get a word, I simply say, "I hear this. Does that mean anything to you?" I am testing that word with the person. They have an opportunity to say no, that it doesn't mean anything to them. I don't insist that I am right, and I don't try to make them feel bad. I simply go back to listening. This is why we test prophecy, because we sometimes get it wrong. We must act in love and humility.

> We test prophecy, because we sometimes get it wrong. We must act in love and humility.

Interpreting the Word

After we receive a word, we need to interpret the word. Usually, if the word is for someone else, I deliver it to them and interpret it with them at the same time. However, I will begin discussing interpretation, and then we will end talking about how to deliver a prophetic word to someone else in a God-honoring way. Many mistakes in the prophetic are made during the interpretation process. We need to approach interpretation humbly, just as we must be humble about receiving a word.

If you are praying for someone and you get a prompting of the Spirit, the person you are receiving the word for should be involved in the interpretation process. The word is for them, and often the meaning of the symbols can only be unlocked by them. Think back to the story I told of the image of a little girl sitting in a basket in a closet. That would have been impossible for me to interpret—but it had very specific meaning to the woman who received it. The best approach is to just present what you have received and begin by asking, "Does that mean anything to you?" If there isn't a clear meaning, wait on the Lord for wisdom to help you with clarity and interpretation. Don't elaborate on what you heard; don't expound on it. If you receive one word, give one word and ask if it means anything.

Many people start with an authentic word from the Spirit, but then they expound on it, and by the time they finish, they have missed the moment with the Spirit. They add all kinds of human words that lack power and distract the person from what was really a nugget from God. If they had stayed with just what God said, the person would have received from the Spirit, but often people talk too much and the person misses the word from the Lord. Too often we make it too much about us, and we feel a need to talk and explain and use too many words. Just give what you receive and nothing more.

Even words that appear to be straightforward sometimes need an interpretation. For example, I was praying for a woman one Sunday at SSCC. The woman's presenting problem was a migraine headache. She was experiencing repeated migraines. I went to pray for her, and I listened for any promptings the Spirit might offer. The word *forgiveness* came to my mind. I followed my own instructions and simply gave exactly what I had received. I said, "I think I hear the word forgiveness. Does that mean anything to you?" She said, "No." I said, "Okay, let's wait some more."

The same word came to my mind again. I simply reported to her, gently, "I still have the word forgiveness. Is it possible you need to forgive someone?" She said, "I'm praying about it. But I don't think so." I don't want to lay guilt or shame on someone, so I said, "It's okay. Don't worry about it. Let's wait some more."

As I waited a little longer, a thought came to my mind that she was struggling to forgive herself. I said, "Could it be you are struggling to forgive yourself?" The tears started flowing, and the story came out that was the root to her shame. I don't remember if she experienced physical healing for her migraines, but the word from the Lord lightened her soul. Give what you receive, and wait on the Lord for interpretation.

> Give what you receive, and wait on the Lord for interpretation.

Pictures are much more difficult to interpret, whether they come from a dream or a vision, because pictures are symbolic, and symbolism is complex and often very personal. I was praying for a young lady one day and I saw a picture of a rough-looking character in a flannel shirt. He had a scraggly beard. I give exactly what I had, and she said, "That's Butch. He abused me." I didn't know what that man represented, but she did. Butch had a scraggly beard, and he always wore flannel shirts. The Lord knew how to convey that to that young woman.

Some symbols are more generic; they don't have a deeply personal meaning—they are unlike the flannel shirt or basket in the closet. Scripture is full of pictures, and it provides us with keys to interpretation of many different symbols. Fire, for example, is used in many different contexts in Scripture. It can be used for judgment. It can also be used for purging, like a purifying fire. It is also used for the Holy Spirit and the presence of God. The symbol of fire is used metaphorically for various things. The context of a symbol can help us interpret it.

Often we can interpret a dream or vision by the way the symbols are used in Scripture. Some things, like cars, obviously won't have a symbolic interpretation from Scripture. But, once again, Theology 101: *God is smart, and He knows stuff we don't know.* We can ask Him to help us. You can also refer to some good books about interpreting prophetic symbols from dreams and visions.

People in dreams are often symbolic representations. Often, they do not represent themselves. So we must ask: what does this person represent to us or to the person we are praying for? Over the years I have had hundreds of people tell me a dream they had with me in it. They thought the dream was for me, but most of the time the dream has no meaning for me at all. The dream was meaningful to them, and I was a symbolic representation of something in the dream.

There are exceptions to these general guidelines, and it requires humility and wisdom to know how to interpret a soulish or prophetic dream. For example, years ago I had a dream about a couple in our church. In the dream I was sitting at a table together with a woman, and we were both sad. She hugged me; we both cried, and then I walked her home. But when we got to her house, it wasn't the house she lived in. It was a new house, and as I looked through the picture window I could see people from our church gathered there.

I woke up and knew the dream was from God. Sometimes I can tell a dream is from God because it disturbs me (soulish dreams can have this effect too). God often gets someone's attention through a disturbing dream; that was true for both Pharaoh and Nebuchadnezzar. I prayed about this dream and had a deep sense that this family was going to leave our church and take others with them; they would be divisive. It was very sad to me.

Some time later, it happened. Every person I saw in that house in the dream eventually left the church because of this couple's influence, just as God warned me. God showed me the way things would go, and I didn't fight to protect my reputation or keep anyone who was being influenced negatively. God gave me the dream to prepare me for what was coming. The dream helped me navigate the difficult season; it provided me strength through that time.

Interpretation is an important part of hearing from God and moving in the prophetic with maturity. Ask the Spirit for wisdom; ask the recipient of the prophetic word if it means anything to them and check with other believers who are walking in the fullness of the Spirit. I often do ministry with people who are very developed in the prophetic. We will still test words with one another.

Let me provide an example from one of the most accurate prophetic people I know, my dear friend Kelvin Walker. On the last Sunday in May of 2015 I gave a message at the church that I had planted and pastored for twenty years. I was excited to preach the message because I had preached it in other locations, and the Lord had been using it dramatically. But when I preached the message that day at my home church, hardly anyone responded, much to my surprise. Every other place I had preached it, more than 90 percent of the audience responded to an altar call; God had moved in power. When I finished preaching that day, I immediately knew in my spirit that my time at SSCC was nearly over. I went out to my car and said, out loud, "I'm done. My time is up." I went home and Jen was sitting on the back porch. I said to her, "My time is up." She said, "That's funny. I said to Danielle [our oldest child] on the way home, 'Dad is done.'" I went in the other room to pray, and I said to the Lord, "If that is you telling me my time is up, then tell Kelvin Walker." I specifically mentioned Kelvin to the Lord because God had given him timely, accurate words for me in the past at key moments.

The next day I received a text from Kelvin. He had just finished my book *River Dwellers,* and he wrote to say how much he appreciated it. I thanked him and responded, "Do you have a word for me?" He wrote back: "I hear three things. One, God is expanding your apostolic calling. Two, you need to start a nonprofit ministry. Three, I hear the word release. Does that mean anything to you?" I wrote back: "Thanks. I agree with the first two. It was the last one I needed." He called me immediately. He said, "Bud, what is going on? I heard that last word from the Lord, and I wrote it and erased it. I didn't want to write that, and for the first time in my life the Lord was stern with me and said, 'You write that!'" I told Kelvin about my experience the day before. He said, "Okay. Let's pray and fast this week and listen for more from the Lord. And then let's connect on Friday." On Friday Kelvin called me and said, "It's going to be two years. Two more years and then you will be done." By the time he said this to me it was June 2015. Two years later, to the month, June of 2017, I left South Shore Community Church.

Kelvin, who has given me and many others accurate, specific, and timely prophetic words like this, still texts me periodically to check a word he has for someone else. He just did it this week. He received a word for a dear friend of ours, and he passed it by me before he sent it on to our friend because he wanted to make sure it was accurate. I thought it was spot-on. Kelvin is a humble, mature leader who hears from God often and accurately, and he still tests his words as the Scripture exhorts him to. I respect that.

As I travel the world one of the things I notice is that often people on prayer teams give prophetic words without testing them humbly with the person who is receiving the word and without bringing that person into the interpretation. Don't fall into this trap. I have been giving prophetic words for nearly thirty-five years, and I still test what I receive. I simply say, "I heard this, or saw this. Does that mean anything to you?" If it resonates with them, then I work with them on interpreting and applying the word to their lives. I don't assume I know what it means. Humility is a prerequisite for effective prophetic ministry.

> Humility is a prerequisite for effective prophetic ministry.

Delivering the Word

When we receive words for someone else, it's important to learn how to deliver the word in a way that honors God and edifies the person. 1 Corinthians chapters 12 through 14 offer the longest teaching on prophecy in the New Testament. Paul writes in 1 Corinthians 14:1-3:

> *Follow the way of love and eagerly desire spiritual gifts, especially the gift of prophecy. For those who speak in a tongue do not speak to other people but to God. Indeed, no one understands them; they utter mysteries by the Spirit. But those who prophesy speak to people for their strengthening, encouragement and comfort.*

Paul tells us to eagerly desire the gift of prophecy because it is a pathway to loving well. 1 Corinthians 13 is "the love chapter." Paul put this chapter directly in the middle of this teaching on spiritual gifts because the Corinthians were trying to one-up one another with spiritual gifts.

Paul was saying spiritual gifts are a pathway to loving one another well, not to promoting yourself. The Corinthians seemed to favor tongues and acted as though, if a person spoke in tongues, that person had arrived at a new spiritual echelon. Paul taught that tongues are good, and he even mentioned that he speaks in tongues more than any of them, but he said prophecy is better because it edifies others and helps us fulfill the law of love. Therefore, Paul urged them to eagerly desire prophecy as a pathway to loving others.

Prophecy is powerful when it is authentic, because when we offer someone a true word from the Lord, there is a manifestation of the Lord's presence in the prophetic word. It is a powerful doorway to experience Jesus.

1 Corinthians 12:7 reads, "Now to each one the manifestation of the Spirit is given for the common good." Paul then goes through a list of various gifts: words of wisdom, words of knowledge, faith, gifts of healing, miraculous powers, prophecy, discernment, tongues, and interpretation. These are all revelatory gifts. That means two things. First, every time we receive a prophetic word, it is a revelation from the Lord. We receive it; we cannot control it. It isn't like the gift of teaching, which, if you have it, you can use anywhere and anytime on any subject you have knowledge about. You cannot make God speak anytime you want; you can listen. He speaks, we listen, we receive, and we give what we have—that's the nature of prophecy. It is revelatory. Second, each time one of these gifts of the Spirit is manifest, the Lord reveals Himself. It is a revelation or manifestation of the Lord's presence in our midst. It isn't just an edifying word that is offered, the Lord is manifesting Himself in that revelatory word. This is a powerful form of encouragement and strength to the body. When there is an authentic prophetic word, Jesus shows up! Therefore, Paul tells us we need to eagerly desire spiritual gifts, especially prophecy.

This is particularly true for those of us who are trying to help others on the healing journey. The soul is terribly complex, and none of us has the wisdom necessary to help broken humans become whole. We need God, and He has given us His Spirit and offers us revelation so we can minister in His power to help others to wholeness. We desperately need to hear His voice.

> The soul is terribly complex, and none of us has the wisdom necessary to help broken humans become whole. We need God, and He has given us His Spirit and offers us revelation.

The purpose of prophecy is to strengthen, encourage, and comfort (1 Corinthians 14:3). And the motive of prophecy is to love people well. One of the great mistakes made in the prophetic is when people give "angry" words. Anger is a powerful emotion, and it can feel very compelling. So many people assume they are compelled by the Lord to give an angry word, and they proceed to let someone have it, or to "tell it like it is." But that isn't New Testament prophecy.

If you are angry with someone, you may feel compelled to say something to that person, but don't put the blame on God for your angry words. We always have to wrestle with our motives. Consider these questions before giving a word: Do I want this person's best? Can I give this word in a way that strengthens, encourages, and comforts them? Is my motive to love them well? If you are willing to be honest and the answer is no to any of these questions, then don't give the word.

You may also need to consider: Am I hurt or angry with this person? Do I have a conflict with this person? If so, I encourage you to wrestle with why you are hurt or angry. Perhaps you need to forgive the person or have a conflict resolution conversation. But you are not in a place to give them a prophetic word.

The purpose of prophecy is to strengthen, encourage, and comfort. The motive is to love well. Even if I am careful, there are times I will not do prophecy well, but if I have this biblical purpose and motive set firmly in my heart, I have a good chance of operating in the prophetic with maturity.

> The purpose of prophecy is to strengthen, encourage, and comfort. The motive is to love well.

I believe the New Testament teaches that all of God's people can prophesy (Acts 2:17). All of us can hear God's voice; this is because the Spirit of God now lives in each of us. This does mean that we have a lot of spiritual toddlers out there trying to figure out how to live this out. That's what was going on in Corinth. That's why Paul gives such good instruction; let's follow his lead and do prophecy the way he taught. Some people become very proficient at hearing God speak; they are consistent and accurate over the long haul. That is why you see some people in the New Testament, like Agabus, who are called prophets. They have been recognized by the church and have been elevated to the "office" of prophet. This is not a self-appointed office; it is God-appointed and church-recognized. This does not mean that they "own" the gift of prophecy and can turn it on like a faucet. It is still a revelatory gift, and they must operate in it by receiving a word from the Lord.

Delivering a Difficult Word

While the purpose of prophecy is to strengthen, encourage, and comfort, that doesn't mean some prophetic words aren't difficult to give and/or receive. They can be. You can give someone a difficult, corrective word and truly deliver it in love so that it strengthens the person in his or her walk with God. However, we must be careful with these difficult words, and we need to learn how to deliver them with wisdom. If you receive a potentially difficult word, don't just blurt it out. Wait on the Lord for a path to deliver it wisely.

Sometimes we're the ones who receive a prophetic word from others, and we must test that as well. If someone gives me a word, even if I don't think it is the Lord, I still test it. If it is something corrective, I test it with other people who are close to me. I will bring that word to people who love me and are not afraid to tell me the truth. Sometimes I have people who are angry with me give me a word they feel compelled to tell me. I still test it with the Lord, and I test it with those close to me to make sure I am not dismissing something I should be listening to closely. Just because someone gives you a message poorly doesn't mean there isn't something there for you to receive. If those in my trusted circle of discerning friends agree it isn't from God, I "flush it." I hold on to the good, but I don't carry the rest around with me in hurt, anger, or like a weight on my soul. God wants to build us up, not tear us down.

I was teaching a Soul Care class with my friend Martin Sanders about twenty years ago. We decided to end the first class with a prayer time where we modeled prophetic ministry. We asked for a volunteer and a woman raised her hand. She came up and sat on a stool. Martin and I were on either side of her, and we started by simply listening for a word from the Lord. We didn't ask her what she would like prayer for or ask her any personal information. We just listened for a prompting from the Spirit. We had never met the woman and knew nothing about her.

Martin and I were praying with our eyes open, and he looked over at me with an inquisitive look on his face as if to say, "Do you have anything?" I did, but I shook my head. He knew I didn't mean, "No, I don't have anything." But, rather,

"No, I don't want to go there." He held his hands out as if to say, "Come on!" I just kept shaking my head. The reason I was so reluctant to go there was because the word I heard was *whore*. Now stay with me: The purpose of prophecy is to strengthen, comfort, and encourage; the motive of prophecy is to love well. How do you get from "whore" to that end? That's why I didn't want to go there.

As I waited on God, a question formed in my mind. I often ask permission first, and then follow it up with a question as I explore what I am receiving. I said, "Can I ask you a question?" She nodded. I asked, "Did you live a promiscuous lifestyle at one time when you were younger?" She snorted and said, emphatically, "Yes!" Immediately another question formed. "Is there a label you have for yourself as a result of those years?" She blurted out, "Whore!" She burst into tears as deep emotional and spiritual pain came gushing out, and she broke into a demonic manifestation. I looked at Martin as if to say, "See! That's why I didn't want to go there!" We prayed for her, and God met that dear woman in a very special way and took her further on the way to freedom.

Relaying the Messages of God

As leaders in Soul Care ministries, we want to represent the Father well to those we minister to. It is very important not to just receive words from the Lord accurately and deliver them with humility, though we want to do those things. We also want to deliver them in a manner that is worthy of the Lord.

We can receive these divine inspirations for believers and nonbelievers alike. 1 Corinthians 14:24, 25 indicates the power of a prophetic word for an unbeliever: "If an unbeliever or an inquirer comes in while everyone is prophesying, they are convicted of sin and are brought under judgment by all, as the secrets of their hearts are laid bare. They will fall down and worship God, exclaiming, 'God is really among you!'"

Sometimes the Lord will give us a specific word of knowledge we have no human way of knowing for someone who doesn't yet believe, and it will move the person's heart toward Jesus. Jesus has this kind of encounter with the woman at the well in John 4. He gets specific knowledge about her: she was married five times before, and the man she was living with at the time she met Jesus was not her husband. It was a game changer for her, and she ended up believing because of His prophetic insight.

Preparing Ourselves to Listen: Stillness

Every time we sit down to pray for someone as a Soul Care practitioner, our primary job is to get them into the presence of Jesus. Jesus heals, Jesus saves, Jesus delivers. Often the quickest way into His presence is through a prophetic word. So how do we become more sensitive to the Spirit's voice? How do we cultivate a heart ready to hear from God? Let me end this chapter with a few practical pointers.

First, it is easier to hear God's voice on the go **if we have spent time listening in stillness**, in our private space alone with God. If we are going to carry an inner stillness to our outer, noisy worlds, we need to create an atmosphere of outer quiet by sitting before the Lord in solitude on a regular basis. We have to cultivate sensitivity in stillness. When I have practiced hearing God's voice in the private place, I can begin to hear God's voice in the public place.

A.W. Tozer said, "The discipline of silence is the price we pay to get to know God." Psalm 46:10 says, "Be still, and know that I am God." The context is a time of trouble: "God is our refuge and strength, an ever-present help in trouble" (verse 1). During times of stress, difficulty, busyness, and trouble, our minds speed up. We get an adrenaline rush; it is our fight or flight reflex kicking into action. The adrenaline is to help us speed up to get through the trouble and get away from the distress. Busyness, daily troubles, and the stresses of life dull us to the Spirit's voice. Therefore, we need to engage in spiritual practices that help quiet our hearts and make us attuned to His presence and voice.

A hurried soul is not one who is conducive to hearing the voice of God. We need to be still to recognize God's presence and activity in these chaotic times. **Here are a few of the practices I have done that have helped me create inner quiet.** (1) I pray through my agenda every day so I am not distracted by the things I have to do. This moves me toward a quiet heart as I lay these things before the Lord and surrender them to His Hands. (2) I pray through my negative emotions every day. One of the things that most often robs me of my inner peace is my unprocessed emotions. If I am afraid of some upcoming meeting or have some financial concern running in my heart, that is going to disrupt my quietude and hinder me from hearing God's voice. So I process that and surrender it to help my soul come to rest. (3) I also make sure my confessions are current; I remove the hindrances to connecting with Jesus. These first three steps are about emptying the suitcase of my soul, then I move toward cultivating God's presence. (4) I engage in worship, thanksgiving, and Scripture meditation to move my thoughts and heart toward God. I don't necessarily engage in all three of these every day, but usually I find myself in at least one or two of them to draw me Godward. By now my inner being is becoming quieter and more prepared to receive. I want to quiet my soul and become aware of God's presence. (5) I spend time in silence before the Lord. I seek to fix my loving attention on His presence. Either at the beginning of this time of silence or by the end, I will listen to see if the Lord has anything He wants to say to me.

Early on in my spiritual journey, I began **keeping a prayer journal**. I process everything with the Lord in that journal. There I process my emotions, work through my struggles, recall God's faithfulness, and record God's miraculous activity in my life. I spend time listening, and I write down whatever I sense the Lord is speaking to me. I have been doing this for many decades, and it has helped me develop a quiet center and increased my sensitivity to His presence and voice. I highly recommend it.

One final caution: we cannot be effective as a Soul Care practitioner if we are bent toward people-pleasing. Jesus was full of truth and full of grace (John 1:14). Often our unaddressed people-pleasing issues keep us from speaking a direct but kind prophetic word that could set someone free. I cannot tell you how many times the Lord gave me a prophetic prompting that was incredibly direct and required courage to deliver lovingly. And I cannot tell you how many times I have seen that direct and kind word result in a significant breakthrough for the person who received it.

I was doing a deliverance one day and the person had all the symptoms of someone who had sexual abuse spirits, though they themselves were not sexually abused. For example, she had erotic sexual thoughts sometimes during sacred moments, like worship; she felt a dark bullying presence at times in her room at night; she had dark, perverted sexual dreams. It was obvious to me she had inherited sexual abuse spirits, but she had no knowledge of either of her parents being sexually abused, and they were both deceased. I said to her, "I am going to ask you some strange questions about your dreams. I want you to know that none of these questions reflect on you. But your dreams reveal the types of spirits that you may have inherited. Have you ever had dreams about being attracted to children?" She had. I asked, "Have you ever had dreams about being attracted to other family members?" Again, she had. I went through a series of questions like this, and it revealed to me that she had spirits like sexual abuse, perversion, pedophilia, and incest, as well as an Incubus spirit. Asking questions like that is very helpful to get someone free, but you have to be okay with asking bold and awkward questions around difficult topics. That's the nature of this ministry, and you have to work through your issues to do this well.

Many people have experienced prophecy done poorly and are reluctant to venture into this realm. Others seem to gravitate to this all too readily but without any authentic humility. Still others give long words in the name of God, but they are making it too much about them, and their words are more human than they are prophetic. Remember: the right answer to misuse is not disuse, it is right use. Prophecy is biblical, and Scripture has given us wisdom on how to do it well. It is important for us as Soul Care practitioners to learn how to prophesy in a mature way, because doing so is a gateway gift to the Kingdom.

Chapter 5

SPIRITUAL AUTHORITY

When I planted South Shore Community Church I had high expectations. I knew God had called me to fight for revival. I believed God was going to pour out His Spirit quickly and powerfully. I preached on themes of revival, and we saw results. But they were not the sort of results that have characterized authentic revivals through the centuries. I preached on healing and prayed for the sick, but few people were healed. I preached on the filling of the Spirit and prayed for people to be filled, but few people authentically and deeply encountered God with a fresh filling. People were coming to Christ, lives were being changed, occasionally someone was healed, or they met God in a powerful encounter where they were filled with the Spirit. But it wasn't to the level that I had hoped for or expected.

There was a gap between what I read in the Bible or in my study of revivals and what I was experiencing in my life and ministry. Hebrews 13:8 says, "Jesus Christ is the same yesterday and today and forever." So if Jesus hasn't changed, why wasn't I seeing the things Jesus did in the past? Too often we preach on the gospels, and essentially we teach, "This is who Jesus was. This is what Jesus did." But if He really hasn't changed, our true message should be, "This is who Jesus is, and this is what Jesus *does*."

> If He really hasn't changed, our true message should be, "This is who Jesus *is*, and this is what Jesus *does*."

But if we say that without any demonstration of power, some people will not trust Him and follow Him.

I studied revivals, and there have been times in history where this gap was closed. There are times and places where God poured out His Spirit afresh and the things of Acts happened on earth again, and that's what I was expecting to happen. But they didn't.

At first, admittedly, I was too passive. I was waiting around for God to close the gap. I thought if I preached the Word of God faithfully, God would do the rest. But as time went on I began to realize something was missing. How do we close the gap between what we read about in the Bible and what we see in our lives?

Let's look at the disciples. They were ordinary people like us, but they saw an extraordinary move of God. They didn't just witness Jesus move in power, they participated in the miraculous ministry of Jesus. In the beginning of the gospels the disciples were following Jesus. They were listening to His teaching, they were watching him do miracles. But then Jesus sent them out to do the things He had been doing. Matthew

10:1: "Jesus called his twelve disciples to him and gave them authority to drive out evil spirits and to heal every disease and sickness." A few verses later, Jesus gave them these instructions: "As you go, proclaim this message: 'The kingdom of heaven has come near.' Heal the sick, raise the dead, cleanse those who have leprosy, drive out demons. Freely you have received, freely give" (Matthew 10:7, 8). And we know from the Gospels and the book of Acts that the disciples partnered with God in His miraculous kingdom activity. How did these ordinary people get to participate in the works of Jesus?

Let's begin by looking at the message of Jesus. The central message of Jesus is the Gospel of the Kingdom of God. This was the first thing Jesus started preaching about: "Repent, for the kingdom of heaven has come near" (Matthew 4:17). It is the last thing He spoke to His disciples about before His ascension. "He appeared to them over a period of forty days and spoke to them about the kingdom of God" (Acts 1:3). It is the central theme of His teaching, His ministry, and so many of His parables. (In Matthew 13 alone Jesus tells seven parables on the Kingdom of Heaven.) If this is Jesus' central message, we ought to be able to articulate the concepts of the Kingdom of God quickly and concisely. Many people simply say that the Kingdom of God is the rule and reign of God. Personally, I don't like that definition much. I am not convinced it captures what is taking place in Jesus' ministry. And some people may mistakenly be led into passivity, believing that whatever happens in our lives is God's rule and reign. But that isn't the way I see the Kingdom playing out in Jesus' life and ministry. Much of what happens in this broken world is due to the rule and reign of Satan, and Jesus comes preaching and demonstrating the Kingdom of God and dismantling Satan's tyranny.

In Matthew 4:23-25, we come to a summary passage of Jesus' ministry. Matthew writes, "Jesus went throughout Galilee, teaching in their synagogues, proclaiming the good news of the kingdom, and healing every disease and sickness among the people. News about him spread all over Syria, and people brought to him all who were ill with various diseases, those suffering severe pain, the demon-possessed [better translated: *demonized*], those having seizures, and the paralyzed; and he healed them. Large crowds from Galilee, the Decapolis, Jerusalem, Judea, and the region across Jordan followed him." Notice that Jesus preaches the good news of the Kingdom and demonstrates it with healing and deliverance.

As I mentioned earlier, too often we reduce the gospel to only the message of forgiveness of sins. But it was so much more. Jesus inaugurated a fresh invasion: Heaven's breakthrough power dismantling hell's tyrannical reign on earth. That's why I tried to put into words what happened when Jesus preached and demonstrated the coming of the Kingdom.

The Kingdom of God is the reversal of everything that went wrong with the world when sin entered the world. To put it another way: it is the restoration of the way things were supposed to be before sin entered the world. Let's examine that against what Jesus said and did.

> The Kingdom of God is the reversal of everything that went wrong with the world when sin entered it.

The Kingdom of God involves repentance that leads to restoration because sin separated us from God. Sin was rooted in a distrust of God that led to rebellion and separation. We cannot enter the Kingdom of God without repentance because we must repent of our rebellion and come to a trusting relationship with God that leads to submission before we can be reconciled. Jesus provided for our forgiveness by His sinless life, death on the cross, and resurrection. But the Kingdom doesn't stop there. Jesus healed the sick. That is because sickness is an effect of sin. There would be no sickness in the world if sin had never entered the world. I am not saying every sick person is sick because they personally sinned, but I am saying sickness is only in the world because sin impacted the world. When we get to Heaven sin will be eradicated, and so will all the effects of sin, including sickness. No one will be sick in Heaven, and no one was sick before sin entered the world. So when Jesus came preaching the advent of the Kingdom, He healed the sick because Heaven was breaking through sin and Satan's reign.

The Kingdom of God is the reversal of everything that went wrong with the world when sin entered it. Thus, Jesus also cast out demons. There will be no demonized people in Heaven; there were no demonized people before sin. The only reason people are demonized on earth today is because of sin—again, this is not always a direct result of their sin. Sometimes people get demons because of the sins of those against them (for example, sexual abuse). But when sin and all its effects are dealt with, demons can be cast out.

Jesus also came to address justice issues. There will be no injustice in Heaven, and there was no injustice before sin. Thus, Jesus fed the hungry and stood up for the downtrodden. Matthew quotes from Isaiah and describes Jesus in this way: "Here is my servant whom I have chosen, the one I love, in whom I delight; I will put my Spirit on him, and he will proclaim justice to the nations. He will not quarrel or cry out; no one will hear his voice in the streets. A bruised reed he will not break, and a smoldering wick he will not snuff out, till he leads justice to victory" (Matthew 11:18-20). When Jesus came to earth He began leading justice to victory. He came to overturn all the injustices created by sin in the world, but He did not use power inappropriately to overcome the inappropriate use of power which created injustice in the first place. He was gentle: a bruised reed He did not break, a smoldering wick He did not snuff out. I love this description of Jesus. It demonstrates His intention to overcome injustice and shows that His heart is full of love for sinners and those impacted by pain, sin, evil, and injustice.

In Matthew 9 Jesus encounters a man who is paralyzed. Jesus says, "Take heart, son: your sins are forgiven" (9:2). Maybe it was what the man needed to hear. But I am guessing that isn't why the guy came; he came for healing. He might have even been a little disappointed that Jesus opened their encounter with a proclamation of forgiveness. Why did Jesus say this? It could have been because the man's sin led to his paralysis. That's possible, but there is no indication of it in the text. It could have been because the man wrestled with shame—the sense that he was broken, damaged, unlovable, ir-reparable—because of something he had done in his past. It's even possible he felt forgotten by God and that somehow or other he did something wrong that led to this paralyzed state.

But I think it's possible Jesus didn't just say it to the man for the man's sake; he said it to evoke a response from the teachers of the law. After all, that is what happens in the very next verse. "At this, some of the teachers of the law said to themselves, 'This fellow is blaspheming!'" They said this because they knew only God could forgive sin. Theologically, that is true. Forgiveness is a gift granted by the offended party; it is never deserved or earned. All sin is an offense against God's way of love, and only God can forgive the offense. Of course, what the teachers of the law missed was who Jesus was. So Jesus uses this opportunity to reveal something about Himself and the nature of the Kingdom.

Notice what happens next, in Matthew 9:4-7: "Knowing their thoughts, Jesus said, 'Why do you entertain evil thoughts in your hearts? Which is easier to say, "Your sins are forgiven," or to say, "Get up and walk"? But I want you to know that the Son of Man has authority on earth to forgive sins.' So he said to the paralyzed man, 'Get up, take your mat and go home.' Then the man got up and went home." *The ultimate proof that Jesus has authority to forgive sin is the reality that Jesus has power over the effects of sin.* If Jesus is the king of the Kingdom of God, and Jesus has overcome sin, Satan, and the kingdom of darkness, then by necessity Jesus must be able to demonstrate His power over sin and all the effects of sin. That is Jesus' logic. The proof that Jesus is king of the Kingdom of God and that He can forgive sin is that Jesus has power over the effects of sin— in this case, sickness. If He claims to have power to forgive but can't eradicate the effects of sin, then His authority can be questioned. This is His argument with the teachers of the law.

> The ultimate proof that Jesus has authority to forgive sin is the reality that Jesus has power over the effects of sin.

In the New Testament there is no authentic proclamation of the Gospel of the Kingdom without a demonstration of power. It is the demonstration of power that proves the Kingdom has come. Heaven is invading earth, and the power of sin and all its effects are reversed. I think more people are going to come to faith in Christ today because they know they are broken and in need of a Healer than because they know they are sinners in need of a Savior. That is a missiological, not a theological, statement. I believe all people are sinners in need of a Savior. I am simply saying that the greatest gateway to evangelism in our context right now is that people are broken, they know it, and Jesus heals the broken.

If we understand the message of the Kingdom, and we understand the nature of the king, why don't we see more Kingdom breakthroughs happening? The key is authority. Notice in Matthew 10 that Jesus told them to preach and demonstrate the Kingdom (verses 7, 8), but in verse 1 Matthew says, "Jesus called his twelve disciples to him and gave them authority to drive out evil spirits and heal every disease and sickness." Authority is the key. Authority is the right to use someone else's power. Jesus has won the victory, and He has given us authority to enforce Heaven's triumphs over hell's tyranny.

Yet people in the church don't teach about spiritual authority very often. We are more likely to hear teaching about leadership in a church than we are to hear teaching about spiritual authority. Leadership is dependent on human capability; spiritual authority is dependent on God's ability. Most of the time when we teach about leadership, it is a secular leadership model that is presented. Don't get me wrong: I think we can learn from business leadership books. But there is a difference between business leadership and spiritual leadership. And spiritual authority is a critical component of spiritual leadership. If we don't understand that, then we will not likely see a fresh visitation of Heaven's power over hell's tyranny in our generation, and we will miss an opportunity to reap a harvest. We cannot usher in a spiritual movement of God by our best human leadership effort alone.

> We are more likely to hear teaching about leadership in a church than we are to hear teaching about spiritual authority.

Spiritual authority, when it is occasionally talked about in the church, is usually considered from a positional perspective. That is, people teach that spiritual authority is all about your position in Christ, your identity. I agree that spiritual authority is positional, but it is also developmental.

In Matthew 17 Jesus was on the Mount of Transfiguration with Peter, James, and John. The rest of the disciples were down below continuing with Kingdom ministry, and they ran into a problem. A father brought his demonized son to the disciples so they could deliver him. But they couldn't do it. When Jesus returned the father ran to him: "Lord, have mercy on my son. He has seizures and is suffering greatly. He often falls into the fire or into the water. I brought him to your disciples, but they could not heal him" (Matthew 17:15, 16). Jesus gives the nine disciples a pretty tough rebuke: "You unbelieving and perverse generation, how long shall I stay with you? How long shall I put up with you?" (Matthew 17:17). The word *perverse* in Greek means to distort the truth. Their inability to demonstrate the liberating power of Jesus was a distortion of the gospel of the Kingdom. They were proclaiming that Jesus was king of the Kingdom of God, but they couldn't demonstrate that Jesus had defeated the effects of sin because they couldn't deliver the demonized boy. Jesus casts out the demons and sets the boy free. Afterward, the disciples come to Him for a coaching session. They want to know what went wrong.

The gospel of Mark gives the most well-known response from Jesus: "This kind can only come out by prayer" (9:29); some translations add "and fasting." Most of the time when people teach this passage they say, "There are certain kinds of demons that can only come out through prayer and fasting." But that isn't what Jesus meant. How do I know this isn't what Jesus meant? First, because Jesus didn't pray or fast. He simply commanded the demons to go and they left. Second, because Jesus already told us how demons come out: by authority (Matthew 10:1). What Jesus is teaching them is how to develop authority. Their problem is that their spiritual authority is too underdeveloped to overcome the problem. Jesus didn't need to pray or fast because He had plenty of authority.

Let's look at what spiritual authority is so we can see how to develop it. Let me give you an important sentence that sums up spiritual authority, and then I will establish the idea biblically and break it down developmentally piece by piece.

Spiritual Authority: Three Musts

Spiritual authority is rooted in identity, expanded in intimacy, and activated by faith. I wrote an entire book, *Spiritual Authority*, based on that one sentence, so you can read that work for more insight. We'll take a brief look here.

> Spiritual authority is rooted in identity, expanded in intimacy, and activated by faith.

Rooted in Identity

Spiritual authority is rooted in identity. In Luke 10 Jesus sent out seventy-two disciples to do the works of the Kingdom. Jesus instructed them, "When you enter a town and are welcomed, eat what is set before you. Heal the sick who are there and tell them, 'The kingdom of God has come near to you'" (Luke 10:8, 9). Verse 17 tells us, "The seventy-two returned with joy and said, 'Lord, even the demons submit to us in your name.'" Jesus gave authority to these seventy-two believers, not just the twelve apostles, and they too participated in the works of the Kingdom. They cast out demons and healed the sick. And we know they had success because of what they said to Jesus above.

Take careful note of Jesus' response: "I saw Satan fall like lightning from heaven. I have given you authority to trample on snakes and scorpions and to overcome all the power of the enemy; nothing will harm you. However, do not rejoice that the spirits submit to you, but rejoice that your names are written in heaven" (Luke 10:18-20). Jesus has given them authority to reverse the effects of the fall, to enforce Heaven's triumphs over hell's tyrannies. He rejoices with them, but then He grounds them in their identity. Don't rejoice over the demons' defeat, but rejoice over your eternal citizenship.

Doing the works of the Kingdom can be pretty heady stuff. It can make us think too highly of ourselves. The problem is then we start making it too much about us. And if we do this, we will also be limited in what we can do by our own abilities and competencies. If we want to see what only Jesus can do, we must make it about Him and not about us. Spiritual authority is about our union with Christ. We are in Christ, and Christ is in us. It isn't about us.

> If we want to see what only Jesus can do, we must make it about Him and not about us. Spiritual authority is about our union with Christ.

Let me remind us again: the Kingdom isn't really that complicated. It comes down to this: When the king shows up, the Kingdom comes. When Jesus showed up, demons were cast out, sick were healed, lost people were saved, and those in bondage were set free. Heaven's reign visited earth and overcame the reign of sin, Satan, and hell. So if we are going to see more of the kingdom coming, we need to make it less about us and more about Jesus.

Our spiritual authority is rooted in our identity in Christ. In John 15:5, Jesus said, "I am the vine; you are the branches. If you remain in me and I in you, you will bear much fruit; apart from me you can do nothing." We cannot heal the sick or cast out demons by our own power or might or in our own name or by our own authority. Apart from Jesus we cannot do the works of the Kingdom. On our own we can do temporal earthly things—play sports, create businesses, have babies, and work marvels with modern technology and medicine. We can develop church programs and teach the Bible, but we cannot change the human heart. We cannot heal the sick with a word, nor can we cast out demons in our own name or ability, nor can we tear down demonic strongholds over families or regions or build lasting Kingdom influence. For doing works that are of eternal value, we must develop authority, and spiritual authority is rooted in identity.

In the book of Ephesians, more than thirty times Paul uses the phrases "we are in Christ" (or "in Him") or "Christ is in us." We have been united with Christ, and this is where authority begins. All authority on Heaven and earth has been given to Jesus. It is only in Christ that we have authority to enforce Heaven's victories. Let me say it again: the greatest problem in the church today is that we are making it too much about us. It is about our goals, our dreams, our plans, our visions, our strategies, and our programs. It is about our wants, needs, desires, abilities, competencies, and opinions. When we are rooted, truly rooted, in our identity, we make it less about us and more about Him. Only then can we see Kingdom things happen.

> When we are rooted, truly rooted, in our identity, we make it less about us and more about Him. Only then can we see Kingdom things happen.

Let's talk about how to take our identity in Christ deeper. I have talked about this in a variety of ways in my books *Soul Care, Pathways to the King,* and *Spiritual Authority.* You can refer to those for more input on this topic.

The biggest problem with sinking our roots deeper into our identity in Christ is that we already know the truths. We know

> But knowledge is not mastery; far too often we are still thinking, acting, and living like unloved, temporal citizens of earth.

that we are deeply loved by God. We know we were chosen before the foundations of the earth; we know we have been redeemed, chosen, forgiven, and are loved (Ephesians 1). We know that Christ died for us while we were yet sinners (Romans 5). We know our citizenship is in Heaven (Philippians 3). We know these things but, too often, we are not living them out in our daily lives. Sadly, though, because we already know them we think we have mastered them. But knowledge is not mastery; far too often we are still thinking, acting, and living like unloved, temporal citizens of earth. And that is keeping us from living out our true Kingdom potential.

The Western world has taught a knowledge-based discipleship. We sit in classes. We give people information. They fill in the blanks. They memorize answers. But knowledge doesn't change people. We even quote Jesus wrongly, as I provided in my example from John 8 earlier in this book. We quote the John 8 verse as if knowledge transforms, but that isn't true. Jesus wasn't a knowledge-based instructor. Jesus was an obedience-based king. It requires integration to develop authority. Knowledge will only leave us with big gaps in our lives between what we experience and what we say we believe.

In the Sermon on the Mount Jesus lays out some of the cultural values of the Kingdom. We examined the idea that discipleship is really about changing cultures. Changing our culture from our family of origin, nation of origin, region of origin, or church of origin to the culture of the Kingdom. So Jesus laid out these principles that dismantled the culture of religion of His day and expressed the cultural values and norms for the Kingdom, and He even ended this masterful teaching with an important parable. "Therefore everyone who hears these words of mine and puts them into practice is like a wise man who built his house on the rock. The rain came down, the streams rose, and the winds blew and beat against that house; yet it did not fall, because it had its foundation on the rock. But everyone who hears these words of mine and does not put them into practice is like a foolish man who built his house on sand. The rain came down, the streams rose, and the winds blew and beat against that house, and it fell with a great crash" (Matthew 5:24-27). Knowledge of the ways of the Kingdom will not produce life change. Obedience to the king and the ways of the Kingdom will change your life.

It isn't enough to know who we are in Christ. We must integrate these truths into our daily existence, into our every interaction. We must build our lives upon them. Let me give a couple of examples.

First, let's look to Jesus as an example. Peter describes Jesus' deeply rooted identity in 1 Peter 2, and he calls us to model our lives after Jesus. First Peter 2:22, 23: "'He committed no sin, and no deceit was found in his mouth.' When they hurled their insults at him, he did not retaliate; when he suffered, he made no threats. Instead, he entrusted himself to him who judges justly." Jesus never sinned, yet was falsely accused, wrongly tried, and sentenced to an unjust death. Peter wants these suffering people to see how Jesus responded to suffering. He didn't retaliate when they insulted Him; He didn't threaten when they persecuted Him and caused Him pain and suffering. How could Jesus respond so purely, righteously, and humbly to such painful treatment? Peter reveals how: "Instead, he entrusted himself to him who judges justly." There it is. He held onto His Father's eternally just opinion of Him. Jesus' identity was rooted in His Father's opinion of Him. It wasn't dependent upon what the leaders thought; it wasn't dependent upon what the crowds said about Him; it wasn't dependent upon what the disciples thought or said or did. Jesus entrusted Himself to His Father's just judgment. He held to this truth even in the midst of attacks, adverse circumstances, betrayals, denials, and false accusations. He was deeply rooted in His identity. The Father had said, "This is my Son, whom I love, with Him I am well pleased." That's it. Final judgment. Everyone else's judgments about Jesus were false and temporal. Only the Father's eternal opinion held sway over Jesus' life.

Jesus didn't just know that the Father loved Him. Jesus could love His enemies and forgive those who sinned against Him because He integrated His Father's opinion into His daily interactions with those around Him. Knowledge without integration leads to disintegration in our souls. Too many people know that God loves them, but they are still acting like insecure, unloved people. Jesus models for us how to hold onto the Father's opinion and live like a loved, secure person.

Peter goes on to say, "'He himself bore our sins' in his body on the cross, so that we might die to sin and live for righteousness; 'by his wounds you have been healed.' For 'you were like sheep going astray,' but now you have returned to the Shepherd and Overseer of your souls" (1 Peter 2:24, 25). Peter is telling us that just as Jesus held to His Father's just opinion of Him in the midst of life's worst circumstances, we need to do the same. He bore our sins, so we are forgiven. We belong. We are loved. We are clean before God. We have been justified. Now, because of that, we can die to our sin, we can die to our self-life, and we

> Too many people know that God loves them, but they are still acting like insecure, unloved people. Jesus models for us how to hold onto the Father's opinion.

can live like Jesus—we can live for righteousness. When we are hurt we don't need to defend ourselves. When we are criticized we don't need to retaliate. When we are judged we don't need to lash out. We don't need to rely on our self-protection, self-reliance, self-dependence, self-defense. We don't need to rely on what others say about us, what we have, what we do, or what we accomplish to feel good about ourselves. We can rely on our Father's just opinion of us. This becomes our true shield of protection and our sufficiency. He loves us like He loved Jesus. This is who we are in Christ. This is what it looks like to integrate our identity in Christ so that it impacts the way we interact with others.

All the wounds that have been formed in our souls can be healed in Christ. Our self-life is most strongly formed in our greatest area of childhood wounding. When we are young we do not have the ability to process our pain and our suffering, so we learn to develop self-protective walls. Our self-life develops. The problem is this self-life becomes wrapped in our identity and we no longer consider it abnormal. Sometimes we don't even see it as brokenness; this is just who we are and what we do. We build these interior walls of self-protection and self-defense to shield ourselves from further wounding. So when people insult us we retaliate, we defend, we withdraw emotionally into a protective shell, we lash out, we become passive-aggressive, or we choose some other self-protective path. But on the cross Jesus healed those wounds and, therefore, we can dismantle the walls of self-protection and self-reliance. We can die to our self-life and Christ can be formed in us. But this will only happen as we hold to the truth of who we are in Christ and intentionally die to our self-protective ways of living. Dying to our self-life means we must give up these self-depending ways we have learned for Christ to be formed in us. This is what Jesus invites us to do in Him.

Let me provide an example from my life, and you can do some parallel learning. My greatest childhood wounding had to do with not being loved. I had separation anxiety where I felt some rejection over my masculinity. My Dad was angry often when I was young. He has changed over the years, but the anger impacted me when I was little. I also went to a new school when I was in second grade. I didn't know anyone, and during the first week I was playing on the playground with some kids and I got bullied. Three kids attacked me. Two held me down while the third kid kicked me between my legs. I was both hurt and humiliated. I went home and didn't tell a soul, but I realized that if I didn't fight back I was going to be bullied every day. So the next day I went to school and I picked on the biggest of the kids when he started making fun of me. I took all that humiliation and turned it into rage, and I went after him. I tackled him and he happened to land near a convenient pile of dog poop, so I pushed his face in it. He never bullied me again. But something was formed in me. I learned that when I was threatened, I could use power to overcome, protect, and gain respect.

> Something was formed in me. I learned that when I was threatened, I could use power to overcome, protect, and gain respect.

Later in life, of course, I didn't use physical power but emotional power. When Jen and I got married and I felt emotionally threatened I would "power up" on her. I would overcome the perceived threat by the force of my opinions. Forceful opinions became a protective shield around my wounded identity. I would defend myself to protect my fragile sense of self, my insecurity. But she started feeling hurt from the defensiveness and power; she felt emotionally stomped on and began to shut down. I could see she was hurt, angry, and distant. I tried to close the gap. She told me that one of the things hurting her was that when I shared my opinion and she shared a different one, she felt like my opinion always ruled the day. Her opinion got stomped out by the force of my opinion.

Most of the time I didn't know I was doing it, and I certainly didn't know why I was doing it. But the pain of our marriage drove me to figure it out. It was part of the self-protection I had formed because of my greatest childhood wounding. These were the walls I had built to protect myself, and if Christ was going to be formed in me, these were the walls that had to come down.

I had to dismantle the ways of self-protection and self-reliance that formed in me. There were the interior walls I had built around my heart to protect myself from further hurt, but they were hurting others and ultimately keeping me from receiving the love I longed for. The inner walls of self-protection had to be dismantled, and I had to learn to hold onto the truth of who I was in Christ. The issue of my value was not dependent upon what Jen thought of me or whether Jen liked me. I wanted Jen to like me. Life was better when Jen liked me, but even if Jen left me, Jesus loved me and that was enough for me. I had to move that from a concept that I held in my head to *a reality I lived out in my daily interactions* with Jen. I had to drop the self-protective, self-reliant walls of my soul, and I had to learn to rely on God's love day by day, moment by moment, interaction by interaction.

The problem with the shields of our self-life is they are indiscriminate. Not only do they block out the people we perceive are trying to hurt us, they block God from healing us. We can't rely on the love of God if we are relying on self-protection. The only way for Christ to be formed in us is if we die to self, lay down our shields, and dismantle our self-life. As I let the walls down Jesus healed the wounded places in my soul. I became more rooted in the love of God and started having healthier relational interactions.

The Apostle John speaks about our identity and learning to live out who we are in Christ on a daily basis. Beginning in 1 John 4:15: "If anyone acknowledges that Jesus is the Son of God, God lives in them and they in God. And so we know and rely on the love God has for us. God is love. Whoever lives in love lives in God, and God in them." John starts with this truth, one that is all over the New Testament: our faith in Christ creates our union with God. God now lives in us and we live in God. It is more than a theological, heady union. The Spirit of God lives within us and we can commune with Him. Our strength and life are found in the Spirit within us.

John moves from this truth to the implication: "And so we know and rely on the love God has for us." We know God loves us because Jesus died for us on the cross. We do not understand everything that happens in this world, which is tainted by evil, but we know that whatever happens we can be assured of God's love because of the cross. This is God's ultimate display of His deep love for us. But John goes on, writing, "we . . . rely on the love God has for us." This is when we start to integrate the love of God into our daily existence, our every relational interaction. Relying on the love of God is the key to growing deep roots in our identity.

I knew God loved me. I could quote all the appropriate verses, but I had to learn to rely on God's love in all my relational interactions. I had to learn how to rely so deeply on God's love that I started acting like a deeply loved person even when interacting with a woman who no longer loved me. Insecure people defend them-

Insecure people defend themselves because they aren't secure enough to receive critical or corrective feedback.

selves because they aren't secure enough to receive critical or corrective feedback. Jesus didn't retaliate or defend Himself because He was secure in His Father's opinion of Him. Jesus judged what other people said about Him through the lens of His Father's eternally just opinion of Him.

During that season of our first marriage conflict, every night Jen and I would talk. She would tell me what she was upset about and, at first, I would defend myself. One night, alone with God, I heard the Lord say, "Stop defending yourself." I made a commitment to stop defending myself. I got to the place where I stopped defending and retaliating. I realized I needed to let down the wall of self-protection to rely on the love of God. My defensiveness was like a wall that fortified my insecurity and walled out the love of God. I can't rely on my self-life and God's love at the same time.

> I can't rely on my self-life and God's love at the same time.

So I stopped defending and started listening to Jen. I would simply listen and repeat back the things I heard her say in my own words until she agreed I understood her. Then I went upstairs into my study to be alone with God. I held to the truth of who I am in Christ, that I am deeply loved. I held to the Father's opinion of me, just as Jesus did. I quieted my soul and listened to the Spirit's voice remind me that I am a deeply loved child of God (Romans 8:14). I was learning to rely on the love of God in my conflicts with Jen. I asked the Lord: "Of these things that Jen said to me tonight, what is true?" In the security of His love I could receive the truth. My value wasn't dependent upon being right or loved by others, so I could receive what was said in the security of the Father's love. Then I asked, "How would a deeply loved person act right now?" And I would try to live like a deeply loved person: I owned my part, asked Jen to forgive me, and took responsible action. I was learning how to build my house upon the rock, rely on God's love, and take my identity deep. It wasn't merely knowledge anymore; it was being integrated into all the interactions of my daily life. This is how you take your identity in Christ deep.

COVID surfaced so much chaos in our country, as we talked about earlier. I often thought of Psalm 11:3: "When the foundations are being destroyed, what can the righteous do?" Never in my life has it felt more like the foundations are being destroyed. It feels like we are standing on quicksand. Or, to use another image, it feels like we are being "unmoored." We once were in a boat that was tied securely to a dock harbored in safety. But someone came by and cut us loose; our boat is no longer securely tied to the dock. Instead, it is being flung treacherously through the storms on the open seas in rocky water. Those two years were a destabilizing time on so many levels. But God promised to redeem everything that came into our lives to make us more like Jesus.

As I was praying about how God could redeem this COVID crisis, one day I had a thought: *What if God is the one who unmoored us?* What if we were tied to the wrong dock, and that is why God came by and untied us? One thing this season has revealed to us is that we are more rooted in our temporal identities than we are in our eternal citizenship. Many people are more American than they are Christian. Some people are more Republican or Democrat than they are citizens of Heaven. Some people are more white, black, or Asian then they are eternal citizens. This season has revealed that we are not deeply rooted in our eternal citizenship.

Paul said, "So in Christ Jesus you are all children of God through faith, for all of you who were baptized into Christ have clothed yourselves with Christ. There is neither Jew nor Gentile, neither slave nor free, neither male nor female, for you are all one in Christ Jesus" (Galatians 3:26-28). Jesus tore down the barriers that divide humans. He tore down the barriers of race, social standing, political alignment, and gender. He tore down the walls we build between ourselves, because all of these identity labels are rooted in the temporal. They all have a place on earth, they all matter to some extent, but they are not our primary identity. Our most significant, most permanent, most important identity is our eternal citizenship in Heaven. This is the one that must take precedence above all others. But when our opinions on temporary matters take precedence over our eternal citizenship, we end up with walls that divide us. This is a sure indication of our temporal moorings. So God, in His mercy, unmoors us from our temporal docks in an attempt to tie us to our eternal citizenship. He wants us to sink deep roots.

The problem is, the more we are tied to our earthly identities and not deeply rooted in our eternal citizenship, the less effective we are for the Kingdom of God. We can't be people of authority unless we are rooted in eternity. Paul understood this. In Philippians 1, Paul, who was in prison, spoke about people who were preaching the gospel out of false motives. They preached the gospel so Paul would get in trouble with the authorities. Paul responded in this way: "It is true that some preach Christ out of envy and rivalry . . . (They) preach Christ out of selfish ambition, not sincerely, supposing that they can stir up trouble for me while I am in chains. But what does it matter? The important thing is that in every way, whether from false motives or true, Christ is preached. And because of this I rejoice" (Philippians 1:15-18). What do you do with this guy? You can't stop him! He is an unstoppable force for the Kingdom of Heaven because his roots are so deep. Paul has so prioritized his heavenly citizenship that his desire to see the Kingdom of Heaven advance is stronger than his desire to protect his own life here in the temporal realm of earth. His eternal roots are so deep that he goes on to say: "For to me, to live is Christ and to die is gain" (Philippians 1:21). Paul is saying: if I go on living, I am going to live wholeheartedly for Jesus, because this is the only thing that matters in light of eternity. This is the only thing worth living for while in this temporal assignment on planet earth. But if I die, that is even better. If I die, I will wake up in the arms of Jesus and be in the place where there is no more sickness, death, heartache, pain, sin, or evil.

Are you deeply rooted in your heavenly citizenship? Is your eternal citizenship truly your first identity? Spiritual authority is rooted in your identity in Christ; temporal identities never lead to spiritual empowerment. Some of you have read *Soul Care*; you have gone to a conference or gone through the e-course. But you still haven't integrated your identity deeply into your daily interactions. Too often you are still living like an unloved person, and this is vastly limiting the development of your spiritual authority. If this is true, it is time for you to go back and do the work. Live it. Learn to truly rely on the love of God.

Let me end this section with some very practical things you can do to take your identity in Christ deeper. (1) Meditate on passages that speak of your identity in Christ. Meditate through Ephesians; most of the first three chapters talk about our identity in Christ. Meditate on Romans 8. Meditate on 1 Peter 2:22, 23. Read these passages slowly. Ask the Holy Spirit to illuminate them into your hearts. Ask the Spirit to show you where you are not living them out effectively, and bring yourself into alignment with God in those areas. Learn how to rely on the love of God. (2) Listen for the Spirit's witness about the love of God. Romans 8:14-17 is a great passage to meditate on. Paul said, "The Spirit testifies with our spirit that we are God's children." The Spirit is speaking to us about the Father's love. We need to create space in our lives to hear the testimony of the Spirit, to receive the revelation of God that we are deeply loved. (3) At the end of each day take a few minutes alone with God to examine your heart. Ask yourself this question: In every relational interaction today, did I act like a deeply loved child of God? Where you didn't, where you picked up your old shields to defend yourself, own it. Apologize. Humbly invite people to hold you accountable to act like the deeply loved person you are in Christ. (4) Identify the self-protective shields you use. How was your self-life formed? What was your earliest childhood wounding? How do you rely on self, protect yourself, defend yourself? Willingly lay down these shields. Choose to dismantle the walls of self-protection. Choose to die to self so Christ can be formed in you.

Expanded in Intimacy

Spiritual authority is rooted in identity and **expanded in intimacy**. If we are going to grow in our spiritual authority, we need to deepen our intimacy with God. When we expand our intimacy, our lives are marked by Jesus' presence. In Mark's Gospel, when the disciples asked Jesus why they couldn't cast out the demon from the young boy, Jesus responded, "This kind can come out only by prayer" (Mark 9:29). (Some translations add "and fasting.") As I said earlier, many people interpret this passage by saying, "There are certain kinds of demons that only come out by prayer and fasting." But that isn't what Jesus was teaching. Demons come out by authority—and Jesus is teaching them how to develop authority.

Though Jesus calls them to pray (and fast), Jesus doesn't need to pray or fast in order to cast demons out. He simply commands the spirit to leave because Jesus has plenty of authority for the assignment. He isn't making a universal statement about certain types of demons; He is making a statement about the development of authority.

I have done well over ten thousand deliverances in my lifetime because I have done Soul Care conferences for many years; I am often involved in fifty or more deliverances in a week. I can tell you from personal experience there are times I have gotten stuck in a deliverance and had no idea what to do. So I prayed and fasted and waited on the Lord for revelation. Once I received revelation about that particular type of demon, I never needed to pray and fast over that situation again. It was as if Jesus handed me a key to the Kingdom for that particular demonic reality, and the next time I ran into it, all I had to do was pull out the key on my Kingdom key ring and unlock the shackles. Prayer and fasting helped me draw near to God, hear His voice, and depend on Him for the wisdom and revelation needed. It taught me humility and gave me confidence that God would give me all the help I needed to set captives free in Jesus' name. But I didn't need to keep fasting over that situation every time I confronted it.

Let me give a specific example. Sexual abuse spirits are some of the most difficult spirits to get rid of because they are very adept at hiding. Every sexual spirit has a blocking spirit; they are the only type of spirits with blocking spirits. The blocking spirit's main function is to keep the sexual abuse spirit from being discovered. Let's say you have a blocking spirit named Anxiety and his leader is actually a spirit of Sexual Abuse. When you ask Anxiety, "Do you have a leader?" Anxiety will say no. The blocking spirit's goal is to leave the sexual abuse spirits behind in hopes that they will all be able to return. I discovered this in prayer and fasting. For years, unless the sexual abuse spirits presented themselves, I unwittingly left them behind because I didn't know how blocking spirits functioned. Once I discovered it, I never had to pray and fast about casting out sexual abuse spirits again. I had the key on my Kingdom key ring, and I knew what to do to unshackle those prisoners.

Let me cover two areas essential for going deeper with God. First, let's talk about our spiritual rhythm. I covered our spiritual rhythm in the first chapter of this book. But I want to add a vital component here. I want to talk about sacrificial acts and particularly spiritual retreats. I said earlier that one of the things that helps me when I am plateaued is sacrifice. When I hit a spiritual plateau I change my rhythm, and usually the first thing I do is some act of sacrifice. I mentioned that my three favorite acts of sacrifice to revitalize my walk with God are fasting, watching (praying in the middle of the night), and retreat. These three sacrificial spiritual activities have greatly helped me develop intimacy with God and expand my spiritual authority.

Fasting has played a key role on my road to greater depths with God. When I sensed God calling me to seek His face, not just His hands, one of the first things I did was go on a three-week fast. I drank whatever I wanted; I just didn't eat any foods. Some people say, "You can't have coffee on a fast." Why? There isn't anything in the Bible about that; that is just a man-made rule. If God asks me to go on a fast and drink water only, I will do it. But generally, when I fast, I drink coffee or tea and water; I fast to seek His face. The first three-week fast I participated in was as though I was living in a spiritual floodgate of

> We don't fast for the immediate benefits; we fast because He is worth it.

revelation. I sensed His presence like few times in my life and heard His voice with frequency and clarity. It was beautiful. The next three-week fast I did there was no sense of this deep connection; I was hungry and a little more irritated most of the three weeks. Someone said to me, "If it wasn't working, why did you keep fasting?" Because He is worth it! We don't fast for the immediate benefits; we fast because He is worth it. We fast for the long-term development of intimacy.

The first book I wrote was *Pathways to the King*. When I went to write my second book, I intended to write *Soul Care*. But I couldn't get it to come together. So I wrote *River Dwellers* instead and it flowed easily. The next year I sat down to write *Soul Care* again, but again I couldn't put to paper what I had taught so often. So I prayed and fasted for the next few weeks as I wrote, and I sensed the Lord's anointing and His direction. Prayer and fasting has often helped me hear from the Lord, deepen my intimacy, and expand my authority. Now it has become my regular practice to pray and fast while writing. When I get stuck in my spiritual journey, I pray and fast.

For many years I prayed, "Lord, give me the ability to impart your Spirit—*if* my character and intimacy can sustain it." I prayed this because I read Acts of the Apostles and they laid hands on people and people were healed, people were filled with the Spirit, gifts were imparted, and the Kingdom advanced. I saw this same pattern in various revivals in history. So I prayed for this ability to impart His Spirit, but only if my character and intimacy could handle it, because I didn't want to dishonor Jesus. After many long years God answered the prayer. I went through an entire year of my life where the vast majority of people I prayed for encountered God in deep and significant ways. They were filled with the Spirit, and there was a visible manifestation of the Spirit's presence. But then after about a year, it dried up. Fortunately, as I mentioned previously, I had read Charles Finney's writings, and I knew what to do.

Every time I see the power start to dry up and the anointing start to wane, I pray and fast until it returns. I think God intentionally allows the power to dry up to remind us that it isn't about us. It is about Jesus.

Watching—staying up in the night to pray—has also been a key sacrificial discipline to help me go deeper in intimacy with God. I went to the monastery one time to spend two days with the Lord, and I sensed the Lord calling me to stay up all night and pray. It became a regular weekly event for a long season in my life. At

Watching–staying up in the night to pray– has also been a key sacrificial discipline to help me go deeper in intimacy with God.

first a few friends joined me, but it grew, and eventually we had several dozen people coming up on a Friday night to stay up half the night and pray. We spent long hours just soaking in God's presence. We often ended with prayer together, letting the Spirit lead and direct our times of prayer together. It was rich. We saw healing, freedom, and many people encountered God. I no longer do a prayer watch once per week. But sometimes, especially when I travel, the Lord wakes me in the middle of the night and I pray. Sometimes when I feel plateaued in my spiritual journey, I combine fasting and watching to breathe fresh life into my spiritual journey.

I want to end this section about going deeper in intimacy with God by talking about the importance of sacrifice through spiritual retreats. Jesus practiced spiritual retreats regularly, and He taught His disciples to retreat. In Mark 6:30, 31, after the disciples came back from a ministry assignment, Jesus gathered them together to hear what they had been doing. "The apostles gathered around Jesus and told him all that they had done and taught. He said to them, 'Come away to a deserted place all by yourselves and rest a while.' For many were coming and going, and they had no leisure even to eat" (NRSV). Notice a couple of things: first, how busy they were; they had no leisure even to eat. Sometimes I hear people say,

"Jesus wasn't busy." Nonsense. Jesus was in constant demand. He was busy, but He wasn't hurried. He was busy, but He wasn't frazzled or preoccupied. Jesus was busy but rested. In my book *Spiritual Authority* I write a good deal about Jesus' retreat life, and I say, "Jesus was busy, but rested, because He did what the Father told Him to do, and He retreated for refueling. Retreats are refueling centers for the soul" (*Spiritual Authority*, p.149).

It is a lifestyle of retreating that allows us to sustain a ministry of high demand. The more authority you carry, the more likely you will be in high demand, and the more essential it is that you sustain a lifestyle of retreats.

Jesus practiced retreats regularly. Mark 1:35: "In the morning, while it was still very dark, he got up and went out to a deserted place, and there he prayed." Jesus often prayed while it was dark. He got alone with the Father in the middle of the night or the wee hours of the morning. He also used mountains and seas as an escape route to a quiet place to restore His soul (Mark 3:7, 13, 14; Luke 6:12; Mark 6:45, 46; Mark 9:2). Luke 5:16: "Jesus often withdrew to lonely places and prayed." If Jesus, the sinless Son of God, needed to go on spiritual retreats, how much more the rest of us?

Jesus practiced retreats frequently. Jesus called His disciples to retreat, and Jesus calls us to get alone with Him. I think there are some depths we cannot get to with God without the regular, consistent practice of spiritual retreating. Nothing has helped me go deeper with God like the regular, consistent practice of spiritual retreats.

I have been doing spiritual retreats for two decades. At first I went away to a monastery once a year for a week to be alone with God. But after a couple of years of that, one day as I drove onto the monastery campus, I sensed the Lord's presence. As I breathed a deep sigh of relief, I heard the Spirit beckoning me to come every other month. I did that for more than a decade; I went to the monastery for at least 30 hours every other month. I do not believe I could have survived the darkest seasons of ministry without spiritual retreats. I do not believe I could have experienced the life and power of Christ as I have without the regular practice of spiritual retreats.

I am currently taking one retreat day each month on my porch. I miss the monastery where I have encountered God so many times, but due to my extensive travel I had to limit my days away from home. I wasn't willing to dispense with retreats because they are vital to my spiritual well-being. If you have never taken a spiritual retreat, I want to encourage you to set aside a day to get alone with God. Put it on your calendar or you won't do it. Life has a way of crowding out everything but the urgent.

It was only after years of fasting, watching, retreating, and pursuing God's face that I began to see the results. There was a dramatic and significant increase in God's manifest presence and power in my ministry. These are practices I cannot recommend highly enough.

There is one other thing I want to talk about regarding our intimacy with God: Jesus needs to be our first love. Jesus said the most important thing is to love God with all our heart, soul, mind, and strength (Matthew 22:37). We cannot live a revived life if Jesus is not our first love.

Remember the church at Ephesus in Revelation 2? Jesus told them, "I know your good deeds, your hard work and your perseverance. I know that you cannot tolerate wicked people, that you have tested those who claim to be apostles but are not and have found them false. You have persevered and endured hardships for my name and have not grown weary" (2:2, 3). This is a good church. They are doing good deeds. They believe sound doctrine. They are working hard for the king and his Kingdom. They have persevered through hardship. They have not fallen for false teachers. They are hitting it on every mark—except one.

Jesus goes on to say, "Yet I hold this against you: You have forsaken the love you had at first. Consider how far you have fallen! Repent and do the things you did at first" (2:4, 5). They had lost their passion for Jesus. Jesus was no longer their primary passion, their main obsession, their heart's preoccupation. When you first fall in love, you become obsessed with the object of your affection. That person preoccupies your mind. You can't stop thinking about the one you love. When you have children, you find the same obsession strikes you again. You can't get them out of your mind. I am at the age where a lot of my friends have grandchildren, and they become obsessed with those little ones. They show me the pictures; they arrange their life around being with those little ones. This is what love does to you.

When Jesus ceases to be our heart's obsession, we have lost our first love and need to recapture it. You cannot maintain spiritual vitality when Jesus is not your primary affection. There are three simple things you can do to recapture your first love. First, admit that you have lost it. Be honest. Don't spin, blame, excuse, justify, rationalize, or deny it. Own it. Second, remember. Remember the heights from which you have fallen. Remember the things Jesus has done for you. Remember your history with God. I remember how Jesus redeemed my marriage crisis to heal my soul—and from that place Soul Care developed and hundreds of thousands of lives around the world have been impacted. I remember

> Remember your history with God. And if you don't yet have much of a personal history with God, then remember that you are part of the family of God.

how Jesus met me in my most severe ministry crisis and how He redeemed it to make me a man of authority and take me deeper in intimacy. I remember where Jesus has met me on life's journey. I remember visits with Him in the monastery and on retreat. Remember your history with God. And if you don't yet have much of a personal history with God, then remember that you are part of the family of God and the stories of God's people are part of your family history. Remember how God has met His people through the centuries, in the Bible and throughout church history. That is your heritage. Third, repent and do the things you did at first. When I first surrendered my life to Christ, no one told me I needed to spend time with God; I did it out of a heart full of love. Sacrifice because of who He is and what He has done; let who He is reignite your passion. Set your heart and your mind on things above (Colossians 3:1).

In 2021 I decided I wanted to make Jesus my main obsession again. Too often our minds have been preoccupied with COVID, economic crisis, political strife, division and hatred, and racism. But I decided I want my mind to be preoccupied with Jesus, not with the problems of the world. I want Jesus to be my main obsession, my first love. Whatever is your heart obsession becomes your mind's preoccupation. Is Jesus your first love? Is Jesus your heart's obsession? Is Jesus your mind's preoccupation?

I read books about Jesus throughout the year 2021. Of course, I began with the Gospels and have been meditating through the Gospels. To continue to stir my heart, I have been reading other books written about Jesus. I read a book by Kathryn Kuhlman in February 2021. I was listening to it on Audible and what most struck me was her obsession with Jesus. I drove home one night from Manhattan and wept because of her obsession with Jesus. That is when the people of God are at our best: when Jesus is our passion and focus. Is it true of you? If you want to develop your authority, you have to expand your intimacy. You can't do it without once again becoming obsessed with Jesus.

Activated By Faith

Spiritual authority is rooted in identity, expanded in intimacy, and **activated by faith**. It is hard to overestimate the importance of faith in the Kingdom of God. Jesus is only amazed two times in the Gospels. He is amazed by the centurion's great faith (Matthew 8:10) and by His hometown's lack of faith (Mark 6:6). The centurion made the connection between military authority and spiritual authority. He was a man under authority, with people under him. They all responded to their superior's commands. They did what they were told to do and went where they were told to go. This man realized Jesus had authority in the spiritual realm like he had authority in the military. Jesus commanded sickness to go, and people were healed. He commanded demons to leave, and people were set free. Jesus was amazed at this man's great faith, and He granted the man's request without even going to his home. But the people of Jesus' hometown did not believe. Jesus could do few miracles there, and He was amazed at their lack of faith. Great faith produces great results; little faith produces little Kingdom activity. This is a Kingdom reality.

There is no credit for skepticism in the Kingdom. Jesus calls out our "little faith" and rebukes our unbelief. Little faith is a faith saturated in doubt. Doubt isn't a sin, but it is underdeveloped faith, and we must take responsibility for developing our faith. This is

Unbelief is a refusal to trust God, and this frequently ends with disobedience. We need to repent of our unbelief and develop our little faith.

why Jesus often chides His disciples for their little faith. But unbelief is a sin. Unbelief is a refusal to trust God, and this frequently ends with disobedience. We need to repent of our unbelief and develop our little faith. Today in the Evangelical Church, too often we take pride in skepticism, but there is no honor for the skeptic in the Gospels. The credit only goes to those who believe. Great faith pleases God.

So how do we develop faith? I wrote an entire book on this subject, *Deep Faith*. The book outlines my journey of developing my faith. I wanted to see Jesus do the things Jesus did in the Bible, so I preached on healing, but as I said at the beginning, few people got healed. I came to realize that my faith, like that of the disciples, was "little faith." I needed to grow my faith into a mature and deep faith. It was a long, hard, painful journey to develop faith, but it was worth the trip. I refer you to that book for a more in-depth analysis, but let me give a couple of key learnings.

First, reading can help us deepen our faith. Obviously, we begin by reading Scripture. Read and meditate on the works of Jesus, on the person of Jesus. I never get very far from the Gospels. I follow Jesus, so I want my reading to be saturated with the life of Jesus. I have to shift my thinking from "this is who Jesus was, and this is what Jesus did" to "this is who Jesus *is*, and this is what Jesus *does*." Jesus hasn't changed.

It also helps to read Christian biographies from people who have experienced more than we have. We all belong to the family of God. The stories of the people in the Bible and stories of people in church history are all part of our heritage as a member of the family of God. Knowing these things can help build our faith.

At one point in my spiritual journey I realized I had more faith for deliverance than I had for healing. I was reading Matthew 10, and Matthew writes here that Jesus gave them authority to drive out demons and heal all diseases. I had faith to believe Jesus for casting out demons; I had been involved in many powerful deliverances. But I didn't have the same depth of faith for healing. I realized that day that my faith for healing the sick was "little faith." So I decided I needed to grow my faith. I went after it. I read books on healing from some of the older saints like A.B. Simpson, Andrew Murray, and others. I read books from modern writers on healing—most of them were Pentecostal or Charismatics. Sadly, I found few modern writers in my Evangelical camp who wrote about healing.

Second, expand your experiences. I sought to expand my experiences in healing. I went to conferences on healing. I preached more on healing and intentionally spent more time praying with the sick. At one point I had read a bunch of books on healing and been to several conferences on healing, and I said to Jen, "I can't keep just reading or going to conferences. I need to experience things I've never experienced before. I need to go to a country where they experience more healing than we experience in the U.S. And I need to go with someone who sees more healing than I see." I was driving home from a healing conference when I said that to Jen, and a few minutes later I received an email from someone who said they felt led by God to send me and my family on a missions trip with Randy Clark to Brazil. Sounded like an answer to prayer to me! They sent us a check for $20,000, and we went to Brazil. I saw healings every day. The last day of the conference I saw a tumor shrink beneath my hand as I prayed. When you see stuff like that, it changes you and deepens your faith. It's one thing to hear about it, it's another thing to be involved in a verifiable, visible miraculous healing.

Finally, if you are going to develop your faith, you will have to take risks. You are going to have to risk more than you're comfortable with. I was 25 years old when I did my first deliverance, and I had never seen a successful deliverance. All I knew was that Jesus didn't want anyone to have demons, and that I didn't get a junior Holy Spirit—the same Spirit that lived in Jesus lived in me. So I took the risk and Jesus delivered!

One Sunday morning I was scheduled to give a sermon on James 5 about healing. I had never seen a divine healing, but we don't preach our experience, we preach God's Word. I had prepared the talk and was ready to go. I got up early on Sunday, and I sat alone with the Lord and said, "Is there anything you want me to add to this talk?" I thought God might want to tweak something a little, but I was in for a surprise. I heard a faint whisper of the Spirit: "Give the talk like you have prepared it. Just add one sentence at the end: the Lord told me to give this talk because He wants to heal many people today." I said, "Lord, that's a big sentence! If no one gets healed, I look like a fool! Can you confirm that this thought comes from you?" Nothing. I went to church; I was hoping someone would give me a confirming word. Nothing. I sat through worship. I didn't sing, I just waited for the Lord to confirm that this was from Him. Nothing. Finally, I stood up and gave the talk. I came to the end, and I took the big risk. I told them what I sensed the Lord saying to me that morning, and more than a dozen people were miraculously healed that morning. One man was scheduled to go in for surgery that week, but God miraculously healed him, and he never needed the surgery. One woman was healed without anyone praying for her. When I spoke that word, she believed and felt electricity start at her shoulder, shoot down through her body, and she was instantly healed. It was a powerful day, but it wouldn't have happened without the faith risk. When I spoke that word it inspired faith in the hearts of people, and God responds to people full of faith.

Let me end by sharing my personal journey with you. Developing spiritual authority is not easy; nor is it a single event. It is a long-term commitment, an arduous trip, one full of many ups and downs, tests and trials, triumphs and tragedies—but one that is worth it. I mentioned earlier that I prayed this prayer since I was in my mid-twenties: "Lord, give me the ability to impart your Spirit—*if* my character and intimacy can sustain it." A few years into the prayer I went to a Leanne Payne Conference. At one point, Leanne asked people to stand if they needed prayer for something specific, and a woman stood in front of me. Leanne asked the rest of us to lay hands on the people who had stood around us. She instructed us not to pray, that she would pray; we were just to lay hands on them. I did as she asked. There were a lot of other people who joined in the prayer session. (Many of them felt the need to pray aloud, even though Leanne had told us not to. We do tend to make it too much about us.) When the prayer time ended, the woman we were praying for turned and asked me, "Did you have your hand on my shoulder?" I acknowledged I did. She said, "Did you feel that?" I had no idea what she was referring to. She went on to explain that she felt divine heat coming through my hand as I prayed. That was the first time that ever happened. I thought to myself: *Here it comes! God is answering my prayer.* But that was the last time it happened for more than five years.

I sensed the Lord telling me to pursue His presence. I always spent time with God, but I turned up the heat. I went on my first long fast; I started a prayer watch every Friday night praying into the wee hours of the morning. I started going on a monastery retreat every other month. I was pressing into God like never before. For years I pursued like that, but still there was little increase. I did, however, experience a greater sense of intimacy with God. Something was happening in me even if I couldn't see it in visible demonstrations of God's power.

My goal wasn't simply to see the power of God. I wanted to see revival. That was my calling and my passion. In the midst of this season of pursuit I sensed the Lord say to me that I was to preach revival until it came. So I preached, and I pursued with passion. Naively, I thought I would preach on revival and everyone in the church would enthusiastically follow. But I started getting resistance and attacks. I had someone create an imaginary Facebook profile and friend people in the church and begin to write against me. I had blogs written against me. A handful of Christian radio shows in our area were done against me. In the midst of these attacks, I went to the monastery one day and laid face down on the floor and said to the Lord, "Why? I am not complaining. I just don't get it. Why are people attacking me?" I heard the Lord, and He said, "I'm answering your prayer." To be honest, I had no idea what He was talking about. I said, "Lord, I have no idea what I have been praying, but if you tell me, I promise I'll stop!" He said, "For over a dozen years you have prayed, 'Lord, give me the ability to impart your Spirit—if my character and intimacy can sustain it.' This is what it takes."

I laid on the floor, surrendered, and said to the Lord, "Then answer my prayer."

For many more years the attacks continued, and I still didn't see a huge increase. The outpouring of the Spirit I longed for did not come. And I became deeply discouraged. I was beat up and weary. I wanted to quit every day, but God had called me, and I wouldn't quit unless God released me, so I persevered. There were many tears of heartache, and by 2013 I was wrestling with something I had never struggled with before. I was wrestling with the question, "Does God lie?" It wasn't a theological question; it was an emotional question. I said to Jen at one point that year, "If I can't settle this, I will have to quit ministry. I can't keep preaching this, if I don't believe." I grieved. I processed with people like Jen and my friend Ron Walborn. They were supportive and helpful.

The breakthrough occurred one day when I was reading Hebrews 11. I told the story earlier in the book. The important lesson God revealed to me was that sometimes He gives us a promise that we do not get to see fulfilled. Many of the people in Hebrews 11 received a promise from God, but it was not for them.

It was for a future generation. He could have told them it wasn't for them. He could have told them it was for a future generation. But He didn't. He trusted them. He trusted that they would fight for the promise like it was their own, that they would overcome all external obstacles and internal struggles and be faithful so that, one day, a future generation would live out the promise they had battled for. And all at once, in spite of the dark night of the soul, I knew what God was asking me: "Would you be willing to fight for revival if you never saw it? Would you be willing to fight for revival if only a future generation got to experience the fruits of what you give your life to battle for?" I surrendered. I said, "Lord, I will fight for revival with my dying breath even if I never see it. I will fight for the future generations." Every one of you who is reading this and is younger than me, know that I am fighting for revival for you. Every day I battle for you, that you might stand on the promise God has given me and taste its fruit.

The dark night of the soul didn't lift that day, but there was a breakthrough in my heart as I surrendered. There is no peace without surrender. I stopped wrestling with God that day; I stopped fighting. I stopped taking offense, and peace came.

It took several more months before the dark night of the soul lifted. One day I was sitting in my living room, and ever so gently I sensed the presence of God again. It wasn't dramatic or powerful. It was just this gentle touch from His tangible presence for the first time in many months. As I wrote earlier, I wept. I had missed Him so much.

After that gentle reentry of his presence, I saw a dramatic increase in the power of God. I spoke at a conference in California right after His presence returned, and as I prayed for people, they encountered God. Several people were filled with the Spirit and fell down under the weighty presence of God. This happens to people in the Bible. John the Apostle, for example, after he encounters the risen Christ in Revelation 1, falls down like a dead man. Ezekiel encounters God's glory multiple times and falls under the weight of God's presence. But these people were Evangelicals; they had never experienced this phenomenon before. They didn't grow up in Pentecostal circles, and this wasn't a learned behavior. This was a clear and real demonstration of God's power. And despite the years of pursuit of His presence, when His power was manifest regularly, I was surprised by it.

For an entire year, everywhere I went I saw God's power manifest. People were healed, delivered, and especially filled with the Spirit, and the presence and power of God were visibly displayed. I did a Holy Spirit weekend at one church in New York, and I taught on the filling of the Spirit. After the talk I simply prayed, "Come, Holy Spirit." People started falling all over the auditorium as the presence of God came with power. Again, this wasn't a learned behavior; these weren't Pentecostals who had learned to fall when a "holy" person prayed for them. These were people who had never seen anything like this, but God came in power. By the time we finished walking through that room and praying for people, God had met nearly everyone in the room in a powerful way.

> And all at once, in spite of the dark night of the soul, I knew what God was asking me: "Would you be willing to fight for revival if you never saw it?"

I had been to church my whole life, and I had never seen anything like it. It happened conference after conference.

Thousands and thousands of people were touched by the presence and power of God. I was moved, humbled, touched, awed, grateful, surprised, and overwhelmed. But I just rode the wave.

Then after a year of God's steady demonstrations of power . . . they dried up. I went to a conference one day and did what I had been doing for the past year, but this time only a few people encountered God. But I had learned from Charles Finney, so I prayed and fasted and sought God's face, and the power returned. That has been the pattern ever since. There will be waves of God's power and presence visiting His people, then it will dry up, and I pray and fast and pursue God's presence. And the power of God will return once again.

It is hard to overestimate the importance of persistence in this pursuit of God's presence and the development of authority. I needed to persist in the pursuit of God's face. I needed to persist in deepening my identity in Christ. I needed to persist in developing faith. I needed to persist through soul-shaping hardship. I needed to persist through attacks. I needed to persist in blessing those who cursed me. I needed to persist through times of spiritual dryness, through disappointment, through the dark night of the soul. It was all critically important to helping me to die to self so Christ could be formed more deeply in me. Truly, the biggest problem in the church today is that we are making it too much about us. And that was true for me and, sadly, too often is still true for me today. I need to die to self

> The church today is marked too much by our presence and too little by His presence. When the people of the church are filled with the Spirit, the church is dangerous to hell.

for Christ to be formed in me. I need to make it less about me, my gifts, my talents, my abilities, my ideas, and make it all about Jesus and His presence. I'm still learning. When Jesus shows up, the Kingdom comes. When I show up, nothing happens. I need to be marked by the presence of Jesus.

The church today is marked too much by our presence and too little by His presence. When the people of the church are filled with the Spirit, the church is dangerous to hell. When we are not filled with the Spirit, we are dangerous to the church.

Chapter 6

TALKING VERSUS PROCESSING

Some people keep talking about the same issues over and over, but the issues never get any better. If we are talking about the same issue we were talking about three years ago, then we are just talking but aren't processing through the issue. How do we process our pain and our issues so that we get through to the other side? Processing is developmental, and it leads to breakthrough. Talking without processing leaves us trapped in bondage. Let's talk about some key principles that can help shift from talking to processing.

Dealing with Root Issues

First, if we are going to shift from talking to processing, **we have to deal with root issues and not merely symptoms.** In Matthew 12:34 Jesus said, "Out of the overflow of the heart the mouth speaks." One of my favorite Soul Care questions is: What's underneath that? What is driving that presenting problem? We have to deal with the heart and soul, not merely behavior. Too often people focus on behavior modification and sin management, but Jesus was focused on the heart and soul.

Here's an example. Let's say a man comes to church and he is wrestling with pornography. He is full of shame. He awkwardly and painfully confesses his struggle. The person he confesses to essentially gives him this advice: "Stop that." *Thank you. I never thought of that. I feel healed.* It doesn't help, of course. The real question is why does he struggle with pornography? What is underneath that? It is possible he is struggling with pornography because he has toxic shame. He feels unlovable because of the painful abuse in his childhood. He uses pornography to soothe his soul and comfort himself. Of course, it doesn't work. All it does is compound his shame. Now, rather than just having the primary shame of his childhood abuse, he also has the secondary shame of his behavior. As he participates in porn, the enemy condemns him: "You call yourself a Christian! How can you do that? Look at what you did." And now his shame comes back on him with compound interest.

It is equally possible that what is motivating him to use pornography is anger. He is hurt in one or more of his relationships. He hasn't processed the hurt and forgiven the people who have sinned against him, and he is medicating the pain and hurt with pornography. Forgiving those who sin against him will help him break free from his pattern of pornography.

Maybe the reason he is struggling with pornography is because he lacks the courage to press into true intimacy with his wife and is settling for the false intimacy of the woman on the screen who always loves him. He tried to talk to his wife about something he needed or wanted, but she didn't receive him compassionately. Rather than pressing through the conflict with truth and grace, he avoids the conflict, backs down, stuffs his emotions, and turns to the woman on the screen. He has to develop the courage and skills to cultivate true intimacy.

Or it may be that he has an intimacy barrier in his soul due to his upbringing and choices. His soul craves true intimacy, but his avoidant attachment style and fear of intimacy keeps him at emotional arm's length from everyone around him. There is an emptiness in his soul, so he begins to turn to pornography to fill the void.

Of course, it may be that he struggles with any combination of these issues, or even all of them.

In these scenarios, behavior modification won't address the issues of the heart. If he addresses the heart issues, it will be a lot easier to change his behavior. If he doesn't deal with the root causes, he will be talking about this same struggle with lust five years from now. There will be ups and downs, short-term gains, and many losses. We must get to the root issues. Jesus came to heal our hearts and souls, but we have to give Him access.

When I am processing an issue, I always begin in prayer, in my time alone with God. I talk to God about the issue, but I don't stop there. If I am struggling with a persistent presenting issue like lust, fear, anger, or control, I wrestle with the questions: Why? What is underneath? What is triggering that? I write out my prayers in a prayer journal. I talk to God about what I am struggling with; I listen for the insight and wisdom of the Holy Spirit. Reflection in the presence of the Holy Spirit often leads me to the insight I need. Of course, it often does not become clear to me without persistence. I pray and wrestle and journal and process these things sometimes for months before I finally come to clarity about the root issue or issues.

I also include other close confidants in my processing. I process with Jen and my friends what I am thinking about, wrestling with, what may be at the root of the issue, and so forth. I usually do this after I have wrestled with God some, so I have some insights and reflections to bring to the discussion. I want to walk in the light with God and others (1 John 1), and often they can give me an insight that can help me on the path to freedom. But even if they don't have any insights, I want to make sure I am not walking in darkness with a struggle. Satan always tries to shame us and keep us from being honest. There is no victory in darkness. You cannot use the tools of the kingdom of darkness to gain freedom in the Kingdom of light.

In the next chapter we will talk about some of the most common root issues. It will certainly not be an all-inclusive list, but it will help us wrestle with these things more effectively, both for ourselves and others.

Encounters with the Presence of God

Second, if we are going to shift from talking to processing, **we need encounters with the presence of God.** Beginning in 2 Corinthians 3:17, Paul writes, "Now the Lord is the Spirit, and where the Spirit of the Lord is, there is freedom. And we all, who with unveiled faces contemplate the Lord's glory, are being transformed into his image with ever increasing glory, which comes from the Lord, who is the Spirit." Paul was comparing us to Moses. When Moses entered the manifest presence of God, he came out with his face shining, but the glory that shone on his face faded away, so Moses put a veil over his face so the people wouldn't see the glory fade. But Paul says we are not like Moses; we don't have to go into and out of the presence of God because now the presence of God is within us. We are the temple of God. We house His presence, and where the Spirit of the Lord is, there is freedom. In the presence of God there is transformation that leads to breakthrough.

> As Brother Lawrence said, we need to practice the presence of God. The Lord is always present, but we are not always aware of His presence.

Paul says that "with unveiled faces" we "contemplate the Lord's glory." We need to intentionally access the presence of God so we can experience His transformational power. Only God can change the heart; only God can heal the soul. Only God can transform a life from the inside out. To access God's presence, we need to contemplate the Lord's glory. We need to cultivate an awareness of God's presence or, as Brother Lawrence said, we need to practice the presence of God. The Lord is always present, but we are not always aware of His presence. But as we learn to cultivate an awareness of His presence, and attend to His presence, we begin to access His transformational work in our inner being. Talking will not produce transformation, but the presence of God will.

I was praying for a woman one day who had a great deal of anxiety. As I listened to her story, I realized that it stemmed from separation anxiety. If you have been through *Soul Care,* you know that I had separation anxiety, and I experienced the Lord's transformative presence at a Leanne Payne Conference. After I listened to her story, I simply prayed for this young lady: "Now may the peace of Christ come upon you." And then I waited. I have learned over the years to pray less wordy prayers, to make them less about me and more about Jesus. I simply enter Jesus' presence while I am with the person, and I wait on Jesus to do what only Jesus can do. I wait for Him to speak, to lead, to act, to move, to show up. When Jesus shows up, transforming power is often displayed, and He came that day on that young lady. His presence visibly descended upon her, and you could watch peace descend upon her. Her anxiety was healed, just as mine had been many years ago in my own encounter with God. Such is the power of Jesus' presence.

We don't just need good theology about Jesus; we need an authentic encounter with the risen Christ. How do we access the presence of God ourselves and with others?

The first way to access God's presence is in our private time alone with God through the practice of spiritual disciplines. We talked earlier about our spiritual rhythm. Our rhythm is what we do on a daily, weekly, monthly, and yearly basis to stay vitally connected to Jesus. The key questions you must regularly evaluate are these: Is your rhythm working? Are you experiencing God's presence? Are you hearing God's voice? Are you experiencing the Lord's tender love washing over your soul? Are you drawing nearer to God and going deeper in intimacy with Him?

Sometimes when I am stuck in my spiritual journey, in a sin pattern, in fear or anxiety, or feeling plateaued in my intimacy with God, I need a larger block of time to access God's presence and process these things. I have advocated for taking spiritual retreats. There are things that can be accomplished in a large block of time with God that cannot be accessed in a daily devotional. There are intimate places I can get to on a retreat that I cannot get to in my regular daily time with God. There are breakthroughs I can get to in a day alone with God that I cannot reach in an hour alone with God. So when I am stuck and can't break through, I schedule a retreat to be alone with God and process at a more intense, deeper level. It has often led me to the breakthrough that I need.

It seems to me that most life change occurs alone with God. It isn't that people don't have a part; they do. I have already advocated for walking in the light with God and others; I believe in the impor-

> It seems to me
> that most life
> change occurs
> alone with God.

tance of true community. But every time I've experienced significant life change there was some place along the journey where I heard God's voice, I encountered God's presence, I experienced God's power, or in some way I met God in a real and tangible way that led to a breakthrough. I can look at every breakthrough scenario in my life and see this pattern.

In my early marriage crisis, I was alone with God late one night; I cried out to Him for help. Jen and I had been talking and talking, but we were not making any progress. It felt dark and desperate. That night in the wee hours, I cried out to God in my heartache, and He said to me, "Never defend yourself again." Every time Jen told me what she was angry and hurt about, I defended myself. She didn't feel heard, and we both tried to express ourselves more forcefully, which only increased the hurt. That one phrase—"Never defend yourself again"—changed our dynamic. It led me to start listening and stop defending.

I was stuck in that marriage pain and in a pattern of lust, so I set aside a block of time with God on another late night. As I cried out to the Lord, I heard the Him say, "There is a book up on top of that eight-foot bookshelf. Reach up and get it." It was *Continuous Revival* by Norman Grubb. God taught me to walk in the light with Him and others; it changed me. Walking in the light was a key principle to breaking free from the grip of darkness.

It was a prompting of the Spirit that led me to read Leanne Payne and the Spirit's voice that told me to go to a Leanne Payne Conference. There, God met me and changed me forever. Repeatedly, my transformational moments have been marked by God's presence. God spoke, revealed, healed, released His power, and I was changed. But all those transformational moments happened at a time when I was pursuing God. Desperation is often the platform to breakthrough because desperation motivates us to pursue God and opens our hearts to listen to new solutions.

When you are in a need of a breakthrough, when you have been talking about something far too long, and it is time to really process the issue and get to a solution, carve out a block of time for God. Spend a day alone with God; stay up through the night to seek Him. Give God access; pursue God's presence and see what God can do. There have been times I had to persist in pursuit for many months, over multiple retreats, but eventually a divine shift occurred. God spoke, and something within me shifted and breakthrough came. Don't let go; keep pursuing God's presence until the breakthrough comes.

When we are working with others to help them through soul care issues, one of the most important things we can do is to make sure they are setting up a regular time with God. I used to take people with me on monastery retreats regularly. I taught them how to spend a day alone with God, and then let them spend the day in His presence. At night I got together with the men that I brought (the monastery only had male guests), and we prayed together. I taught them how to hear God's voice and listen prophetically for one another. Many men had breakthroughs on those monastery retreats because they encountered God's presence.

Not only can we access God's presence in our personal time with God, we can also access God's presence with others. We were created in the image of God; God is community—Father, Son, and Holy Spirit. We were born for community, and often we cannot access the breakthrough we need from God without the help, support, love, and prayer of others. We need others to talk to, confess to, process with, and pray with. We need people to pray for us, pray with us, lay hands on us, and listen to God on our behalf. I have been the beneficiary of community like this, and I have been used by God in the lives of others to help them access His presence for breakthrough.

When I was processing that first marriage crisis, I called my friend Rich Schmidt. It was one of the hardest calls I ever made in my life. I called to tell him that we were in the middle of a marriage crisis and my wife didn't like me anymore. I had previously told Rich I was struggling with lust, but I felt much greater shame over my struggling marriage. The thing we most need to tell someone else is the thing we least want anyone to know. That is the thing we keep in the dark, and the darkness holds us prisoner. We need to bring it into the light. That day Rich shared with me that he too was struggling in his marriage, and we began to journey together on the road to self-awareness and healing.

> The thing we most need to tell someone else is the thing we least want anyone to know. That is the thing we keep in the dark, and the darkness holds us prisoner.

I called my great friend Martin Sanders one day. He was the professor of the last class I took in seminary, and I had stayed in touch with him over the years. We started doing some ministry together as he invited me to teach some classes with him at Alliance Theological Seminary. As I explored my family sin patterns, I began to see how much sexual immorality had plagued my family. I was afraid that one day I would blow up my ministry and my family with sexual sin. So I called Martin and said, "I need to process some stuff with you. Would you come and preach on a Sunday, and then I will take you out to lunch and we can process some stuff from my life and family?" He agreed. I sat with him in the car for several hours and walked him through my family history and my own struggles with lust. I told him I was afraid I would end up taking the path of so many who had gone before me. He said,

"You will finish well, and I will walk with you all your days." He listened, he prayed, he encouraged, and we have walked together for more than three decades. I have always remained faithful to my wife.

I have helped many people process their issues through the years. I have received people's confessions, prayed for them, and seen many breakthroughs. I have cast out demons from thousands who have been set free. I have prayed over people's trauma and seen God release them from grief, pain, and heartache. My approach is very simple: I listen to the person and listen to the Holy Spirit. I wait on His presence and listen for the leadings of the Spirit, and I courageously and humbly try to follow wherever He leads. Repeatedly, I have watched Jesus show up and do what only Jesus can do.

I was doing a deliverance recently with someone who was a psychologist. The person had been sexually abused and had battled with symptoms of demonic attacks, condemnation, and anxiety. I led this person through the deliverance. Every time I asked the demonic spirit if it had any ground, the spirit told me that, yes, it had ground. I kept saying to the person, "It has to be specific, unconfessed sin. If the spirit brings up anything that you have already confessed, that isn't ground. That's just condemnation." Time after time the spirit brought up something that the person had already confessed, and I assured them they didn't need to confess it again; they were forgiven. Finally, after more than a dozen times, the person looked at me, utterly exasperated, and said, "I have been living under condemnation my whole life!" Indeed, this person had. But that day they were delivered from demonic forces, and they were freed from shame, guilt, and condemnation. At the end of our time together the person said to me, "I had processed all this stuff. I had done the work. I thought I was free. I didn't realize that all of these evil things were still living in me, doing this dirty work in me." That's the power of community. That's why Jesus asked us to do this with others.

I was doing a conference in Redding, California with my friend, and dean of the seminary, Ron Walborn. Ron had to leave early, but before he left, he said to me, "Will you meet with Ruth? She is stuck and needs some help." I agreed and wandered over to where he told me she was sitting. I asked her to tell me her story.

The most important part of her story: as a little girl, Ruth's mother used to say to her, "Women are just oppressed. That's just the way it is. There is nothing you can do about it."

Ruth learned to stuff her emotions. She thought: *No one cares. No one will love me. No one will nurture me in my pain.* So she just stuffed them—all of them. When something bad happened she went into her room and sat quietly. She didn't pray, she didn't listen to music, she didn't journal. She just sat in her room and stuffed her pain into the basement of her soul. And eventually she didn't feel much of anything at all; she just felt numb.

As she told her story, an image came to my mind. I said, "Ruth, it is like you are sitting in a steel room. There are no windows. And you can't get out. You are in this dark and lonely place. But Jesus stands outside at the door, and He knocks. He wants you to open the door and let Him in."

She said, "Why doesn't He just open it Himself? He can come in if He wants to."

I said, "He is a gentleman. He won't force himself upon you. He is not an oppressor. You must choose to let Him in." I could see that she was reluctant, so I said to her, "I won't force you, either. We have one more service tonight. If you want prayer after this service, if you're ready to open the door, then come up to me and I'll pray with you."

At the end of that service, Ruth was first in line, and she simply said, "I'm ready." I laid my hand on her head and said,

"Just picture yourself in that steel room, and open the door to let Jesus in." Then I prayed, "Come in, Lord Jesus."

The presence of God was so strong upon her that she just fell over under the weight of His presence. She stayed on the floor for about 45 minutes. When she got up she was radically changed. Over the next several months she experienced many long overdue tears and much joy. She experienced grieving and healing and, most importantly, God's loving presence.

Today, Ruth no longer lives in a small box. She has full range of her emotions because Jesus has set her free. If we are going to experience breakthrough, we need to access God's presence by ourselves and with others, because only Jesus heals the soul.

Some of you are trying to pray with others, but you aren't seeing God move with power. Don't be discouraged. When I started in ministry, I saw far less of God's power demonstrated than I do today. Keep cultivating intimacy with God. Develop increased levels of sensitivity to His presence and His voice. Keep reminding yourself that it is not about you; stay focused on Jesus. When you go to minister to a person, always listen for the promptings of the Spirit. If you don't receive any specific wisdom to help, do your best to make the person feel loved. You can't make God show up. You can't make God speak prophetic words of insight. You can't manufacture God's power. But you can always do your best to make the person feel loved. And love is healing.

Grieve Your Losses

Third, if we are going to shift from talking to processing, **we need to grieve our losses.** Sometimes we get stuck in sadness, but we don't process our grief. Some people think they are grieving because they feel sadness, but feeling sadness and grieving are not the same thing.

In June 2017 Jen and I transitioned out of the long-term pastorate. We had planted South Shore Community and been there for more than twenty years. We had to process a lot of grief with our departure. In February of that year Jen came to me one day and said, "Are you angry with me?" I said, "No. Why do you ask? Have I been treating you badly?" She said, "No. You're just kind of radiating anger." I knew I was. I was processing it and trying to figure out what was underneath.

It is sometimes difficult for me to access "weak emotions." Usually I feel anger instead. When I am sad, I often don't feel sadness; I feel anger. When I am fearful, I don't feel fear; I feel anger. The good news is when I feel angry, I know I have something I need to process. The bad news is I often do not know what is underneath that anger, and I have to figure it out. In this case, the first level of anger was connected with loss. I was grieving the loss of many friends that we had done life with for a long time as we were getting ready to depart.

Let me give a few key principles for processing grief. First, pray the lament Psalms. A little less than half the Psalms are laments, and they are helpful guides to grieving well. Let's look at one of these Psalms. David writes in Psalm 142:1-7:

> *I cry aloud to the Lord; I lift up my voice to the Lord for mercy. I pour out before him my complaint; before him I tell my trouble. When my spirit grows faint within me, it is you who watch over my way. In the path where I walk people have hidden a snare for me. Look and see, there is no one at my right hand; no one is concerned for me. I have no refuge; no one cares for my life. I cry to you, Lord; I say, "You are my refuge, my portion in the land of the living." Listen to my cry, for I am in desperate need; rescue me from those who pursue me, for they are too strong for me. Set me free from my prison, that I may praise your*

name. Then the righteous will gather about me because of your goodness to me.

When I pray the lament Psalms, I read through a handful of them until I find one that resonates with my emotional state of being. Then I pray it back to God in my own words. They guide me through the grieving process.

Second, if we are going to grieve well, we need to bring our pain honorably and honestly before the Lord. This is what the psalmists did. We need to be raw but reverent, honest but honorable. In Psalm 142 David brings his complaint before the Lord. He complains to God about his troubles. We cannot simply cloak our pain with religious phrases. In my book *Calm in the Storm*, I wrote, "If we don't process our grief, our trust will be diminished. We can't whitewash pain and heartache with pithy religious phrases or a memorized verse from the Bible. This is what a religious person does—they take a truth and put it on like an outer garment, but they fail to internalize it in their inner being so that it becomes part of their life. They have the right words, but religion is skin-deep. Religious people often fail to internalize eternal truths and they face life with a thin soul. True trust is developed when hardships are authentically processed and the pain-stricken heart comes to restful surrender in the eternal arms of the Man of Sorrows."

> If we don't process our grief, our trust will be diminished. We can't whitewash pain and heartache with pithy religious phrases or a memorized verse from the Bible.

COVID introduced all of us to one of the more bizarre times in human history. It produced a lot of grief. We were faced with all sorts of losses. Some people lost loved ones; others lost nearly all human contact. Many faced economic hardships and others lost jobs. As I wrote, I wasn't able to see my aging parents for more than a year. I had spent many years building up my ministry as a conference speaker and author, and it was instantly dismantled. We found ourselves suddenly cut off from life as we knew it: from social interaction, travel, eating out at restaurants, and all sorts of other pleasures. I found myself wrestling with grief and sadness and, once again, I turned to the Psalms.

I found Psalms that resonated with my heart, and I prayed them back to God in my own words. I unpacked the emotional distress and grief in the suitcase of my soul. We cannot be healthy with unprocessed pain in our soul. Throughout the pandemic I continued to process the sadness in my soul. Often I sat with my friend Martin or my wife Jen and simply talked with them about the sadness I felt.

When I am grieving I seek to identify and express the feelings that are within me: sadness, hurt, disappointment, anger, loss, grief, betrayal, sorrow, and whatever else I discover. I pour out my complaint to God along with David. But in the end, I always remember the goodness of God. I want to be honorable and reverent with the Lord because He is worthy. I do not always understand why things happen as they do, but I know I can trust God because of the cross. On the cross of Christ God demonstrates His goodness and love. He entered our suffering with us, and He suffered for us. He didn't stand aloof from our suffering. He became one of us and joined in the pain and sorrow of this fallen world. This is how we know we can trust Him. We must separate our life from God. Life is life, and life is sometimes harsh. But God is God, and God is good. Life is tainted by sin, but God is only understood through the lens of the cross, not through the lens of sin. The cross makes sense of a world marred by sin.

There is a pattern to the lament Psalms. They mostly sound like this: "Life is really bad. I am in pain. Why, God? Where are you? Why don't you help? It's okay. I know you love me. I know you're with me. I trust you. I surrender." They sound a little schizophrenic at times, but they are raw but reverent, honest but honorable. They are getting up, and out, all of the emotions while still looking to God in trust. This is critically important to processing. You won't process with someone you don't trust. You might talk to them, but you won't really open your soul to them with true vulnerability. That requires a level of trust. If we don't process our pain, we can't get to a place of deep trust with God.

Third, if we are going to grieve well, we need to look up and out of our pain and look to God. By the end of the lament Psalms, the psalmists always look up and out of their pain and look to God in surrender and trust. They nearly always end with some form of, "I trust you. I surrender." That is essential to processing. Grief is the great exaggerator. It makes us feel things deeply; even though they may not be true, they feel true. David said in Psalm 142, "No one cares for me." But that wasn't true. His mother still loved him. He had some mighty men who were willing to lay down their lives for him. He had many people who cared for him, but *this emotion was how he felt in the moment, and he expressed it.* There is nothing wrong with expressing how we feel even if it isn't accurate. If we are going to grieve well, we must get in touch with our pain and express it. We can right-size our feelings later,

> There is nothing wrong with expressing how we feel even if it isn't accurate. If we are going to grieve well, we must get in touch with our pain and express it.

but it is important to first get them up and out of the suitcase of our souls.

Some people have a hard time looking up and out of their pain to trust God because of previous victimization. Some people get stuck in sadness because of the bent will. They feel powerless, and so they wait for someone to rescue them. They may have been abused—physically, emotionally, or sexually. They may have been bullied. They may have grown up in an extremely controlling home and felt disempowered. But somehow their will has been weakened, and now they feel powerless in the face of this pain and grief. So they get stuck in sadness.

We may have been victimized in life, but we are not a victim. Not in Christ we aren't. Too often we fail to take this crucial step of looking up and out of the sadness and looking to God with a trusting heart. This is one of the reasons I pray the Psalms when I am processing grief. These people were masters at processing pain, and most of us from a Western worldview are not very good at this. We medicate pain, but we don't process it as well as they did. So let them be our guide, and make sure you take the crucial step of looking up and out of our pain and surrendering to God.

You can only have three responses to God. You can rebel, you can resign, or you can surrender. Rebellion is a "shake your fist in the face of God" attitude. We go our own way. Resignation is sometimes confused with surrender, but it is not. Resignation is a powerless position. We feel overwhelmed and overcome; we feel weak, and we give in. "There's nothing I can do. It's just the way it is." Both rebellion and resignation are rooted in distrust. Only surrender is rooted in trust. There is no peace without surrender.

You are the only one responsible for you. Even if you got abused, you are responsible to address the weakened will, and to strengthen your identity. No one else can do that for you.

God and others can help you in the process, but you must take responsibility. You must choose to trust God and surrender. You have more than ample reason to trust him because of the cross. As Soul Care practitioners, we have to help people who struggle with a victim mentality by helping them take responsibility for their lives. We cannot be enablers.

Here is a fourth tip for grieving well: practice expectation management. There are times we cannot get out of disappointment and sadness unless we manage our expectations. Let me illustrate. Let's say you are in relationship with someone else—it could be your spouse, your parent, your child, or a friend—and you have an expectation of that person. It may be an expectation of how they are going to express love to you or how much time they will spend with you. You express your expectation to that person clearly, and they hear you and understand it, but they refuse your request. You only have a few choices. First, you can hold on to that expectation, and if the person continues to refuse your desire you can choose to become resentful, angry, and bitter. It's an option, but not a great one for your well-being. Second, you can hold on to your expectation and continue to be denied and forgive that person for all the ways you feel hurt . . . but live with perpetual disappointment and sadness. It is an option, and many people choose it, but once again it isn't productive to your soul. Third, you can manage your expectations. You can choose to die to your desires, die to self, and lower your expectation of what the person is willing to give you so you aren't constantly hurt, disappointed, and tempted toward anger.

> As Soul Care practitioners, we have to help people who struggle with a victim mentality by helping them take responsibility for their lives.

For example, I have had people who told me they wanted to be my best friend and were angry at me because I wasn't meeting their expectation. Someone can have that desire, but I have the right to say no. If I say no and that person refuses to adjust their expectation, then they are going to be continually hurt, and they will be angry or disappointed.

We cannot have a goal in life that requires someone else to be or do something to meet that goal. I will have no control over that goal because it involves the will of another. That's a goal that is going to leave us hurt, angry, and frustrated. I know lots of people who are walking around hurt because of denying this principle. They simply haven't practiced expectation management, and they are carrying hurt because they refuse to adjust their expectations to another person's will. They keep talking about the problem, but they aren't doing what they need to do to process it.

> We cannot have a goal in life that requires someone else to be or do something to meet that goal.

Let's say I want Jen to articulate more frequently what she appreciates about me. I have a right to ask for what I desire. But I don't have a right to demand her to change and withhold love from her or punish her in some way if she doesn't meet my expectation. If I did that, I would not be loving my wife as Christ loved the church. To do this would be manipulative, cajoling, and immature. And it would also leave me in perpetual anger, hurt, sadness, or disappointment. The only person I am responsible for is me. So I must choose a response that honors God, honors Jen, and helps me move forward in a healthy way. That means I must manage my expectations.

We all need to practice expectation management or we will be talking about the same issues five years from now that we are talking about today. I have read Fenelon's book, *Let Go,* more than any other book other than my Bible. No one in the history of the church has understood death to self and its benefits like Fenelon. Every time I feel disappointed, sad, hurt, or angry because I am not getting something I want, I pick up Fenelon to help me die to self. I express my expectations and desires to God and others; sometimes they fulfill my desires. But sometimes I just need to manage my expectations, die to self, and grow up—or I won't get free.

My fifth tip for grieving well: learn how to reframe and redeem the losses of life. The Bible promises us that God can redeem everything that comes into our lives to make us more like Jesus. Romans 8:28, 29: "And we know that in all things God works for the good of those who love him, who have been called according to his purpose. For those God foreknew he also predestined to be conformed to the image of his Son, that he might be the firstborn among many brothers and sisters." It isn't that God brings everything into our life; there are plenty of evil things that happen in this world, like rape. God doesn't bring rape into anyone's life; He has no evil to give. But God is so good that when evil touches our life and God touches that area, God can create good from it. This gives us hope to face every trial and tribulation. This gives us a path forward with purpose even in the darkest hours of life. We must learn to reframe and redeem our heartaches and losses.

> God is so good that when evil touches our life and God touches that area, God can create good from it. This gives us hope to face every trial and tribulation.

When I was leaving South Shore Community Church, as I was processing the grief of leaving, I discovered that I was also feeling unwanted. They were moving on from me, and they needed to, but it left me feeling unwanted. I knew it was strange to feel that way since I knew God was calling me to something new, and I was the one moving on by my own choice. But still, I felt it. One night I was processing my departure with the board; we were taking time to grieve, and one of the board members expressed that he was feeling rejected. He said, "I know that it isn't true, but I feel like you are rejecting us to go to something better." I laughed and said, "I am feeling unwanted." We expressed our hearts of love to one another, and we processed our emotions together. But then I knew it was time to reframe our perspective. I said, "I am not rejecting you and I am not unwanted. God is in this. He is calling me to travel around the world to fight for revival. This is part of my apostolic calling, and we all knew that. And you are sending me as part of your commitment to God and his Kingdom." That brought a new perspective to the moment. Grief has a way of distracting us from God's perspective. We have to process the grief, but then as we look up and out to God, we need to reframe and redeem the pain. We need to see God in it and see how God can redeem it in our lives to advance his Kingdom.

> Grief has a way of distracting us from God's perspective. We have to process the grief, but then as we look up and out to God, we need to reframe and redeem the pain.

My sixth and final tip for grieving well is we must process our shame. Sometimes we have shame mingled with grief because of what someone has done to us. For example, if you are married and your spouse commits adultery, you have to grieve the betrayal, but you will also feel shame that your spouse rejected you for another. And if you don't process the shame, you will likely be talking about it for a long time. The same thing is true when your grief is associated with failure. It could be moral failure, marriage failure, parental failure, or career failure. Failure produces shame, and we must grieve our losses and process our shame to experience breakthrough.

Let's illustrate this with the life of Moses. Moses had a suitcase full of shame. The first time Moses encountered God is in Exodus 3. God appeared to Moses in a burning bush, but Moses did not realize it was God. Moses went over to look at the bush and God revealed himself. In Exodus 3:6 God says, "'I am the God of your fathers' . . . At this, Moses hid his face because he was afraid to look at God." Moses hid his face because he was steeped in shame.

Remember when Adam and Eve first sinned? What did they do? They hid themselves. Shame always hides because shame is fear-based. Shame fears: *if you knew me, you wouldn't love me or accept me.* I teach Soul Care around the world, and I call people to walk in the light with God and others; I am honest and vulnerable. As a result, a lot of people confess sin to me. They come up and say, "I have never told anyone this before . . ." And then they tell me their misdeed. But no one has ever said that to me and looked me in the eye. Secrets produce shame and shame produces hiding. That's why Moses hid his face.

Where did Moses develop shame? We know he committed murder, and he never really processed what he did; he just ran. The problem with the suitcase of your soul is wherever you go, there it is. He also had shame because his parents abandoned him. They did it for noble purposes, but when you are little, you can't figure that out. You just feel abandoned, rejected, unwanted, and unloved. The voice of shame says, "I am not lovable. I am not wanted. There is something wrong with me." Then he is adopted by a royal Egyptian household. Egyptians hated Hebrews; they wouldn't even eat with them. Moses grew up in a prejudiced environment, and this piled on more shame. So by the time Moses encountered God he had a suitcase full of shame. And when God revealed himself to Moses, Moses hid his face because he was steeped in shame.

A lot of that shame is addressed as Moses grows in intimacy with God. But at the end of his life, we see new symptomatic expressions of Moses' shame. Deuteronomy is Moses' final words to the people of Israel. He is saying farewell to them and giving them final words of instructions. There, in his final words, his shame leaks out in blame and anger. Shame always blames—it either blames God, blames others, or blames self with self-incrimination.

> Shame always blames—it either blames God, blames others, or blames self with self-incrimination.

Moses' shame this time is connected to the failure of the mission. Moses had a twofold mission: (1) he was to lead the people out of the land of Egypt; (2) he was to lead them into the Promised Land. Part one was a success, but part two was a failure, and that triggered shame in Moses. It was proof to himself that all his self-doubts were warranted. He didn't have what it takes; he was a failure. So his anger flared.

In Deuteronomy 1:37 Moses said, "Because of you the Lord became angry with me also and said, 'You shall not enter it [the Promised Land] either.'" That is not true. He is blaming the people, but that isn't why Moses couldn't enter. Then in Deuteronomy 3:25, 26 Moses says that he pleaded with the Lord: "Let me go over and see the good land beyond the Jordan—that fine hill country and Lebanon. But because of you the Lord was angry with me and would not listen to me." Again, in Deuteronomy 4:21, Moses says, "The Lord was angry with me because of you, and he solemnly swore that I would not cross the Jordan and enter the good land." Moses blamed them three times for his failure to enter the land.

Shame always blames because shame isn't secure enough to take responsibility. Self-blame isn't responsible ownership that leads to life change; rather, it is a victimized self-blame. "I'm no good. I will never get it right. I'm just a loser." But there is no responsibility, no ownership, no change. And this is the point of this chapter: it doesn't lead to processing that creates breakthrough; it leads to talking that leaves us stuck. In Moses' case he was angry, and he blamed the Israelites—and God some, too. But he doesn't own his part.

Finally, at the very end, God sheds light on the subject and Moses' shame is broken and his blame ends. The Lord says, "There on the mountain that you have climbed you will die and be gathered to your people, just as your brother Aaron died on Mount Hor . . . This is because both of you broke faith with me in the presence of the Israelites at the waters of Meribah" (Deuteronomy 32:48). There lies the truth. Moses didn't get to go into the Promised Land because of his angry response—not because of the people, and not because of God. And here in the presence of God, there is no more blaming, no more pleading. Finally, Moses accepts responsibility. God buries him, then, with His own hand.

We will not move past talking without responsibility, and we won't take responsibility as long as we are living in shame because shame always blames. When I left South Shore, I spent several weeks processing the grief of my departure with my people. One week I processed the loss of relationships. I had every person who played a significant role at SSCC over the years stand up and I blessed them, thanked them, and told them how much I loved them. It was moving; I couldn't get through it without many tears. There wasn't a dry eye in the house. But it helped all of us to say goodbye, to access grief, and to process our separation.

One of the weeks I stood up and talked about all the things we set out to do but never accomplished. If you are still the leader, there is hope that one day you will accomplish those goals and see those visions come to fruition. But when you are leaving, you realize that you will not see those things through. I grieved the things that we set out to accomplish but did not. I took responsibility for the leadership mistakes and failures I made. I owned my part and apologized. Afterward, someone came up to me and said, "That must have been so hard. I never could have done that." But truthfully, it wasn't hard to publicly own it because I had already processed my shame, grieved my losses, and owned my part with God. It was only natural to do it with others—and it was freeing and liberating.

When I left SSCC, I grieved everything I needed to grieve, and I was ready to move on to the next season in my life. I embraced it wholeheartedly and have enjoyed it thoroughly. I have had more fun and born more fruit in this last season of my life, since I left SSCC, than in any other season. That's the power of grieving well. It allows you to truly process and move on in victory.

One of the things we need to do as Soul Care practitioners is help people grieve well. We must create opportunities for them to grieve. We must learn how to access the sadness in their souls with wisdom. For example, one of the things I have often done to help people access grief is apologize to them for something they have experienced in life. If someone was abused by their father, I will say, "As a dad, I want to say I am so sorry for the way your father treated you." Tears will often gush forth as I validate their pain and apologize on behalf of a father who never did. I have often apologized to my students who have experienced racism. I have apologized to women who experienced misogyny at the hands of men.

I mentioned that when I left South Shore, I had all the key leaders who had served faithfully stand up, and I blessed them publicly, face to face. This process tempted the grief in them to come forth, and that is why I did it. When my kids graduated, I had everyone in the family write letters to them as they went off to college. We told the departing child how much we loved them and what they meant to us. Then we had a big send-off dinner and read the letters and prayed a prayer of blessing over them. Again, I am creating an opportunity for grieving. As everyone expresses their love for this person, they experience the sadness and grief of the parting. If you don't grieve the season you are leaving, you can't fully embrace the season you are entering.

> If you don't grieve the season you are leaving, you can't fully embrace the season you are entering.

In our doctoral classes we have our students write a grief journal. They record the events they need to grieve. Then they get in groups and talk through those grief journals. People listen, validate their pain, and pray for them. They express love and compassion, and the grief begins to get emptied from the suitcase of the soul. As ministers of the soul, we need to do this for people.

Change Takes Time

Fourth, if we are going to shift from talking to processing, **we need to accept that change takes time.** We live in an instant gratification society, one with fast lanes, microwaves, and online shopping with overnight delivery. We want what we want, and we want it now. Sitcoms introduce a problem and solve it within a half-hour. We expect to resolve things quickly, but sadly that isn't the norm for life change. Many of the images that Jesus uses for spiritual growth are agricultural. Jesus speaks of seeds being sown and eventually sprouting to produce a harvest. But there is a long delay between the sowing and the harvesting. Farming isn't a sow-today-and-reap-tomorrow world.

Merely knowing the truth does not produce transformation. It is in the holding on that freedom is discovered, and holding on involves perseverance.

As we said earlier, discipleship is about changing cultures. We are changing culture from our culture of origin, our family of origin, and our nation and region of origin to the culture of the Kingdom. Our culture has been deeply assimilated and integrated over time; to take on a new set of cultural norms requires intentional choice over time.

I often teach on identity, who we are in Christ. People come to me and say, "I know I am loved by God." And they do know it: cognitively. But they are still living like unloved people in many of their interactions. Their knowledge has not made its way into their living; it has not become the new normal. They know they are loved, and they can quote all the verses that say so, but they have not yet learned to rely on the love of God in all their daily interactions (1 John 4:16). When someone criticizes them they struggle with imaginary conversations and defensiveness. They get hurt, angry, and behave insecurely. When someone is angry with them, they still walk on eggshells and feel anxious. When they mess up, they feel shame and struggle with condemning thoughts and self-incrimination. They are still living under the old cultural norms.

People are often too passive about their own development. They think change is going to come about magically. It doesn't. It reminds me of this Proverb, from chapter 24: "I went past the field of a sluggard, past the vineyard of someone who has no sense; thorns had come up everywhere, the ground was covered with weeds, and the stone wall was in ruins. I applied my heart to what I observed and learned a lesson from what I saw: A little sleep, a little slumber, a little folding of the hands to rest—and poverty will come on you like a thief and scarcity like an armed man" (vv. 30-34). The wise man walks past a field that is overgrown. The law of entropy has come to full effect. Where there was once a thriving vineyard there are thorns, thistles, weeds, and dilapidated walls. The writer's point is powerful: no one wants to strive toward a state of entropy. Entropy is the natural state of a fallen world. If you leave a field unattended, it will not thrive with fruitfulness. It will become overgrown and unproductive.

The Proverb writer is not merely concerned with fruitful fields. He is concerned with well-tended souls. A life that is not well cared for is a life that will tend toward spiritual entropy. We cannot be passive about spiritual development and expect to magically grow up. We cannot be passive about our maturity and expect to hold soul entropy at bay. If you want to grow, you have to do the work.

> We cannot be passive about our maturity and expect to hold soul entropy at bay. If you want to grow, you have to do the work.

At the very beginning of our church plant, I had a young man come to my church. He had a messy life, a painful story. It was a story of abuse—all different types of abuse, some of it longstanding. He ended up on the streets as a child prostitute and suffered at the hands of many evil men. One day he tried to escape the streets and showed up at a church for help; the priest took him in and abused him. I have listened to thousands of stories, and it is one of the worst stories I have ever heard. By the time he came to faith in Christ his life was a mess. He needed intensive care, discipleship, love, and deliverance. I used to say to him, on a regular basis: "Those who show up, grow up." I knew he constantly felt the pull to regress to his previous vices, to quit on his arduous journey toward wholeness. But I kept encouraging him to show up. Show up, even if you are drunk. Show up even if you slept in the wrong bed the night before. Keep showing up. He did. And he grew up.

Over the years, this man who had started life in a huge hole passed many people on the spiritual journey who had a much better start in life than he did. They started with better families, had more emotional support, and had more love and care than he did. Yet he grew more mature than many of them; he became healthier, emotionally and spiritually, than many. "A little sleep, a little slumber, a little folding of the hands to rest—and poverty will come on you like a thief and scarcity like an armed man." Many others have been robbed of their potential by their passivity. You cannot maintain passivity and mature properly.

Humility begins with honesty and ends with responsibility. No one matures without authentic humility. You must take an honest look at yourself and see what God sees. When God shines light into the suitcase of your soul, you need to humbly receive the light as a gift. You cannot grow up if you spin, blame, excuse, justify, rationalize, or deny. You must own it. This is where change begins. We will never rise above our level of self-awareness. Self-awareness is the gateway to transformation; it doesn't guarantee it, but you can't get there without it. So we begin with honesty and must take responsibility. We must take responsibility for our life, our part, our motives, attitudes, and behaviors. If we are going to continue to blame, we will continue to live with a chaotic soul. Entropy rules the life of the irresponsible. You are the only one responsible for you. Own whatever you need to own. Take responsibility for your part. There is no other way to become a grown-up.

You are not responsible for what happens to you in life, but you are responsible for how you respond. You may have been victimized in life, but you are not a victim. You are more than a conqueror (Romans 8:37). You can do all things through Christ who strengthens you (Philippians 4:13). You are in Christ; Christ is in you (Ephesians chapters 1-3). You have the power in Christ to overcome. But if you see yourself as a victim, you will remain powerless to change.

In the old days, when they were training an elephant for the circus, they would tie the baby elephant to a large tree. The baby elephant learned that no matter how hard it pulled and fought against the restraints, it could not get free. Finally, the elephant quit trying. Later they would simply tie the fully grown elephant to a little stake in the ground. It was a stake that would have been nearly effortless for the elephant to pull up, but the huge animal was convinced it couldn't overcome being tied down. They call that an "elephant stake."

Many people have been victimized in life and they feel powerless; they feel like they have no control over their lives. People like this often come to me and say, "Why won't God help me? Why won't God do something? Why doesn't anyone help me?" They are tied to their past by an elephant stake. They remain passive, waiting for God or someone else to come and rescue them, to do what only they can do. Just like the baby elephant, they had a mindset formed from their past that limits them in their present and robs them of their potentially best future. They must pull up the elephant stake—but they can't do it without taking responsibility.

Change takes time and change takes effort. We cannot passively wait for God to do our part. If we find ourselves passively waiting for God and others to rescue us, we will end up taking offense, and the law of spiritual entropy will continue to rule our souls. The offense will harden our hearts. The victim mentality is often linked to an identity wound; we need to break that before we can begin to take responsibility for our life and experience breakthrough. If we don't break the victim mentality we will be talking for years in a broken-down field and complaining that no one will help us take care of our field.

People often get discouraged in their developmental journey. They feel stuck, defeated, and are on the edge of quitting. We need to encourage them to persevere. I often say to people, "You are not where you want to be, but you are not where you used to be either. Look at the long run. Don't just look at this present moment in time where you feel stuck. Look at the last five years and see how far you have come." If someone has been working the process, not just talking, there is maturity taking place. Help them see where they have come from, where they are, and where they are going in Christ. It's too soon to quit. I am often vulnerable when encouraging people who feel stuck on their journey. There were times I felt like quitting, but look at what has happened because of the perseverance. If I had quit during the marriage crisis, I never would have discovered the principles of Soul Care, and hundreds of thousands of people who have benefited from them would have been robbed of the opportunity. Who knows what

> If someone has been working the process, not just talking, there is maturity taking place.

will come of our perseverance? Who knows how it will change us and impact others around us?

Learn to Grow Deeper

Fifth, if we are going to move from talking to processing, **we need to learn how to grow deeper in knowledge, wisdom, and self-awareness.** We need to learn how to connect the dots of our life. Why do we do what we do? Why do we think the way we think? Why do we feel what we feel? How are the lies that we believe connected to our fears, our wounds, and our family sin patterns? What is underneath that behavior? Connecting these dots is crucial to our personal freedom and to helping others walk in freedom.

As I teach at the doctoral program for Alliance Theological Seminary, I often push the students to process their issues and go deeper. Sadly, too often in today's world the levels of self-awareness are frighteningly low. Most people battle with their presenting symptoms, and they focus on their behaviors. They want to eliminate lust, or break free from anxiety, or stop feeling sad or bad or angry or hurt, or they want to resolve a relational conflict. Too often we get wrapped up in sin management and behavior modification, but we don't deal with the issues of the heart and soul. It is like having a surface pain that is caused by cancer and yet only addressing the symptomatic surface pain. If you continue to ignore the cancer, it will cause catastrophic results.

Jesus said, "For the mouth speaks what the heart is full of. A good man brings good things out of the good stored up in him, and an evil man brings evil things out of the evil stored up in him" (Matthew 12:34, 35). We must address the issues of the heart. When our heart is full of bitterness, for example, we may begin to spill out anger or we may become depressed. We must begin to recognize what is going on under the surface if we are going to be good Soul Care practitioners.

I am very good at listening to a story and helping someone get to their root issues. But I didn't come by this naturally; I developed this wisdom over time. I read many soul care books, have listened to plenty of stories, reflected on what I read and observed, and started seeing patterns in life. All of this enabled me to connect the dots. I saw connections between what happens to someone in life and the way they think, feel, act, and relate to others. I didn't start as a practitioner. I started in desperate need of the redeeming work of Jesus, and I did the work in my own soul.

Developing wisdom begins with self-awareness. We cannot lead others where we have not been. We only have authority over that which we walk in victory. So if we want to be Soul Care practitioners, we must be able to connect the dots in our own life or we will never be able to help others. Remember, when Jen and I hit that early marriage crisis, at first I was resistant to change. I wanted her to change; after all, she was the one who was upset! One day I was alone with God and complaining that we weren't getting anywhere. I heard the Lord say, "The law of the harvest, Galatians 6." I knew the passage: a person reaps what they sow. I sensed the Lord saying, "You are standing in a field of weeds. You can blame Jen if you want to; you can blame me if you want to. But it is your field. You have sown seeds of pride, selfishness, and anger into your marriage, and you have reaped a field of weeds. If you sow new seeds, you can reap a new harvest." That day I took responsibility for my life. I was ready to change, but the truth was, I didn't know how to.

I knew I was angry, but I didn't know why. I knew I was struggling with lust, but I didn't know what was underneath that or how to overcome. I knew I was selfish, but what was driving that? And then there were other things I didn't even know about myself: I had a root fear of not being loved that was dictating many of my relational choices and much of my defensiveness. I started wrestling with these things before God. I read books I had never read before as the Lord directed me. I went to conferences, like Leanne Payne's, and I started experiencing breakthrough. I got to the roots of bitterness, pain, wounding, hurt, and selfishness. After I started to change, and things got better in my marriage, I didn't stop. I kept reading, reflecting, processing, and learning. After things got better, within the first year, I had read more than fifty books on these topics. I wanted to go deeper, learn more, grow more, and gain more wisdom. I started nuancing my understanding of these things of the soul.

We need to live in the light if we are going to be wise Soul Care ministers. The deeper you go in self-awareness and freedom, the more effective you will be helping others.

Wisdom begins with self-awareness, but it deepens with reflective learning. I must reflect on what I experience through life, pain, conflict, and hardship. I must consider what I am gleaning from Scripture, reading, and others. I have to connect my life to these life lessons, and then I can begin to see clearly for others. Jesus said, "Why do you look at the speck of sawdust in someone else's eye and pay no attention to the plank in your own eye? How can you say, 'Let me take the speck out of your eye,' when all the time there is a plank in your own eye? You hypocrite, first take the plank out of your own eye, and then you will see clearly to remove the speck from the other person's eye" (Matthew 7:3-5). Get your house in order before you start a construction project in your neighbor's yard. You teach what you know, you reproduce who you are. We cannot operate with wisdom about other people's soul issues when we lack self-awareness.

We also develop wisdom by listening to the stories of others and observing patterns. For example, I started noticing that all addicts have three things in common. First, their addiction is rooted in shame. They feel some primary shame in their life—one that often comes from abuse, or some other painful childhood development—and they begin to mask the pain of their soul with some addiction. Sometimes their shame is formed from a trauma, at other times it is formed from not attaching properly to their parents; they were not loved with sensitivity and tenderness, and they began to feel unwanted, rejected, and unlovable. These traumatic wounds and attachment issues are the roots of shame, and they cause the person to lean toward an addictive behavior as a form of comfort. And the addiction leads to a secondary shame. Not only do they feel bad for who they are, now they also feel bad for what they do—for the addictive behavior.

Second, all addicts lie. Because of the shame, addicts cover up. We already feel bad about ourselves due to shame, and when we behave badly, we don't want anyone to know and confirm that we are broken, damaged, and unlovable. So we hide, lie, and cover up like Adam and Eve in the Garden.

Third, all addicts are selfish. Shame is an "eyes on me" disease of the soul. When I talk to someone in shame, and they say, "I've never told anyone this before," their head is down, and they don't make eye contact. If you put your chin down to your chest, the only person you can see is you, and you have a distorted view of yourself. That's shame. We get our eyes on ourselves and make it too much about us. The more we feed the addiction, the more selfish we become.

I made these observations from reading, reflecting, listening to people's stories, and talking to many people who

> If you put your chin down to your chest, the only person you can see is you, and you have a distorted view of yourself. That's shame.

struggle or have struggled with addiction. From there I began to realize that if we are going to help addicts get free, we need to address these issues. So a plan emerged: (1) We had to help people break free from shame. We had to help people deal with the formational roots of shame, which often involves significant identity work and deliverance. (2) The person needed to make a commitment to ruthless honesty. No more lying. No more hiding. They have to reach out for help when they feel the pull of the addiction, not after they fall. Too often our accountability is limited to telling people after we screw up, but that is too late. (3) The person needs to engage in spiritual disciplines that counteract their selfish tendencies. They need to engage in things like fasting on a regular basis. Fasting fosters self-denial; addiction feeds our self-centeredness.

This is an example of how wisdom is formed by engaging in deep reflection, reading, listening to people's stories, and prayer. Processing requires deep thinking, honest conversations, reflection, hard work, prayer, and journaling. There is no easy path to self-awareness and maturity for any of us. One of the problems with religion is that it is too simplistic. Simplistic solutions will not lead to breakthroughs when we are dealing with the complexities of the soul. When I was a kid growing up, it seemed like the solution to every problem was "read your Bible and pray." No offense, but that advice is lousy. I was reading my Bible; I had read it through dozens of times. I *was* praying—every day and with great vigor. But I wasn't experiencing breakthroughs. I can't tell you how many addicts I have known who went to church, read their Bible, and prayed yet still wrestled with the addiction. We have to get beyond simplistic solutions, behavior modifications, and religious answers. We have to get to matters of the heart.

One of the keys to developing self-awareness is monitoring our self-talk. What do we say to ourselves, about ourselves? What are the imaginary conversations we find ourselves having with others? When do you engage in that self-talk? Why does it happen? What triggers it? Why do we tell ourselves the things we tell ourselves? Our self-talk is incredibly revealing about the things happening in our hearts. What runs through your head unfiltered reveals what is in your heart undealt with. Pay attention and figure out what is going on inside of you. Journal on it, reflect about it, pray over it, and talk to others about it.

> **What runs through your head unfiltered reveals what is in your heart undealt with.**

I was talking with a person recently who insisted to me that they were self-aware. They were aware of the presenting symptoms, and they were aware of their feelings. But they had no idea why they felt the way they felt or even what was underneath those feelings. They were aware of surface issues and had been talking about those presenting issues for years, but they weren't breaking free. They were just talking, not processing. That is not the kind of self-awareness that leads to victorious living.

Grant God Full Access

Sixth, if we want to shift from talking to processing, **we need to give God full access.** This means we are going to have to break down our points of resistance and our walls of self-protection. I said earlier that our self-life is most strongly formed in our greatest area of childhood wounding. We build those interior walls of the soul to protect ourselves, but not only do they wall out people who we perceive are trying to hurt us, they also wall out God from healing us. These walls are so normal to us that we often assume they are normal for everyone, and therefore we do not see that they are part of our brokenness. Other times we assume they are just part of our personality ("That's just the way I am"), so we excuse them, even though doing so ensures our dysfunction.

The one thing God most wants is access. He wants access to our heart and soul, but He cannot get access unless the interior walls of self-protection come down. When we give God access, He can deal with the heart issues and help us break free. He can pull up the weed by the roots. So what does God do to gain access? And how can we cooperate with Him and help others to work with God so He has access?

First, God uses conviction. Jesus said the Holy Spirit convicts the world regarding sin (John 16:8). 1 John 1 says, "God is light; in him there is no darkness at all. If we claim to have fellowship with him and yet walk in the darkness, we lie and do not live out the truth" (1 John 1:5, 6). God shines light into the suitcase of your soul to show you what is there. Light does not change reality; light reveals reality. God never shines light to make you feel bad. God shines the light, shows you this issue, so He can gain access to that area of your life so He can get you free.

For example, when I started processing my marriage conflict with Jen, I became aware that I was angry, and I knew it was hurting our relationship. God was showing me my anger so I could change, but I had to admit I was angry. My father's anger was a temper, but my anger was more of a frozen anger, and I was in denial about it. Next, I had to figure out where the anger was coming from—there was unforgiveness I needed to unpack. But even after I forgave those who sinned against me, there was still anger. I discovered there was also hurt contributing to my anger. Anger was a shield I carried to protect myself from more hurt. I had to choose to lay down the shield of anger and begin to rely on God's love, love meant to heal me and protect me. That helped me drain a lot more anger, but there was still some left over because of shame. Until I became aware of shame and pulled it up by the roots, I couldn't find the level of freedom I needed.

God's role in this process was to shine light. My role was to accept the light as a gift. I have to confess: I am pretty sure God was doing His part all along, but I wasn't always as good at my part. I can remember times when I said something with unhealthy passion that was fueled by anger, and afterward I felt uneasy. But I didn't reflect about it or ask what was going on in my soul. I didn't process it well, and I allowed the anger to go on in my soul undetected and undealt with for too long. Sadly, too much of the time I didn't even know I was ignoring the Holy Spirit's conviction. I wasn't self-aware enough to pick up on His signals.

The second way God attempts to gain access to our heart and soul is through the law of the harvest. Starting in Galatians 6:7, Paul writes, "Do not be deceived: God cannot be mocked. People reap what they sow. Those who sow to please their sinful nature, from that nature will reap destruction; those who sow to please the Spirit, from the spirit will reap eternal life." When we continually blow past the stop sign of conviction, we end up creating a destructive seed-sowing habit in our lives that will eventually reap an unwanted harvest. In my case, I had ignored the promptings of the Spirit to deal with issues like selfishness and anger, and I had sowed many weed seeds in my marriage; eventually those seeds came to fruition. The law of the harvest is inevitable and unavoidable. It is as sure and real as the law of gravity. If you jump off a building, there is only one possible outcome: you will fall. In the same way, there are certain inviolable laws of the soul and, when you violate them, you will absolutely experience the consequences. You keep sowing anger, you will reap relational problems. Guaranteed.

There are a couple of critical truths about the law of the harvest we need to explore. First, it is not God doing this thing *to* you. It is a cause and effect. Sow weed seeds, reap a field of weeds. You can't sow weed seeds and expect to reap apples. You can't sow anger and expect to reap tenderness from your spouse. Second, the law of the harvest is not punitive; it is restorative. The Lord isn't doing this to you, and the Lord is not allowing this to happen as a punishment. God wants to redeem the consequences of our life choices to make us more like Jesus. He wants to use the painful results of our bad decisions as a wakeup call in our lives so we will bring our lives back in alignment with Him. In my case, the marriage pain was the thing God used to turn my life around. I didn't feel His judgment during the pain of my marriage crisis. I simply sensed His tender love at work making the gentle corrections I needed. He was very much like a good Father.

> We don't get to choose *if* we suffer in life; we only get to choose *how* we suffer in life. We must choose to suffer wisely.

We need to learn how to suffer wisely. I claim Romans 8 and James 1 every time I am in a time of pain and suffering. These passages promise us God will redeem that pain to make us like Jesus. We don't get to choose *if* we suffer in life; we only get to choose *how* we suffer in life. We must choose to suffer wisely. When I am going through a painful season of life, I get alone with God and ask Him to show me how He can redeem this difficulty in my life to make me more like Jesus. I keep asking until it becomes clear to me, and then I follow God's path with all my heart.

The third way God attempts to gain access to our hearts is through discipline. Let's take a look at a longer passage from Hebrews 12, starting in verse 4:

> *In your struggle against sin, you have not yet resisted to the point of shedding your blood. And have you completely forgotten this word of encouragement that addresses you as children? It says, 'My son, do not make light of the Lord's discipline, and do not lose heart when he rebukes you, because the Lord disciplines those he loves, and he chastens everyone he accepts as his child.' Endure hardship as discipline; God is treating you as children. For what children are not disciplined by their father? If you are not disciplined—and everyone undergoes discipline—then you are not legitimate children at all. Moreover, we have all had parents who disciplined us and we respected them for it. How much more should we submit to the Father of our spirits and live! Our parents disciplined us for a little while as they thought best; but God disciplines us for our good, that we may share in his holiness. No discipline seems pleasant at the time, but painful. Later on, however, it produces a harvest of righteousness and peace for those who have been trained by it.*

Let me make several observations from this rich passage. First, notice again that discipline is restorative, not punitive. The purpose of God's discipline is to make us holy. He isn't punishing us. He is training us in peace and righteousness. He is seeking to gain access to our heart and soul so He can form Christ in us. He isn't like our parents, who disciplined us imperfectly, and as they thought best. He is our perfectly loving Father, who is only good all the time, and He only disciplines us for our good that we might share in His holiness.

Second, I love that the author says, "Endure hardship as discipline." Listen, he isn't saying that all hardship is discipline; he is saying endure it as discipline. In other words, when you are going through a hardship, don't ask, "Why?" or "Is this from God?" Instead, endure this hardship as a tool that God can use to shape your life and make you more like Jesus. Endure it as an excellent training ground; this is a place where God is equipping and training you to live a Kingdom life. This attitude about hardship has made a huge difference in my life. I stopped asking God "Why?" and I started asking God "How?" How can He use this hardship to train me, equip me, and make me more like Jesus? I have found God always answers the question, "How can you redeem this in my life to make me more like Jesus?" See James 1:2-5.

> This attitude about hardship has made a huge difference in my life. I stopped asking God "Why?" and I started asking God "How?"

Third, when you are going through a season of discipline, don't lose heart. Discipline isn't fun! "No discipline seems pleasant at the time, but painful." Amen! But look back at the hardships in your life. I have grown the most in the worst of times. I grew healthier during my most painful marriage crisis. I developed intimacy and authority during my worst attacks in the ministry. I died to self and developed faith in the dark night of the soul when I could sense nothing from God at all. Repeatedly, I can look at my life and see how God has used the darkness to shape me. There are things I have discovered about God in the darkness that I never could have discovered in the light.

My fourth observation about discipline in Hebrews 12 is that we overvalue comfort and undervalue holiness. God values holiness. Holiness is better for us, for God, and for the cause of Christ. When we are in alignment with God, life works better for us. God doesn't make arbitrary rules because He wants to see if we will trust and obey Him. God makes the rules that work best because He created us, loves us, and knows what is best. When I buy a car, I follow the car care instructions laid out by the creator of the car. Why? Because they made it and thus know how to ensure it is operating at its optimum. Holiness is the path that leads us to the most fullness, fruitfulness, joy, and relational connection with God and others.

My final observation about discipline is that discipline is a result of God's hand, not consequences. When I eat poorly and don't exercise, I am going to have more health problems. That isn't discipline from the Lord; that is just the consequences of my choices. It isn't punitive; it is cause and effect. But God can redeem it. However, some things come into our lives for our development, and they aren't the result of our choices. It is God's hand at work to do a deeper work in us. When I went through that season of attacks, I prayed like Paul, asking God to remove this thorn from me. But the Lord didn't remove Paul's thorn, and He didn't remove the attacks I suffered either. That season of attacks, and then the dark night of the soul, were used by the Lord to form something deep in me. So I embraced the attacks and the dark night of the soul; I chose to "endure hardship as discipline." We have a good Father. I think the attacks were just people being people, not that God sent them. He could have put a stop to them, but He didn't because He wanted to train me for higher Kingdom service. I think the dark night of the soul was the discipline of the Lord: it was God's training ground for my development as a person of spiritual authority.

If we want to experience true transformation, we need to give God access. This is how God seeks to gain access: conviction, consequences, and discipline. We can trust Him. We can give Him access to ever deeper places in our heart and soul. If we don't give Him access, then we will find ourselves just talking about the same things over and over without life change. Only God can change the heart. We need to let Him in.

Press In and Press Through

Seventh, if we are going to move from talking to processing, **we must press in and press through.** James said, "Consider it pure joy, my brothers and sisters, whenever you face trials of many kinds, because you know that the testing of your faith develops perseverance. Perseverance must finish its work in you so that you may be mature and complete, not lacking anything" (James 1:2-4). James invites us into a counterintuitive response to pain. He tells us to rejoice, or consider it pure joy, when we face difficulty. That is not our natural reaction to pain and suffering, trials, and tribulations! If James is going to invite us to respond in this most unnatural way, then surely he will tell us why we should do it. His very next word is: the testing our faith develops perseverance, and perseverance is necessary for maturity and completeness so that we lack nothing.

Perseverance always seems to be a big deal to God. For those of us in a comfort-based society, perseverance is far less valued than happiness or comfort. But in God's economy, it is hard to overestimate the value of perseverance. Perseverance is necessary for maturity. There are qualities that cannot develop in us without persevering through pain. There are depths we cannot achieve without persevering through trials.

When I went through the prolonged season of attacks, I was carrying a lot of pain in my soul from the rejection and public humiliation. One day during that season I met with some staff members, and we were preparing for a service. I was preaching on perseverance and someone brought a video clip for us to watch as a potential illustration. It was from the football-based movie *Facing the Giants*. A football coach is preparing his team for a game with a superior opponent. His star player, Brock, doesn't think they have a chance. Brock is a leader, and his defeatist attitude is negatively impacting the team. The coach knows he must address it, so the coach asks Brock to give him his best in a "death crawl." The assignment is this: Brock has to crawl on his feet and hands—without his knees touching the ground—with another player on his back. He starts in one of the end zones, and the coach makes Brock promise to give him his very best. Then the coach asks him how far he thinks he can go; Brock says he can make it to the 20-yard line. The coach says he thinks he can make it to the 50, halfway across the field, and the players laugh. He puts a blindfold on Brock and tells him to give his very best. Brock begins to crawl with another player on his back. The coach encourages him to keep going. He calls out to Brock: "Give me your best, your very best. Don't quit on me. Keep driving! Don't quit till you have nothing left. Keep going! I want everything you got. Keep going!" At one point Brock yells, "It hurts! He is heavy." The coach is down on his hands and knees next to Brock and shouts, "I know he is heavy. Do not quit on me. You keep going. It's all heart from here. You keep going! Keep going! You promised me your best. Keep going!" Brock ends up making it all the way from one end zone to the other—a full 100 yards—as dramatic music plays.

That day as I watched that scene, I sobbed. I couldn't help it. I was going through the most difficult test of my life, and I wanted to quit every day. My staff sobbed with me; they knew the trial I was going through. Quitting wasn't an option. I had committed myself to do Jesus' bidding, to give Him my best, my very best.

Now I see what that season has done for me. I see how the Lord redeemed it. In the middle of that season of life, my faith felt so weak. My strength felt so spent. But I learned to persevere, and Jesus did a deep work in me that couldn't have been done without that trial. I emerged out of that season with a new level of faith. There was less of me and more of Him. I was freshly marked with His presence and power. I wouldn't change it for anything in the world. I never would be where I am now without persevering through what I went through then. That's the power of perseverance.

We must learn to press in and press through in our darkest times for all that God has for us, and to gain more of His Spirit's presence and fullness. Too often the problem is that we have the wrong goal. Our goal is to feel better. So we face a crisis—a marriage crisis, ministry crisis, parenting crisis, or emotional crisis—and we press in just far enough and long enough until our pain is alleviated and our crisis averted. We just want to overcome the pain. But we don't press in and press through to all that God has for us because we had the wrong goal. Our goal was simply to feel better.

I said earlier that when I went to the monastery during that season of attacks, I said to the Lord, "Why is this happening?" He said, "I'm answering your prayers." He told me that this is what it took for me to see my lifelong prayer answered: "Lord, give me the ability to impart your Spirit—*if* my character and intimacy can sustain it." I laid on the monastery floor and prayed, "Then answer my prayer." Years of attacks. Years of perseverance. Years of formation without being able to see what was happening in the depths of my soul. But I wouldn't quit. I wouldn't quit pursuing God. I wouldn't quit the assignment God had given me. I wouldn't quit blessing those who cursed me. I wouldn't quit coming and asking God to redeem all the pain and form Christ in me. I wouldn't quit praying that lifelong prayer. I wouldn't quit because my goal wasn't

I wanted to see all that God had for me fulfilled. The only way to get there is to press in and press through.

to feel better. My goal was to become whole in Christ, to mature in Christ, to grow deep in Christ, to be intimate with Christ, and to see revival come no matter the cost. I wanted to see all that God had for me fulfilled. The only way to get there is to press in and press through. You don't press in until the pain is relieved. You press in and press through until the goal of God is accomplished in your life.

This is what it takes to move from talking to processing. This is what it takes to help others get there. When it is your life, you need to take responsibility. When it is someone else's life, you are the coach. You call out the best in people. You speak the words of Jesus to them, as best as you can, full of truth and full of grace. You exhort them to be honest and take responsibility for their part. You assure them of God's goodness and represent Him well to them. You inspire faith in them to never quit, to keep going, to draw all that they need from God to finish the race. To give God their best, their very best, because the stakes are eternal.

Chapter 7

DIGGING UP THE ROOTS

I wrestled with discouragement for two years of my life. I couldn't get rid of it. I was able to overcome it for a day or a week, but it always came back. One day I was in my backyard and I said to the Lord, "This is the only time in my life I have not been able to surrender my way through an issue." As soon as I said that it hit me: disappointment wasn't the issue, it was simply a symptom. You cannot surrender a symptom and gain freedom from it. You have to get to the roots. Why is this symptom presenting? Why do you do what you do? What's underneath that?

I went inside and said to Jen, "I finally figured out what is going on with this discouragement. I've been trying to surrender a symptom; it's not the disease. It's not the root of the problem." She said, "Oh good! So what is the root?" I said, "I have no idea. But when I figure it out, I will surrender it, and the victory will come."

Two weeks later I came home from work and started talking with Jen as she prepared dinner. I said, "If I had been called anywhere else, other than New England, I would have seen more fruit. I feel like I am wasting my life." As soon as I said that phrase—"I feel like I am wasting my life"—I knew that was the root. I said, "That's it. That's the root of my discouragement." I went off into the other room and surrendered it to God. If God wanted to call me to New England, He could. If God wanted me to waste my life, that was His prerogative. He could do with my life as He chose; I was His. I surrendered that to the Lord, and the discouragement lifted. I have not had more than a day of discouragement since—and this after two years of battling against it. This is why we need to get to the root issues.

When we get to the root of the matter, we can chop out the weeds and keep the fruit from manifesting in our lives any longer. But if we keep lopping off the head of the weed and leaving the root behind, the weed will grow back. Winston Churchill called Harry Hopkins, a key advisor to Franklin Roosevelt, "Lord Root of the Matter" for his keen ability to cut to the chase and get to the heart of an issue. If we are going to be wise Soul Care ministers, we need to learn how to do this.

Too often we do sin management or behavior modification, and we fail to find the breakthrough we need. Jesus said, "The things that come out of the mouth come from the heart, and these defile you. For out of the heart come evil thoughts, murder, adultery, sexual immorality, theft, false testimony, slander. These are what defile you; but eating with unwashed hands does not defile you" (Matthew 15:17-20).

Self-awareness is the gateway to transformation. It doesn't guarantee it, but you can't get there without it. Self-awareness is like a lid on your life. Unless you come to understand what is in the heart that is blocking your freedom, that heart issue will become a limitation in your life. We can't take people where we have not been. So if we are going to become insightful at helping people address the root issues, we must become self-aware about our own root issues and first gain victory over those in Christ. Then we need to go beyond our own story and gain wisdom and understanding about issues of the soul that haven't impacted our lives but are impacting the lives of those we seek to help.

In this next section I want to talk about some of the major root issues that need to be addressed to access freedom. I can't cover all of the root issues, but this will address some of the major ones, and it will help you as a Soul Care practitioner to identify what may be driving someone's presenting problems. These root issues can lead to emotional pain, dysfunction, sin, and a host of presenting issues. Of course, many times there are multiple roots to the same symptom, and we will have to address more than one thing to experience freedom.

My Root Issues

In the last chapter, for example, I wrote about moving in 2017. We left behind our church of more than twenty years. Jen came to me and asked, "Are you angry with me?" I wasn't angry with her, but I was wrestling with anger floating around in my soul. I started processing, journaling, and talking to God and others about it. The key question I was wrestling with was: *What's underneath that?* The first layer was grief. One of the stages of grieving is anger. I processed my grief, but I was still angry. So I went back to the Lord again. I processed some more, and I discovered fear. I was leaving a secure job that paid me well and taking a job at the seminary that was nearly half the salary. Yet the area we were moving to had a much higher cost of living—more than $20,000 per year higher. I was over 50 years old, we had not put away enough money for retirement, we had three kids in college, and my wife was finishing grad school. It just seemed like a bad idea from a financial perspective.

Once I identified the fear, I brought it to the Lord. I said to Him, "I will make this move if you are in this and promise that you will provide." I heard a faint whisper of the Spirit: "You will make more money than you've ever made before." I thought, *Is that really you, Lord?* I waited. No confirmation. I said, "Can you send a check along with that promise?" No check. But I surrendered my fear and chose to trust God to provide. (By the way, we ended up making more money than we ever had through conferences and book sales.)

The anger, however, did not lift. There was one more layer: shame. The shame was connected to the things we set out to accomplish and yet failed at completing. Now that I was leaving, they were not going to get accomplished on my watch, and I had to wrestle with this sense of failure. After I processed the shame, the anger lifted. There were three root issues underneath that anger: grief, fear, and shame. Each needed to be addressed to clear the symptom. You can't get free from anger by counting to ten or memorizing some verses about anger management.

If I am going to be a savvy Soul Care practitioner, I need to understand how to connect the dots between a symptomatic expression and a root issue. I need to become a Harry Hopkins of the soul, Lord Root of the Matter. Let's talk about some key root issues.

Identity Roots

First, **we have to deal with identity roots**. This is one of the most important root issues to address. Your identity is like the foundation of a house. If the foundation is not properly set, no matter how good the builder, no matter how good the building material, the house is in jeopardy. So it is with the soul. You cannot build a healthy soul on a faulty foundation.

Let me give some examples. Many people wrestle with anxiety. It is the number one mental health problem in North America. More people are on anxiety medications than any other form of medication. There are many different reasons for anxiety, but one of the reasons some people wrestle with anxiety is identity related. For example, people sometimes wrestle with anxiety because they have performance anxiety. I had a friend in college who froze when he took an exam. He was intelligent, but he always underperformed on tests because of performance anxiety. Other people have people-pleasing anxiety. The issue of their value is dependent upon whether certain people love and accept them. When they displease people or fall out of favor with them, it creates anxiety for them. Other people have control issues; the issue of their value is dependent upon whether they are in control. When they can't control their circumstances, relationships, or outcomes, anxiety stirs within them.

Many people will not address their identity issues to clear up a symptom like anxiety. They won't make that connection themselves. And often they will feel they don't need to work on their identity in Christ because they think to themselves, *I know God loves me.* Yes, but are you living like a deeply loved person in all your interactions?

Some people haven't done the work to renew their mind. Some have done declarations—they declare who they are in Christ. But declaration without integration leads to disintegration of the soul. Faith without deeds is dead. It isn't enough to declare; we must start integrating the truth into the way we live. I had to hold onto the truth and start acting, in faith, like a deeply loved person in my interactions with Jen. I had to stop holding onto the lies—the issue of my value is not dependent upon whether Jen likes me. I refused to have imaginary conversations with people in my head because that was feeding the lie. It takes real soul work to shift your foundation. It doesn't happen because you go to church or read your Bible or make declarations.

I had to identify when I was standing on the faulty foundation. These three questions helped me grow in self-awareness and identify when I was standing on a false foundation. (1) What do I think when I am standing on a lie? What runs through my head? That which runs through your head unfiltered reveals what is in your heart undealt with. (2) What do I feel when I am standing on the lie? What do I feel emotionally? Viscerally? (3) How do I act when I am living off the lie?

As I identified the answer to these questions, it gave me the self-awareness I needed to quickly identify when I was living out a lie. That's when I need to renew my mind and act in a way that is consistent with the truth of who I am in Christ. For example, when Jen and I had a conflict resolution conversation and she told me what she was upset about, I went upstairs after the conversation to do the soul work. I felt anxious and defensive. I knew it was because I believed a lie—a lie that said the issue of my value was dependent upon whether Jen loved me. So I refused to defend myself or act on my fear or angst. I needed to reconcile my temporal earthly experience with my eternal heavenly reality. I held on to Scriptures and the phrases I received from the Spirit (Romans 8:14-17): "I have been chosen before the foundations of the earth" (Ephesians 1); "the issue of my value was settled at the cross."

Doing this exercise helped settle my heart some, and the anxiety lessened. I then listened to the Spirit's voice. Romans 8:14-17 promises us that the Spirit will testify with our Spirit that we are God's children. I claimed the promise, sat quietly before the Lord, and waited for the testimony of the Spirit. The voice of the Spirit echoed over the restlessness of my soul and brought peace—like the voice of Jesus speaking calm to the stormy sea. Finally, I asked myself the key question: Now, how would a deeply loved person act? I owned what I needed to own; I did what a deeply loved person would do. The more I lived out of this truth, the more I felt secure. The foundation of God's love was being set in my inner being, but it didn't happen without the work.

Lots of people get stuck in identity roots because they have an identity wound. Let me use an image to help illustrate. Your soul is like a bucket, and people with an identity wound have a hole in the bottom of their bucket. They experience God's living water poured over them, but it doesn't stick; it flows out the hole in the bucket. They encounter God, but it doesn't stick. Everything goes out the hole in the bucket. They live with an inner emptiness inside. This is an identity wound.

Identity wounds are largely formed in two ways. First, the person has some sort of traumatic experience or experiences. For example, there was physical, emotional, or sexual abuse— or all of the above. Second, the person didn't attach securely to their parents. There was some sort of attachment disconnect. Their parents were not loving, sensitive parents. There may have been abuse, neglect, abandonment, criticism, harshness, smothering, or high control, but the parenting they received left them with an insecurity that hindered their ability to attach properly to others. Tim Clinton and Gary Sibcy wrote a helpful book called *Attachments*. I do a whole seminar on identity wounds, which I don't have room to cover here. But you can look for it on our website, and you can read *Attachments* to help deepen your wisdom on the subject.

Fear Roots

Second, sometimes people are struggling with **a root of fear**. The number one command in Scripture is "fear not" or "do not be afraid." Fear is a primary emotion and dominant issue in many people's lives. It is a particular hazard for faith-based people because the root of religion is fear. Legalism is fear-based. The Bible says that we are not to get drunk, but often people are afraid and think, "If people drink, they are going to get drunk. Especially our teenagers. Then something really bad might happen to them." So they lay down the law and one-up God on his holiness standard: "you cannot drink!" But that isn't what God said; that's what fear said.

Lots of strict religious parenting is fear-based. So when we grow up in a fear-based atmosphere, fear becomes part of our core and, sadly, most of the time we don't even know it. It leads to a lack of integration of the truth, but we don't realize it.

My grandmother was a godly woman, but she was also a very fearful woman. When someone in our family was in crisis, my grandmother would fast. She wasn't just fasting, though, because she was spiritual; she fasted because she was so nervous she couldn't eat! Often she would stay up in the night and pray during a time of crisis. But, again, she didn't stay up because she was spiritual; she was so upset she couldn't sleep. Fear often ruled her heart. These acts of apparent devotion were not purely faith-based; they were motivated, in part, by fear. Now, part of what made her a woman of faith was that she learned to rely on God in her fierce battle against fear. But she never actually overcame the fear, and that is likely because she never dealt with the roots. So she passed on fear to our family as she parented in fear.

In my case, I didn't recognize that I was afraid because I didn't feel afraid. When I am afraid, I feel anger or power. I had to learn what fear felt like in my body. I felt a tightening in my chest, my mind raced, the adrenalin surge in my body gave me a sense of power, and my heart rate kicked up when I was afraid. Learning how my body reacted to fear helped me identify when I was afraid so I could act in faith instead of fear. We can either act on faith or we can act on fear, but we cannot act on both at the same time. We must choose. I wanted to be a man of faith, so I had to learn when fear was driving me off course with God.

When Jen disagreed with me in the early days of our marriage, I felt afraid; it was the fear of not being loved. But I didn't know that then, so I frequently acted on fear. I was defensive and I powered up. She felt like her opinions didn't matter, and she felt stomped on. I had to address the fear of not being loved; I had to pull it up by the roots so I could break the fear-based behaviors that were damaging our marriage. God revealed the roots of this fear at a Leanne Payne Conference, and I experienced a significant healing in a prayer time. But it didn't entirely eliminate fear in my life. I had to learn to rely on the love of God to overcome my fears. I still have to rely on the love of God to overcome fear; I am more aware of fear in my life now, so that makes it easier to access victory.

As I travel around the world and do Soul Care Conferences, I often do question and answer times with the audiences. These made me realize how fear-based many Christians are. I cannot tell you how many times I have listened to someone ask a question at a conference and said to them, "That's a fear-based question." They had no idea. At one conference I must have received six or seven questions in a row that were entirely rooted in fear. And time after time I said, "That's a fear-based question. Can you hear it?" Finally, the last guy stood up to ask a question and he started by saying, "After listening to you, I suspect you are going to say that this is a fear-based question." Then he launched his question, which was entirely fear-based, and I just smiled and held out my hands wide. Everyone laughed. This is why God says, more than anything else, "Do not be afraid." Fear often rules our heads and hearts and dictates our choices.

I receive a lot of fear-based questions around spiritual warfare and deliverance. My mother called me one night in the early stages of our church plant. She casually asked, "What are you doing tonight?" I told her I was about to do a deliverance. She exclaimed, with her pitch rising, "In your house?" I didn't have an office space; we were a church plant. So I said, "Yes. In the basement." She shrieked, "With the baby in the house? What if they go into the baby?" I said, "Mom! Jesus isn't going to let the demons go into the baby. Listen to yourself. That's fear-based." That's religious; religion is fear-based. I've had people at conferences ask me that same question hundreds of times over the years. Pay attention to what is going through your mind. Is it fear-based? Then it isn't of God; it's religious.

Here is another fear-based question I get quite often: "How do you protect yourself from the attacks of the enemy when you are doing so much deliverance?" Now, really, think about it. Do you think Jesus was nervous about attacks of the enemy because He was doing deliverance? That's fear-based. I make sure I am walking in step with the Spirit. I regularly spend time with the Lord, in the Word, in prayer, in silence, and on retreat. In other words, I do the things I need to do to abide in Christ. Then I make it about Jesus, and not about me, and I do the work of Jesus without fear.

Perhaps the biggest problem with fear is that it makes life too much about us. Think about how people responded at the beginning of the COVID crisis. Jen and I went to the grocery store one day and there was no meat, no pasta, no toilet paper, no paper towels; the place was barren. People were freaking out. (That's a very technical Hebrew expression!) There were signs up in stores telling people not to hoard. If they didn't hoard, there would be enough to go around. But people were hoarding. Why? Because of fear. Fear makes us selfish. Fear makes us put our focus on ourselves, and self-focus robs us of faith.

Before you can help someone break free from fear-based living, you have to be free. And you have to help them recognize how big a role fear plays in their lives. What does it feel like when you are acting out on fear? How does fear manifest in your life?

It really helps to identify the root fears you struggle with. People always want a list of root fears. But the easiest way to identify your root fear is simply to pay attention to your story. You didn't just choose a random fear in your life; your root fear, or fears, are based on what has happened to you. Was there abandonment or rejection? That is going to create a fear in you. Was there a lot of abuse? That may create a fear of not being loved or not being safe. Was there a lot of pressure placed on you to succeed? You may have a fear of failure or a fear of disappointing people. You also could have a fear of failure formed from living in a family that has suffered a lot of failure, or from controlling, fear-based parents who never let you risk anything. Listen to someone's story and learn how to connect the dots.

What are your core fears? How did they get formed in you? Where do you see these fears forming in your family tree? How are your fears connected to the wounds you've suffered? How are your fears entangled with the lies you believe about yourself? These are the kinds of things you have to wrestle with, journal on, reflect about, pray through, and seek wise counsel on. Sometimes you can talk through these things with wise friends, and there are other times you may need a therapist.

Root of Bitterness

Third, sometimes people struggle with **a root of bitterness**. Roots of bitterness create many symptomatic problems in people's lives. Hebrews 12:15 says, "See to it that no one misses the grace of God and that no bitter root grows up to cause trouble and defile many." When a bitter root grows up there are many consequences. The first consequence is we miss out on the grace of God. We fail to experience God's favor in our lives, particularly in the places of our wounding. Anger is a shield we use to protect ourselves. When we get hurt, we pick up the shield of anger to keep ourselves from getting hurt again. Not only do they block out those we perceive are hurting us, they block out God from healing us. We are left carrying around our bitterness and pain.

Anger, if processed quickly and properly, does not develop roots. Anger is a secondary emotion, but it can become a primary problem, a root problem, when it is allowed to fester in the soul unaddressed. Sadly, that leads us to cause trouble and defile many. We end up with bitter root judgments. We start looking at other people through the lens of our unaddressed wounding and bitterness, and we have a negative interpretation of them. We often judge others through the lens of our unprocessed wounds. Where grace has not healed us, judgment afflicts us.

In our early marriage struggles I hurt Jen through my selfishness and anger, and this was often displayed in silent treatments. She became cold and distant. This motivated me to begin having conversations with her about why she was angry. In the beginning, she shared what she was angry about, and I defended myself. We weren't getting anywhere. Eventually, I stopped defending myself and started owning my part. With God's help, I developed new life patterns. We were months down the road in this process when, one night, Jen and I were having a conversation as we did the dishes. I told her something I was upset about at work, but she was unmoved and unsympathetic to my plight. I said, "Do you know what negative interpretation means?" After she answered no, I said, "It is a term used in psychology. It basically means you think

I am only evil all the time." She burst out laughing because she knew it was true. I said to her gently, "Sweetheart, I have hurt you in our marriage. But over the last few months I have sincerely worked on changing. And you haven't given me any credit. It's time for you to forgive me." She said, "You're absolutely right." That night began a turnaround for us.

Bitter roots result in negative interpretation that causes us to judge other people; we judge their actions, their motives, their heart. And our judgment keeps us from drawing near to them. It is a shield to keep us from trusting them again, and keep them from getting close, so we won't get hurt anymore. But it causes trouble and defiles many because our interpretation is not accurate. Our view is tainted by our hurt and bitterness. The problem is we are convinced our opinion is accurate because we feel it so strongly, and we often tell others and spread the poison. We do not want to be a poisonous agent of the enemy in the community of God, so we have to deal with our anger before it becomes a root issue that causes trouble.

Bitterness doesn't just cause trouble for our relationships; bitterness often leads to trouble in our own lives. Sometimes bitterness causes physical problems. A New York City doctor, John Sarno, wrote a book called *Healing Back Pain*. Sarno discovered that he had many patients who had back pain and were going for surgery, but the root of their back pain was unprocessed negative emotions, particularly bitterness. When they sorted through their negative emotions and bitterness, their back pain went away, and they no longer required surgery.

A young woman came to me one day after church. She told me she was suffering intense back pain and asked if I could pray for her. I said, "Of course. Let's just wait on the Lord for a minute in silence and see if He has anything for us." As I waited, I heard the word *bitterness*. I said to her, "I hear the word 'bitterness.' Does that mean anything to you?" She said, "I hate my husband." I said, "That would count. Are you willing to forgive him?" She prayed a blessing over him and forgave him. We prayed for her back pain, and it went away.

I was in Brazil on a missions trip and we did a healing service. A man with a frozen shoulder came forward for prayer. Every time he attempted to move his shoulder he winced in pain. I waited on God, but didn't hear anything, so I prayed for healing. I asked him to try to move the shoulder and he instantly winced in pain. I went back to listening. This time I heard the word *bitterness*. I said, "I hear the word 'bitterness.' Does that mean anything to you?" He told me his son had wronged him in business, and he was bitter at him. Then he dropped to his knees and began to sob as he prayed for his son and blessed him. After this heart-wrenching prayer time he stood up, threw his arms in the air, and began to jump up and down! God had healed him as he released his son from his bitterness.

I have also seen bitter roots lead to emotional problems. I have prayed for people who were freed from depression, anxiety, and panic attacks after they forgave the people who sinned against them.

Now, a word of caution. Not all back pain is caused by bitterness; neither is all depression. These are complex issues, and over-simplification can lead to a formulaic approach that leaves people in bondage. We need to discern with humility the root cause of a presenting problem. It is possible that back pain is simply a physical problem.

One of the benefits of leading people to apply all the principles of Soul Care is that it helps people discover freedom from all sorts of symptomatic expressions. When we forgive those who sin against us, we have more freedom and less issues in life.

We also need to be aware of our family patterns of anger and bitterness. When our family has generational patterns of anger and bitterness, we give the enemy access to our souls. Sometimes it results in demonization; other times the enemy gains a stronghold of bitterness in our family. It becomes a curse, a demonically reinforced pattern of behavior that is hard to break. We all have susceptibility to family sin patterns. A root of bitterness that has pervaded a family needs to be broken or it will lead to many dysfunctional issues.

If you or a person you are ministering to has bitterness, you have to work through the process of forgiveness laid out in *Soul Care*. Do the work. Get free from the snare of Satan; bitterness is often the root cause of trouble in our lives.

Unhealed Wounds

Fourth, sometimes the root issue has to do with **pain, wounds, and trauma that are unprocessed and unhealed**. The root can be a significant traumatic event: sexual abuse or witnessing a murder as a child or growing up in a home with severe emotional neglect. At a conference I was praying for a woman who was suffering from panic attacks and a severely elevated heart rate. As I waited on God, I sensed that these symptoms were connected to an abandonment wound. I asked her about that, and she shared she was abandoned as a child and that her husband recently left her for another woman. I prayed over the wounds and asked the Lord to release His restorative presence over the woman's wounded heart. I watched as the peace of Christ supernaturally descended on her. Her heart rate returned to normal.

Trauma can leave us with many presenting issues. But when Jesus touches our traumatic experiences with His healing presence, sometimes these symptoms can melt away. We looked at 1 Peter 2 earlier; Peter was talking to a church that was suffering. Sometimes we suffer because we make a bad choice, and we suffer the consequences of our decision, but the good news is God can redeem the consequences of our bad choices. This can be the impetus for change. Other times, though, we suffer from doing good. Jesus, of course, suffered this way. But Peter notes that this can curry God's favor in our lives—if we endure the suffering with magnanimity. Then Peter says, "To this [suffering wisely for doing good] you were called, because Christ suffered for you, leaving you an example, that you should follow in his steps. He committed no sin, and no deceit was found in his mouth. When they hurled their insults at him, he did not retaliate; when he suffered, he made no threats. Instead, he entrusted himself to him who judges justly. He himself bore our sins in his body on the cross, so that we might die to sins and live for righteousness; 'by his wounds you have been healed'" (1 Peter 2:21-24).

Jesus was falsely accused, mistreated, and abused, but He did not retaliate. He simply entrusted Himself to the Father's just judgments. The Greek word here is literally the same word used for Judas' betrayal. Judas "handed Jesus over" to Pilate for Pilate's judgment. Jesus handed Himself over to His Father for His judgment. Jesus accepted the Father's word as final, one that canceled all other judgments as false. He bore our sins so we could live in victory over sin. And then this line, from verse 24: "By his wounds you have been healed." This is written to a people who were suffering unjustly like Jesus. Peter is saying to them that when you suffer unjustly, like a child who has been abused or abandoned through no fault of their own, Jesus' unjust suffering is your path to healing. When you are touched by Jesus' presence in your place of pain, there is healing for your soul.

Healing prayer comes down to this: I want to get the person I am praying for into the presence of Jesus. When Jesus touches them, they are healed. Jesus took up our pain and our suffering on the cross, and He can heal the places where sin has damaged our souls. His grace, favor, and presence can heal our souls and redeem our pain to make us more like Jesus and more effective in His service.

In my story, my greatest childhood wounding had to do with not being loved. It began with separation anxiety, was reinforced through some angry parenting, and included some bullying. It created issues in my soul: anxiety, anger, and self-ishness. I sowed seeds of selfishness and anger in my marriage, and I reaped a harvest of weeds. But that harvest led me to deal with the root issues of my soul. I could no longer manage the symptoms; I was forced to find out what was underneath. It led me to a healing encounter with Jesus at a Leanne Payne Conference. By His wounds I was healed. The things I suffered as a child were not my fault. They were unjust sufferings, and Jesus met me in those places and healed my soul and redeemed the wounds to make me a wounded healer. However, the choices I made from my wounding were my responsibilities, and I needed to repent. Our wounding is not an excuse for irresponsible behaviors.

Authority is developed out of these healed places where God's presence and favor begins to mark our lives because we invite Him into the pain and process unjust suffering in His presence. God redeemed the unjust suffering to allow me to develop authority to help many find freedom, many who have suffered from pain and trauma in their lives. But God also redeemed the "just" suffering in my life. I had suffered in my marriage, but I contributed to that suffering. Yet God still redeemed it when I cried out to Him and gave Him access to address the issues of my heart and soul. I experienced His tenderness and healing even in the areas where I had sinfully contributed to pain in my life. He took our sin and pain to the cross. He can redeem it all. There is great hope in Jesus.

Sometimes the root issue of pain in our lives is not connected to a past painful event, like being abused, but is pain and/or disappointment that has accumulated over many years. As I wrote earlier, I think most midlife crisis is simply accumulated disappointment.

Accumulated disappointment leads to displaced passion. We have to process our accumulated pain and disappointment just as much as we need to process our traumatic pain. We need to grieve our losses and disappointments in life, especially as we get into our forties and fifties. That's when life catches up to us and we start to accumulate disappointment. That's when we realize that this temporal world cannot satisfy our hearts that were created for eternity. I don't know anyone in their fifties who isn't at least somewhat disappointed with life. Part of maturity is shifting our focus from our temporal identities, dreams, and attachments to our eternal identity as citizens of Heaven.

This can be a formative season in our lives if we learn to grieve our losses and we sink deeper roots in the eternal. These disappointments are there to remind us that we are merely passing through. This is a temporal world; our true citizenship is in Heaven. This world will never satisfy all the longings of our souls. We will only be satisfied when we are with God in Heaven.

I have prayed with people who were wrestling with depression, and this was at the root. They had accumulated disappointments. They had been to therapy, counselors, experienced inner healing, even deliverance, all done to try to break free from depression. But they had accumulated disappointments they needed to process, and they needed to sink deep roots in Heaven. When they did, the depression lifted, and they were filled with joy again in their walk with God. I have prayed with people who were struggling with lust; some had experienced victory over lust in the past, but now they were struggling again. The root was accumulated disappointments; once they processed the grief and sank deep roots in Heaven, they broke free. We have to get to the roots.

Let me end this point with two final thoughts. First, I have noticed that some people over-rely on healing prayer. When all you have is a hammer, everything looks like a nail. Inner healing is a good tool, but it isn't a cure-all. We need the right tool for the right problem. Second, I want to take a minute to discuss adoption. Many times people approach me at a conference and ask me how family sin patterns impact those who are adopted. Sadly, they have to wrestle with three things: (1) Some of their issues have been inherited from biological parents. For example, if their biological mother was a prostitute, they are going to inherit demonic spirits. (2) They have learned behaviors from their adoptive parents. Those things, too, must be addressed. (3) Sadly, they also have an identity wound from being abandoned, and that must be addressed for healing to be appropriated. You cannot address these issues with a simplistic approach or only one tool in your tool bag.

Unsurrendered Issues

Fifth, sometimes the root issue to our troubles is **something in our life we have not surrendered**. There is no peace without surrender; there is no victory without death to self. Jesus said, "Whoever wants to be my disciple must deny themselves and take up their cross and follow me. For whoever wants to save their life will lose it, but whoever loses their life for me will find it" (Matthew 16:24, 25). We cannot access the abundant life of Jesus without surrender, without death to self.

We are spiritual beings in a spiritual world; we are always giving away spiritual access. We do not get to choose if we give away access; we only get to choose *to whom* we give away access. If we pick up the tools of the kingdom of darkness, we give access to the evil one. But if we surrender to God and pick up the tools of the Kingdom of light, we give access to God and gain access to God's victories.

I have noticed a pattern in my life. The only time I am miserable is when I am making it too much about me. For example, the only time I am miserable in my marriage is when I am thinking too much about myself. *What about me? What about my needs, my wants, my desires?* But when I die to self and make it about Jesus and Jen, the misery lifts. When my will is out of alignment with God's will, Satan gets access and my soul is troubled. When I die to self, surrender to God, and my will comes back into alignment with God's will, I am free.

Let me give an example of how this works in my life. Magnanimity may be my favorite character trait in a person. I admire people who display this rare human quality—a large-hearted person, one who is noble, generous, and gracious in spirit, especially to those who offend them. But it doesn't come easily or naturally, at least not to me. I wish it did. I have experienced my share of attacks and criticisms, both public and private. Sadly, my base instinct is still too often to defend myself, or even to counterattack. I don't act on that ignoble desire very often, but I still feel it within myself. I have to choose magnanimity. I must choose to die to that base instinct, surrender to Jesus, and bless those who curse me. I hope one day that I will abound in grace so deeply that it will overflow easily. I hope that one day I will hardly ever be offended but instead be filled with the kind of magnanimity that Jesus displayed with His enemies. But in the meantime, I will choose to act in magnanimity even when I don't feel it in hopes that I may become the man I long to be. I must choose, once again, to die to my self-life for Christ to be formed in me.

There have been times I struggled with anger or anxiety because I did not surrender an issue. The moment the issue was surrendered, the anger or anxiety lifted. There have been times I have prayed with people who were struggling with anxiety and fear, but the Lord revealed there was some unsurrendered issue at the root of it, and when they surrendered, the anxiety and fear lifted.

Again, these things must be applied with wisdom. I am not suggesting that someone who is being physically abused in their marriage simply learn to submit and surrender. They will have to take their identity deeper and learn to create boundaries.

Mental Health Issues

Sixth, sometimes the root of our troubles is **a mental health issue**. People are sometimes born with physical disabilities, and they can also be born with something not working properly in their brains which creates problems for them on the road to health and wholeness. There are some issues that are physical issues, and the person needs a miraculous healing or a doctor's care. There are other problems that are soul issues; the person needs to work through a process like Soul Care. These problems require human responsibility to be overcome. There are some problems that are demonic at their root, and no amount of therapy or medical treatment will resolve that. But there are other problems that are psychological, and this person may need a therapist or some medicine to help them overcome. You can't counsel demons, and you can't cast out human.

One of the most common questions I receive is this: "How do you discern if something is a demonic issue or a mental health issue?" I do a whole talk around discerning between soul and spirit issues, and I hope to write about this a great deal more when I publish a manual on how to do deliverance. But let me cover a bit here.

The place to begin is with the reality test. Is the person living in reality? For example, on multiple occasions I have been doing a deliverance with someone who told me another person was practicing witchcraft and controlling their mind. I believe in witchcraft. I believe in demons. I believe demons can communicate to people, and they can influence people. But you still have choice. They cannot control you. You were created in the image of God, and that means you have a degree of sovereignty since God is sovereign.

There are at least two implications of this sovereign image-bearing: first, you have choice. You don't have unlimited choice, but you do have choice. You can't do *anything* you want, but you do have choice over certain things. You are a responsible moral agent.

Victor Frankl was forced into a Nazi concentration camp. They took away his possessions, they took away his food, they took away his family, they took away his health. But Frankl realized the one thing they could not take away was his right to respond. He could still choose his attitude. He could choose kindness in an unkind atmosphere. He could choose to honor others in an atmosphere of abuse. He could choose love in an atmosphere of hatred. That is the power of being created in the sovereign image of God.

The second ramification of being created in the image of a sovereign God is that we have authority. A sovereign has authority. God has ultimate authority, and we have limited authority. But we have authority over the demonic realm that seeks to influence us because God has given us authority. The end result is that mind control isn't true; it doesn't pass the reality test. People who have been through severe witchcraft are going to have a harder time overcoming the influence of demons, but they can still make choices.

Another time I was dealing with someone who was convinced certain famous people of extreme power were after them. Now this person grew up and lived in a very small town. These famous people didn't know this individual existed, and they certainly were not after them. That's not reality. Please hear me for a second: the person may have had demons, but unless I could help that person get back to reality, I wasn't going to be able to get rid of the demons because the lies the person believed gave the demons ground to stay and keep the person from taking responsibility for their life.

Once I was doing deliverance with a person who had been kidnapped as a child. They were in a conference setting, and they manifested. I knew it was real, and it was demonic, because I had seen many manifestations like it, and the demon responded to commands in Jesus' name. I helped the person get free from the demonic spirits that were present. But the person was also experiencing hallucinations. They saw people coming to abduct them even when no one was there. Even after the deliverance, the hallucinations continued. These images were not demonic; they were part of the traumatic experience of their youth, and they needed a psychiatrist or clinical psychologist to help them get free. I prayed for a miracle: that God would heal the trauma and the hallucinations would stop. But they didn't go away, so I sent the individual to get help from a specialist.

Often through the years I have had people bring me someone with autism hoping the condition was demonic. I have been around people who were autistic when they were hitting themselves. I waited on the Lord as I observed the behavior. I even commanded the behavior to stop in Jesus' name, to test to see if it was demonic. But multiple times now, as I have tested autism, it hasn't been demonic. I am not saying that it could never be demonic. I suppose there are times when demons could imitate autistic behaviors and a deliverance could bring some definite relief, though I have never seen that. However, in the cases I have tested, it was not demonic, and they needed medical and psychological care.

I have also done multiple deliverances involving people with dissociative identity disorder (DID)—what used to be called multiple personalities. I have seen cases where there were five personalities, and they were all demonic; after the deliverance the person was "cured" of their DID. I have seen other cases where there were seven personalities—six of the personalities were demonic but one was a personality that was formed in a traumatic childhood experience to help them cope with the trauma. On one such occasion the person was there with their psychiatrist (who was a believer), and I looked at the psychiatrist and said, "That one is on you, Doc. That one is not demonic." You can't counsel demons, and you can't cast out an authentic psychiatric problem.

There are often very good reasons why a person doesn't pass the reality test. It is connected to a trauma of their past, or something is not functioning properly in their brain, at times even from birth. But I don't have the expertise to deal with those issues. Loved ones often bring people with mental health issues to me at a Soul Care Conference. They are hoping the presenting problems are demonic and that I will do a deliverance and make the issues go away. I can see their desperation and I feel compassion, but if it is not demonic there is nothing I can do. You have to discern between soul and spirit. When it is human, you need human solutions—or a miracle. When it is demonic, deliverance is the final answer, and this leads me to my final root category.

Demonic Issues

The seventh and final root issue I want to discuss in this chapter is **demonization**. (Again, this is not an all-inclusive list of every possible root issue. This small compendium is simply designed to help you think broadly and, hopefully, expand your wisdom as you are trying to help other people get free.) Some problems are demonic and can't be resolved with anything but a deliverance.

Jesus was not a country bumpkin who couldn't discern the difference between a psychological problem and a demonic problem. He had perfect discernment, and He did deliverance because He confronted problems for which there were no other solutions. He then commanded His disciples to do deliverance (see Matthew 10), and at the end of Matthew's Gospel He commissioned them to "make disciples of all nations, baptizing them in the name of the Father and of the Son and of the Holy Spirit, and teaching them to obey everything I have commanded you." He commanded them to teach us to obey all His commands, and these would include deliverance. Deliverance is a Kingdom concept, and it is utterly necessary for the King to do his liberating work.

Often people come to me and say, "I have repented of all my sins. I have renounced all my family practices." And they think, therefore, that the demons have left. Repentance and renunciation are tools to help you break ground, but they do not extricate demons. Jesus commanded them to leave. The Greek word Jesus used for delivering people from demonic entities was *ekballo*: "to cast out." In Luke 11 Jesus uses the image of the house; the person is like a house. The demons are inside the house; you must cast the demons out to get rid of them. Repentance, renunciation, and many other tools are useful for disempowering the demons, but they do not get rid of them. You must do deliverance and cast the demons out in Jesus' name.

If you have never taken the Deliverance Training Workshop I offer, and you want to be equipped in deliverance, that is the place to begin. You can find out more information about that at our website, www.renewalinternational.org.

There are three things that can help you diagnose whether something is demonic.

First, I do a quick inventory with people to understand their story. This helps me divide soul and spirit and gives me insight into the possibility of demonic roots. Here are the key questions I ask:

1. Have you or your family been involved in any other religious practices? When people have engaged in witchcraft, demonization is going to result. The more severe the practice, the more likely there will be demonization and the worse it will be.

2. Have you or your family been involved in sexual immorality? Sometimes demons can be transferred through illicit sexual encounters. If a family has a long history of sexual immorality and infidelity, there is a greater possibility of demonization.

3. Is there a lot of anger, bitterness, hatred, and resentment in your life or in your family history? Is there any history of violence, murder, or abortion?

4. Have you or family members suffered from abuse? Physical abuse? Emotional abuse? Sexual abuse? Sexual abuse, especially when there is any form of penetration, most often leads to demonization.

5. Have you or your family struggled with anxiety, depression, suicide, suicide ideations, mental hospitalizations, or mental illness? Often those treating these issues do not have a worldview for the demonic, so they diagnose and treat the symptoms, but the actual source in some cases may be demonic.

6. Is fear, control, manipulation, shame, legalism, or perfectionism a pattern for you or your family?

7. Have you or family members struggled with addiction? Drugs, alcohol, sex, gambling, other addictive behaviors?

The more you answer yes to these questions, the greater the probability of demonization. The worse the story, the more likely demonization is at work. So the first thing is to look at the story.

Second, know the symptoms for demonization. The number one symptom of a demonic presence is anxiety. But not all anxiety is demonic. There can be many causes of anxiety; however, when a demon is present, anxiety is often a presenting symptom. I have seen hundreds of people set free from a lifetime of anxiety after deliverance. People with demons often struggle with condemnation as well. They have many condemning, belittling, demeaning thought patterns. Sadly, they sometimes think it is the Holy Spirit convicting them. But the Holy Spirit's conviction is always about specific, unconfessed sin. He doesn't bring up things from your past you have already confessed, and He doesn't speak to you in generalities.

Often people who have demonic spirits struggle with their thought life. They try to implement James 4:7: "Submit yourselves, then, to God. Resist the devil, and he will flee from you." They submit to God; they resist the devil. And they can overcome the temptation, but the thoughts keep coming like a leaky faucet. They can't shut them off. For example, I did a deliverance on a man who struggled with condemning thoughts. I addressed the spirit of condemnation, made sure it didn't have any ground or access, and commanded it to leave in Jesus' name. The man contacted me a month later and said, "I have struggled with condemning thoughts my entire life. I thought that was normal. I thought everyone had to battle with condemnation every day. But since my deliverance, I haven't had to battle with condemnation at all." He could overcome, but the thoughts kept coming—until the demon was cast out and the leaky faucet shut off.

Some people struggle with suicidal thoughts. They are in a good mood, driving down the street on a sunny day, and suddenly a random thought comes to them: *I should drive into a tree.* That's not normal. That's demonic. Other people have blasphemous thoughts that pop into their mind when they are in worship or reading their Bible. Again, that's not normal; that's demonic.

Many people who have been sexually abused or inherited sexual abuse spirits from a parent have certain symptoms that will immediately clear up after deliverance. Here are the most common sexual abuse symptoms: (1) They have early, prepubescent, erotic sexual thoughts. They start to have lustful thoughts at 5, 6, or 7 years old. That isn't developmentally possible; that's demonic. (2) They have sexual images during sacred moments: Bible reading, prayer, worship, etc. (3) They feel a dark, bullying presence in their room at night, and it frightens them. (4) They have perverse sexual dreams that leave them feeling dirty. Dreams about sexual encounters with a family member, being sexually abused or raped, being a sexual abuser, being a seductress, things of that nature. (5) They wake up in the night and feel as though someone is having sex with them, but no one is there. Sometimes the demon will even leave bruises or scratches on the person. (6) They don't sleep well at night; they struggle with interrupted, disturbed sleep. Often after deliverance they start sleeping through the night for the first time. Again, not all people who struggle with interrupted sleep have sexual abuse spirits, but the more of these symptoms one has, the more likely there are sexual abuse spirits present. I have done deliverances on thousands of people who had these symptoms and, after the deliverance, they never had them again.

This is not an all-inclusive list of symptoms, but these are common. When someone has these symptoms, they need to go through Soul Care, break all of the ground and access points of the enemy, and go through a deliverance.

The final tool we can use to see if someone has demons is to take them through a spiritual test. First John 4:1: "Dear friends, do not believe every spirit, but test the spirits to see whether they are from God." Let me provide an example of how I conduct a spiritual test. I say, "The spirit that Jesus calls to attention, come to attention. Spirit: answer these questions in Jesus' name." Then I proceed to ask the spirit a series of questions that are simple, biblical questions. I command the spirit to speak to the person, and I have the person report to me what they receive. The spirit will speak in one of three ways: through their thoughts, through pictures, or through their feelings (bodily sensations or emotions). So I coach the person not to filter anything, but tell me what they see, what they feel (physically or emotionally), and what they "hear" (words that come to their mind or voices in their head). The questions are very simple: "Is Jesus Christ the Lord?" "Is Jesus Christ your Lord?" "Do you honor the blood of the Lord Jesus Christ?" "Do you love this person?" "What is your purpose in this person?" A list of these questions is in the back of my book *Soul Care*.

The Holy Spirit never gives a wrong answer. So if there is a wrong answer, that is most likely a demonic presence. The Holy Spirit is not confused. So if you get "yes/no," that is demonic (and this is very common). We need to find its name, make sure it doesn't have any ground or access points, and then command it to go where Jesus sends it. The methodology is in the back of the book *Soul Care* and also in the *Soul Care* e-course. But the best training I currently give is in the Deliverance Training Workshop I offer. These are listed under events on our website, www.renewalinternational.org.

If we are going to help people get free, we need to get to the root issues. Otherwise, we will be trying to lop off the head of the weed without pulling it out by the roots, and the weed will return. So how do we pull up the roots? Let me end this chapter with some practical tips on overcoming root issues.

Discover the Roots

First, to pull up the roots, **you must discover what they are with the help of God and others**. You cannot overcome that which you will not admit. This is about welcoming the light of God. We are in a battle between the Kingdom of light and the kingdom of darkness. We must walk in the light with God and others. There is no other path to freedom. Darkness never leads to freedom.

The problem is that finding these root issues is often a complex and messy process. There are frequently multiple root issues beneath a pattern of behavior in our lives. There may be wounding, identity issues, and demonic issues beneath one presenting problem. We need to discover these roots through all the tools at our disposal.

Let me provide a few good tools.

(1) Prayer. Every day I begin by praying through my emotions. This is because, often, the first indication that something is out of alignment in my soul is that something is off in my emotional life. So almost every day I pray through whatever emotions I am experiencing: sadness, anger, grief, hurt, shame, lethargy, and more. I pray through the good emotions, too, but I pay particularly close attention to the emerging negative emotions in my heart. I seek God for insight. I wrestle with God in prayer over what I am struggling with, the emotions I am experiencing, and what is causing them. I think in most life-changing experiences there is some moment where God encounters me, speaks to me, reveals something to me, makes something known to me, or in some other way helps me turn a corner. So I spend plenty of time alone with God, and in those times I am looking for a breakthrough. If need

be, I pray long into the night or I go away on spiritual retreat to give adequate time to process. I do whatever I need to put myself in a position to encounter God, because only God knows the true roots.

(2) Journaling. Often I incorporate journaling directly into my prayers. I type my prayers into my computer, and I process, pray, journal, write, think, and reflect all within that space. No one becomes self-aware without reflection. You might not like journaling, but you have to find your path forward for deep thinking. You can't become self-aware without reflection; you can't get breakthrough without self-awareness. You might be better walking and talking it out with God and then jotting down some bullet points of your discoveries. That's fine. But make sure you are reflecting carefully, getting God's input, and recording your discoveries. That is vital to well-being.

(3) Good conversations with soul savvy friends also can lead to the discovery of root issues. After I have spent time praying and reflecting, I often spend time talking with people. Not anyone, but my closest resource people: my wife and closest friends. They know me; they know my story and they can often offer insight. I don't bring it to them after I have it all figured out. It is often still murky and messy when I discuss it with them. Even if they can't offer insight, they will offer love, prayer, and support that is vital on the journey. Often just articulating something out loud will help me clarify and gain insights into the issue at hand.

(4) Books. Often when I am wrestling with an issue, and I can't find my way through it, I turn to books that offer insight. I will start with one book that addresses an issue I am struggling with, and that book may lead to another book until, eventually, I find my way to the root issue I am seeking to understand. I often try to read the primary sources; that is, there is usually an author or two everyone seems to reference.

(5) Counselors and therapists. Sometimes, to help people come to self-awareness and get to the root issue, that person should see a counselor or therapist. Over the years I have had many people come to me who are in therapy but aren't making progress. I think there are a couple of important things to finding a good therapist. First, you need to feel connected with your therapist; they have to feel like a safe person. Otherwise, you won't completely reveal yourself. Second, they have to begin addressing root issues. If they are only dealing with behavior modification, you aren't going to experience the breakthrough you need. Do they help you discover and address the roots? Are they asking the key questions to help you discern: What's underneath that? Third, are you experiencing breakthroughs? I often talk to people who have been in counseling for ten years. I ask, "Is it helping?" They waffle. "Yeah, I think so." I say, "What breakthroughs have you experienced?" Nothing. Find another therapist. Sometimes you need to find one with a higher skill set. My dad has AML: acute myeloid leukemia. He isn't treated by a general practitioner because he has a complex disease. His AML doctors have several levels of training beyond a GP. That doesn't make a GP bad; they are important and useful. But sometimes you need a higher-level skill set to get the help you need. It is the same with counseling. Sometimes you need a clinical psychologist or psychiatrist to find freedom.

Be Responsible

Second, if we are going to get to the roots, **we need to be responsible for our part**. Humility begins with honesty, and it ends with responsibility. You are the only one responsible for you. No one else can take responsibility for your part and help you get free. God won't. I can't. And neither can anyone else. If you have a root of bitterness, you need to forgive. You need to start blessing those who curse you. If you won't, you will continue to be stuck with the symptoms of bitter roots. If you have demons, you must take responsibility to break the ground. You have to confess your sins. You have to address your bent will, your weakened identity. You have to take responsibility to do the work.

We have become a blaming society. Sadly, we aren't doing anyone any favors if we don't encourage people to take responsibility. We can sit around and blame our parents, the government, our teachers, and our friends all day long, but it will not get us free. We are not responsible for what others have done to us, but we are responsible for ourselves, for our reactions, for our responses. You are not responsible for being abused, but you are responsible to forgive your abuser and begin to repair your wounded identity. If you see yourself as a victim, you will behave like a victim; you will be powerless. You are responsible to break that victim mentality and begin to take responsibility for your life. There is no path forward without responsibility.

Do what you need to do to get free. If you have a root of fear, you may feel like you are powerless over fear, but you have to strengthen your identity in Christ. You have to get to the place where you refuse to act on fear any longer. Part of the victory I gained over fear in my life was refusing to entertain imaginary conversations in my head—never again. I can't stop the feeling of fear, but I can stop entertaining imaginary conversations. They became illegal for me, because I knew they were strengthening fear's grip on my soul. I was feeding my fear and starving my faith. I was strengthening the lies in my soul and weakening my identity in Christ. I came to this decision: no more imaginary conversations. At first, I would catch myself in the middle of one. That's because it was a normal pattern of behavior for me; my mind would just naturally drift in that direction. But once I made the decision that they were illegal for me, as soon as I caught myself in an imaginary conversation, I cut it off. I turned my attention to Jesus and renewed my mind to strengthen my identity in Christ. I prayed about what I needed to do with that situation and what I needed to say to that person in real time. And then I followed through responsibly. That's how I broke the pattern. Eventually I got to the place where I wasn't having imaginary conversations in my head because I was having actual conversations with the person rather than in my mind! That's how you get to be grown up; you become responsible. Life change doesn't take place with irresponsible choices.

The Presence of God

Third, if we are going to gain victory over the root issues in our lives, **we need to bring those roots to the presence of God**. Only Jesus can redeem our circumstances. There is life change in the presence of God. In 2 Corinthians 3:17, Paul writes: "Now the Lord is the Spirit, and where the Spirit of the Lord is, there is freedom. And we all, who with unveiled faces contemplate the Lord's glory, are being transformed into his image with ever-increasing glory, which comes from the Lord, who is the Spirit."

We are different than Moses because the Spirit now lives in us. We can touch the presence of God within us. And where the presence of God is touched, lives are changed. Transformation takes place. The Greek word for transformation is the same word from which we get our word *metamorphosis*. The presence of God leads to a personal metamorphosis. Paul says that we need to "contemplate" the Lord's glory. We need to consciously, intentionally, and actively enter God's presence, because that's where life change takes place.

We can access God's presence through our private time with God. We use spiritual disciplines like prayer, fasting, silence, solitude, meditation, and worship to enter the presence of God. We contemplate the Lord's glory, and we linger in His presence. Therefore, when I am trying to break free from something, I block out time to get alone with God to wrestle in prayer and figure out the roots. Then I block out more time to get alone with God and deal with those roots in His presence. I bring myself to Him so He can bring me to breakthrough.

We can also access God's presence by first going through the prayer and ministry of others. People can lead us through deliverance, inner healing, and prayerful encounters with the presence of God where we access victory. When I went through my marriage crisis, I went to a Leanne Payne Conference, and I had an encounter with God that led me to victory over an identity wound which caused separation anxiety. It was a significant life-altering encounter.

I went through a season in my life where I was attacked, as I mentioned earlier. I blessed those who cursed me and forgave those who sinned against me. But I was still carrying around heaviness and sadness in my heart. One day a woman came to me at church. She was weeping. I thought something must have happened. I pulled her into an embrace. Between gasps she said to me, "I . . . am . . . weeping . . . for you. For what we have done to you." I lost it, and we sobbed together. And God met me. Those powerful Spirit-anointed tears led me into God's healing presence.

Resource People

Fourth, **if you can't find a breakthrough, access a professional who can deal with other possible root issues**. There may be a brain function issue, or some form of mental illness or some medication may be needed. Sometimes we need help discerning a root issue; we cannot find it on our own. There is no shame in getting help.

I have referred people to therapists or other skilled professionals many times, because they are confronting something that is beyond my expertise. I have done all I know to do, and I have prayed for a miracle, but the presenting problem persists. Often, in my case, when I hit a wall and don't know what to do next, I bring in other discerning people to help diagnose the situation. I often do ministry with my friend Martin Sanders. Neither of us is a professional therapist, but we have years of experience and wisdom in deliverance and Soul Care work. There are times, though, when the two of us working together cannot help a person get the breakthrough they are looking for, and we send them to another resource person. There are times I have done my very best. I loved the person; I brought in my best resource people. But in the end, we couldn't get them free from what ailed them. Heaven will resolve all of earth's problems.

I know some of you are desperate to see someone to a breakthrough. You care deeply, you pray and fast, and you are unable to get the person to where they hope to be. You can't always produce the results you long for, but you can always do your best to make sure the person feels loved.

Keep growing in wisdom and intimacy with God. Keep developing discernment and authority. Be loving. Be persistent. Be humble. And leave all the results with God. We are, at our very best, imperfect representatives of Jesus. His grace is sufficient for us in all of our inadequacies and for those we minister to in all manner of brokenness.

Conclusion

THE TENDERNESS OF JESUS

One day a woman came to my office for help. She was new to our church, and she told me she was struggling with depression, anxiety, and panic attacks. I asked her to tell me her story. There was some addiction in her family tree, she had suffered abuse, and her mother struggled with depression. She went on to tell me she thought she had been date-raped when she was 16. She remembered going on a date, the man bought her a coke, which she started to drink, and that was the last thing she remembered. The next day when she woke up, her privates were sore. As this young lady told me her story, she cried softly, and a question popped into my head: *Ask her if she has any unconfessed sin.* I fought against the urge to ask that question. It seemed so insensitive. I prayed: "Lord, *really*? Is that you? That doesn't seem like a very compassionate thing to ask. She is in pain. This is ministry time, not teaching time!" But I have learned to trust the still, small voice of God, even when it doesn't seem to make sense. So I forged ahead: "I don't mean to be insensitive. But can I ask you a question?" She nodded. "Is there any unconfessed sin in your life?" She put her head into her hands and started crying much harder. Of course, that made me realize the Holy Spirit was on to something! And suddenly, I knew what the issue was. She was wrestling with homosexuality. I said to her, "Do you want to tell me what it is?" She kept her head in her hands and shook her head from side to side and cried even harder. I forged ahead again. "It's homosexuality, isn't it?" This shocked her. She stopped crying but didn't look up. I cupped her chin in my hand and raised her head to look at me and said, "The Lord told me what it was because He has already forgiven you. And He wants to help you."

We started working with that young lady on Soul Care principles: identity, healing wounds, confession, and forgiveness. She began finding freedom. We did a round of deliverance with her—more freedom came. She was walking with Jesus and hearing His voice.

A few years down the road, I led the church through Soul Care on Wednesday nights (this was long before the book was written). We went through it over thirteen weeks, with teaching, experience, and triads. Early in the process the woman came to and told me that she started having dreams. The dreams were about the night she believed she was date-raped. In the first dreams, she was in a car, it was pitch-black, she couldn't see anything, she only heard voices. I said to her, "I think God is going to restore this memory to you through dreams. Are you willing for that?" She was a courageous young woman who wanted freedom, so she said yes. I prayed that the memory would be completely restored through dreams. Each night over the next several weeks she dreamed, and the memory was restored bit by bit until it came back completely. The man had drugged her and date-raped her with his friends.

She also started to experience some demonic symptoms, and I knew she needed another round of deliverance, so we set another appointment. We did some deliverance, but we got stuck. I said to her, "Let's pray and fast. We need God's wisdom." When we got together the next week, we got through some more spirits. There was one left. She saw letters, but the spirit was confusing them by swirling them around. She was, though, able to read all the letters. I put them into a descrambler app, and the only word that came out that used all seven letters: Incubus. It was the first time I had broken through with sexual abuse spirits who are notorious hiders. I didn't even know what the Incubus spirit was, so I Googled it and discovered it was a demonic spirit that presented as male and sometimes engaged in sexual contact with people. It was an ancient deity of sexual abuse.

That dear lady is free today. Her life change was beautiful to behold.

This story serves as a great example of the Soul Care journey. Let me close this book with some final reminders for all of us as Soul Care ministers.

First, be humble. When I started doing Soul Care ministry with people, I got stuck frequently! I still get stuck sometimes, but back then I really didn't know what I was doing, and when I didn't know what to do, I simply told people the truth. I often said things like, "I'm not sure what to do. Let's pray and fast, and we can come back to this again." In the early days of deliverance, I frequently said to people, "I'm stuck. I'm not sure where to go from here. But Jesus wants you free, and He has given us the Holy Spirit. Let's pray and fast and get some other people to join us next week." Sometimes the Lord would give me supernatural wisdom while I was praying and fasting. Sometimes I didn't receive any new revelation until I met with the person. And sometimes we had to come back for several more sessions before the wisdom came. The lesson? Just be humble.

The soul is complex. It isn't easy to untangle the messiness of human brokenness. Don't fake it. Admit when you don't know something and humble yourself before the Lord. Fast and pray and seek the Lord for the supernatural revelation you need. Theology 101: God is smart, and He knows stuff you don't know. And He likes to tell you what He knows.

Second, perseverance is critical to freedom. Life change is a journey, not an event. We need to persevere as practitioners;

people need to persevere on their journey. When I was a local church pastor I was walking with people over the long haul. It wasn't about that individual appointment; I didn't need to get everything resolved in one session. We have to take a long view of discipleship. There were some people in my church I did deliverance with in multiple sessions through the course of many years.

One dear woman who was a faithful leader in our church probably had eight or nine rounds of deliverance. Every time she sat through a group test, something demonic would present itself. We would do another round of deliverance and it looked like she was free, but then the next Soul Care Conference came around and she would "fail" the spiritual test again. One day she said to me, "Am I ever going to get free?" I said, "Absolutely. You've had a rough life, with lots of witchcraft in your family, abuse, and all sorts of stuff. It just takes time." One year she came to a Soul Care Conference and she "passed" the test. She came up to me afterward and said, "I'm finally free!" She persevered in her spiritual journey, did the work, walked in the light, and grew deeper. I persevered as the Soul Care minister, and eventually she got free.

Third, lean into the voice of God. I cannot overemphasize how important it is to hear God's voice. Look again at the story I told about the woman at the beginning of the chapter. Notice how often God spoke on her journey to freedom. God said to me, "Ask her if there is any unconfessed sin." God told me what the sin was. God spoke to her through a series of dreams and revealed to her a key piece of knowledge she needed to finalize her deliverance. God speaks, and we need to hear His voice if we are going to help people get free.

When I have worked with a person and got stuck and couldn't discern what I needed, I took time to pray and fast so I could hear God's voice. If I couldn't break through for the revelation I needed by prayer and fasting, I added other people to the ministry team who also knew how to hear God speak. I don't feel like I need to receive all the revelation myself. I am more than happy to expand the team and have someone else get the needed word from the Lord. The goal is the person's freedom; the goal isn't that I get the key that unlocks their shackles. You don't have to have all the answers; you don't need to receive all the revelation. Pray, fast, assemble a team, don't fake it. Just be humble. Give what you have received and test it humbly. Trust God to help you along the way. That's why they call it faith.

Fourth, love people well. You can't always help people experience God's presence or power. You can't always get people to the breakthrough for which they are hoping. You can't always receive the revelation you need in the moment. But you *can* always do your best to make people feel loved. Love is healing. Love is the most important commandment. I want to represent the Father well to the people I am serving. I want to demonstrate His patience, kindness, and tender affections.

If you find you are getting to the place where you are too weary and frustrated to represent the Father's heart well, then take a break from the ministry. Go away on a retreat. Take time to rejuvenate until His presence and His love once again mark your ministry to others. It's hard to help others when they don't feel loved.

Fifth, speak the truth. Jesus was full of grace and full of truth (John 1:14). This is my goal in every human interaction. I certainly don't achieve it, but by keeping that as the goal set before me, I am far more likely to approximate that fullness and far quicker to apologize when I miss it. Many people find it hard to be direct, but Jesus didn't. We can't help people by being dishonest with them about their issues. So often people who get into this ministry do so because they are kind people, but kindness without honesty will not help people get free. We have to learn to discern between ministry moments and teaching times. A ministry moment is when a person needs love, tenderness, compassion, and comfort. We need to listen, care, and minister to their hearts. A teaching time is when a person has received enough that they are ready for a truth principle that can lead to a breakthrough. If we try to speak truth to people during a ministry time, they will often shut down. If we minister to people in a teaching time, we will enable people. Christians are the most dishonest people I know in the name of kindness, but Jesus is the most honest person I know in the name of love. Be more like Jesus and less like Christians (the part about them too often failing to be honest), and the world will be a better place.

Notice in the story at the beginning of the chapter how Jesus gave me direct words He wanted me to convey to that dear woman. He wasn't being mean. Jesus never shines light into our souls to make us feel bad; He shines light to get us free. It takes courage to be direct and honest. When we are dishonest in the name of kindness, we are making it too much about us. We are making it more about our comfort, too much about being liked, and not enough about the person's freedom. Jesus never did that. He said direct things to people because He loved them and wanted them to be free from Satan's snares.

To be a good Soul Care practitioner we need true wisdom. Wisdom is rooted in truth, not opinions. We aren't sharing our opinions. Too often when people are "ministering" to others they resort to advice-giving and opinion-sharing. "Well, if I were you, I'd just . . ." No offense, but no one cares what you would do. Don't confuse your opinions with the truth; don't confuse your opinions with wisdom. This is another reason I begin the process by listening for the Spirit's revelation. The number one job of a spiritual leader is to find the mind of Christ and do it. When we are ministering to others, this is what we are after. We are after the wisdom of God. That's where the breakthrough will be found.

Sixth, don't make it too much about you. When we shrink back from saying the truth because we don't want to offend people or we don't want to be disliked, we are making it too much about us. When we are praying for someone and another ministry team member gets the word from the Lord that unlocks the breakthrough, and we feel jealous or a little disappointed because we didn't receive the word, we are making it too much about us. When we are praying for a person in a group, and the person says, "Who has their hand on my left shoulder? I feel heat . . . " And we realize it isn't *our* hand that carries the presence of God to the person, and we feel disappointed, and ask ourselves, "What's wrong with me?" When we do these things, we are making it too much about us. It's not about you. It's about the person and their freedom. It's about Jesus and His redeeming work. So don't make it about you. Make it about Jesus; make it about others.

I constantly remind myself: *I have nothing.* I hold up my empty hands and remind myself that this is what I bring to this prayer time: absolutely nothing. Apart from Christ, I can do nothing. My goal is to get them into the presence of Jesus. It's about His presence, His insights, His wisdom, His revelations, His power. It's not about me or you. Fight the natural human tendency to make it too much about you. When Jesus shows up, the Kingdom comes. When we show up, nothing happens.

Seventh, remember it is a real spiritual battle. This morning I was meditating on Mark 1 and was reminded again of the battle. Beginning in Mark 1:9: "In those days Jesus came from Nazareth of Galilee and was baptized by John in the Jordan. And just as he was coming up out of the water, he saw the heavens torn apart and the Spirit descending like a dove on him. And a voice came from heaven, 'You are my Son, the Beloved; with you I am well pleased.' And the Spirit immediately drove him out into the wilderness. He was in the wilderness forty days, tempted by Satan; and he was with the wild beasts; and the angels waited on him. . . . Now after John was arrested, Jesus came to Galilee, proclaiming the good news of God, and saying, 'The time is fulfilled, and the kingdom of God has come near; repent, and believe in the good news.'"

Notice the tension in the passage between the raging battle and violent language and the tenderness of God. The heavens were torn apart. In an act of violence, God was breaking through against the prince of the air, the ruler of the age, as Scripture calls Satan. Satan and his evil intentions have marred the planet. He hates people, and he wants to harm and enslave us. To enable us to break free, Jesus entered a violent conflict, a conflict between the Kingdom of Light and the kingdom of darkness.

The Spirit drove Jesus into the wilderness. More violent language: a type of marching into battle. Jesus met Satan there and Satan tempted Him, trying to get Jesus to sin, rebel, and turn away from the Father. Jesus was there with wild beasts in the wilderness. He is in the wild in a violent fight against the prince of darkness. Then Jesus goes out to proclaim the message of the Good News of the Kingdom: Heaven is invading earth and overturning the tyrannical rule of Satan, sin, and evil. To enter this Kingdom, you must repent. You must turn away from all other loyalties and make the King and His Kingdom your new primary loyalty.

It is a violent overthrow. But notice, too, the tenderness of God in the passage. Jesus was baptized. It was a baptism of repentance. Yet Jesus never sinned. He wasn't baptized for His sake; He was baptized for *our* sake. It was identificational repentance. He was identifying with sinful humanity and repenting on our behalf in the same way that Daniel or Nehemiah repented for the sins of their forefathers. In the tenderness of God, Jesus knew that we could not overcome the rule of Satan on our own. So Jesus came.

When the heavens were torn asunder, the Spirit descended on Jesus—like a dove. So gentle. So tender. After He was driven into the wilderness, marching off to war with Satan, the angels came and ministered to Him. The tenderness of the Father is on display. When Jesus started preaching, He proclaimed the Good News that the Kingdom was near, at hand, within reach. He brought the breakthrough to us. More tender compassion.

But perhaps the greatest display of tenderness is in the words of the Father to Jesus: "You are my Son, the Beloved; and with you I am well pleased." He speaks into Jesus' identity: the Son of God. He speaks of His pleasure, His approval; with you I am well pleased. But the most tender phrase of all: "the Beloved."

Behold: the Father's Beloved has come to fight for you! He has come to set the captives free. He has come to disarm Satan, to destroy the works of the devil. He has come to overturn the reign of Satan. He has come to reverse the effects of the fall; He has come to restore things to the way they were supposed to be. Behold: the Father's Beloved has come to fight for you!

That's why we do what we do. And we never do it alone. Jesus, the Father's Beloved, has gone before us. He has won the battle, and He is with us. He knows the ferocity of our enemy, but He is unchallenged in His authority and power. He has overcome the world.

The battle is real. Jesus' victory is secure. Our job is to carry His presence, listen to His voice, and enforce His victories over the enemy of our souls as we set the captives free.

Let me conclude with the story I started with about the woman who was date-raped. After we finished her deliverance, I prayed with her, but I had a sense that Jesus had revealed the memory to her in a dream, and that He wanted to visit her in a dream to complete the healing. I said, "I think Jesus wants to give you one more dream about the car where the rape took place, but this time Jesus is going to show up with His healing touch." I prayed for that, and Jesus delivered. That very night she had a dream, and Jesus opened the car door and took her away from that horrible scene. He led her into a beautiful field full of flowers, and He danced with her. She was dressed in white, like a wedding dress, as He danced with her and delighted over her. It was a beautiful ending to a terrible story.

That's what Jesus does. He makes beautiful endings of terrible stories. He heals our soul. He sets us free. The Father's Beloved is fighting with all His tenderness for you and all those you minister to in His name! That's the main job of a Soul Care minister. Bring everyone to the Father's Beloved!

ABOUT THE AUTHOR

Rev. Dr. Rob Reimer is the founder of Renewal International, which he began to fulfill his call to advance the Kingdom of God through personal and corporate spiritual renewal. His books *Soul Care, Spiritual Authority, Deep Faith, River Dwellers, Pathways to the King,* and *Calm in the Storm* have sold worldwide. Rob mentors Christian leaders, and his conferences have helped thousands of Christians find freedom and fullness in Christ. Personally transparent, Rob relates lessons learned as he has walked with God, responded to His Word, and processed pain in marriage and ministry. These lessons are not only taught, but participants actively begin the process of incorporating them into their lives, walking in the light, practicing hearing from God, and accessing His power for ministry.

Dr. Reimer is the Professor of Pastoral Theology at Alliance Theological Seminary in New York, where he earned his Master of Divinity degree. He also holds a Doctor of Ministry in Preaching from Gordon-Conwell Theological Seminary.

To access the eCourse, listen live, or view video teaching on *Soul Care,* or to explore more of Rob's work, view his itinerary, or to invite him to speak, please visit www.DrRobReimer.com.

ALSO BY DR. ROB REIMER

River Dwellers
Living in the Fullness of the Spirit

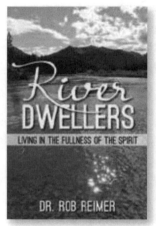

Did you ever wish there was more to your Christian life? Too often the Christian life is reduced to going to church, attending meetings, serving God, and doing devotions. But Jesus promised us abundant life—a deep, intimate, satisfying connection with the living God. How do we access the abundant life that Jesus promised? The key is the presence and life of the Holy Spirit within us.

Jesus said that the Spirit of God flows within us like a river—He is the River of Life. But we need to dwell in the river in order to access the Spirit's fullness.

In *River Dwellers,* Dr. Rob Reimer offers a deep look at life in the Spirit and provides practical strategies for dwelling in the River of Life. We will explore the fullness of the Spirit, tuning into the promptings of the Spirit, walking in step with the Spirit, and developing sensitivity to the presence of God in our lives. This resource will guide you toward becoming a full-time river dweller, even in the midst of life's most difficult seasons when the river seems to run low.

Together let's become River Dwellers, living where the fullness of God flows so that we can carry living water to a world dying of thirst!

Pathways to the King

Living a Life of Spiritual Renewal and Power

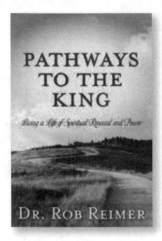

We need revival. The church in America desperately needs revival. There are pockets of it happening right now, but we need another Great Awakening. About forty years ago, the church was impacted by the church growth movement. The goal of the movement was to get the church focused on the Great Commission—taking the Good News about Jesus to the entire world. The church was off mission, and the movement was a necessary course correction. But it didn't work. Many people came to Christ as a result of this outreach emphasis, and I am grateful for that. More churches are now focused on evangelism, helping people come to know Jesus, than they were before the movement. But we have fewer people attending church now (percentage-wise) than ever before in the history of the United States. We need revival.

This book is about how we can usher in revival and also about the price that we must pay to experience it. I believe we have a part to play in seeing the next great spiritual awakening. God wants us to be carriers of His kingdom. He wants us to experience the reality and fullness of His Kingdom, and he wants us to expand the Kingdom to others—just like Jesus did. In order to do that, I believe we must follow 8 Kingdom Pathways of Spiritual Renewal: Personalizing our Identity in Christ, Pursuing God, Purifying Ourselves, Praising, Praying Kingdom Prayers, Claiming Promises, Passing the Tests, and

Persisting. These eight pathways are discussed in great detail, are securely rooted in biblical truths, and are illustrated by compelling examples from Scripture and from my life, the lives of believers in my community, and in the lives of great Christians throughout history.

Available at www.DrRobReimer.com

Deep Faith

Developing Faith that Releases the Power of God

Jesus said, "Very truly I tell you, all who have faith in me will do the works that I have been doing, and they will do even greater things than these" (John 14:12). The extraordinary promise of Jesus is that we can do Kingdom works that He did—cast out demons, heal the sick, save the lost, and set the captives free.

Jesus wants to advance His Kingdom through us. But this promise comes with a condition: the level of our Kingdom activity is dependent upon our faith.

There are promises in Heaven that God wants to release, but they cannot be released without faith. There are miracles that God wants to do that cannot be done without faith. There are answers to prayer that God wants to unleash that cannot be unleashed without faith. There are works of the Kingdom that God wants to accomplish that cannot be accomplished unless the people of God develop deeper faith. But there is hope for all of us, because faith can be developed.

Faith opens doors and creates opportunities for accessing God's power against all odds. Faith is a difference maker, a future shaper, a bondage breaker, a Kingdom mover. In this moving book, Dr. Rob Reimer challenges readers to develop deep faith that can release the works of the Kingdom. Faith is not static; it is dynamic. We can and must take an intentional path toward developing our faith if we want to see the works of the Kingdom in greater measure.

Spiritual Authority

Partnering with God to Release the Kingdom

Jesus gave His disciples authority to preach the good news of the kingdom of God and to cast out demons, heal the sick, save the lost and set the captives free. Everywhere Jesus went, the Kingdom came with power. There was no proclamation of the gospel without a demonstration of power. It was the authentic demonstration of Jesus' power through His followers that ignited the greatest spiritual movements in the first century. Today, we are becoming more like the spiritual climate in the first century then like 1950s America. In a pluralistic, syncretistic society where all deities are considered equal, only the unequal display of Jesus' power will convince people of the supremacy of Christ. The key to demonstrating the power of the King is authority, and authority is not just positional; it is developmental. Spiritual authority is rooted in identity, expanded in intimacy, and activated by faith. This book takes an in-depth look at how we can grow in identity, intimacy and faith so that we can develop our authority and release the kingdom.

Also available in Spanish (Autoridad Espirituald).

Calm in the Storm

How God Can Redeem a Crisis to Advance His Kingdom

There is nothing like a crisis to reveal the cracks in the walls of our soul. But God promises to redeem all things that come into our lives to make us more like Jesus. We are experiencing a unique crisis in our day and age, COVID-19. It has created fear, death, and will leave economic disaster in its wake. In this book, I don't just talk about how we can survive this crisis, or how we can access the peace of God in tumultuous times. I talk about how God can redeem a crisis in our personal lives to take us deeper into maturity and intimacy with Christ. And how this particular crisis could potentially lead to revival if the church processes it well. We stand on the precipice of an unprecedented opportunity to be purified and mobilized on mission to advance the Kingdom of God in our generation.